"There are many books on the market on the topic of SOA and SOA's business and technology value. This book focuses on one of the key technical values of SOA and does an excellent job of describing SOA-based application integration by clarifying the relationship and patterns of SOA with other integration technologies in a distributed computing environment."

—Sandra Carter, IBM Vice President for SOA, BPM, and WebSphere Marketing

"Service-Oriented Architectures present many challenges today in the integration of existing systems and new systems, along with many times old legacy mainframe applications. This book successfully addresses many of the complexities we see in the integration of SOA and mainframe legacy applications, presenting options and approaches to integrate the applications with the rest of the enterprise. The author takes a clearly defined pattern-based approach discussing the advantages, tools, and methods. Readers will benefit from the insights in this book whether they play the architect role or a developer role on a SOA project."

—Sue Miller-Sylvia, IBM Fellow and Application Development Service Area Leader

ABOUT THE AUTHOR

DR. WASEEM ROSHEN has a PhD from Ohio State University, Columbus, Ohio (USA), and has over 18 years of practical experience in the Information Technology (IT) field. Currently Dr. Roshen works as an IT Architect in the Enterprise Architecture and Technology Center of Excellence at the IBM Corporation. Previously, he has worked at the GE Global Research Center in Niskayuna, New York, the ITT Technical Center in Tucson, Arizona, the GIK Institute of Science and Technology, Ohio State University, and the University of Virginia. He has extensive experience with distributed computing, including Service-Oriented Architecture (SOA). In addition, he has expertise in custom development, integration architecture, and J2EE (now known as JEE). His current interests include quantum computers and cloud computing. Dr. Roshen has over 60 publications and 29 patents and is a member of IEEE and the IEEE Computer Society.

ABOUT THE TECHNICAL EDITOR

Currently, TIMOTHY FROMMEYER is an IT Architect for IBM, where he works with customers and their Service-Oriented Integration and Architecture projects. Prior to working at IBM, Tim worked 20 years at AT&T Laboratories, where he received hands-on experience with many distributed computing technologies through the design and coding of distributed applications for telecommunications systems. Also at AT&T Laboratories, Tim spent three years as a representative to the Object Management Group (OMG), the organization responsible for the CORBA standard. Tim's work at the OMG involved ORB inoperability issues. The technologies and techniques described in this book provide a short biography and timeline of Tim's career. He has designed and coded applications using many of the technologies described in the book, everything from RPC to CORBA and message queues to SOAP. Tim received a BS from Eastern Kentucky University, a MBA in finance from Indiana University, and an MS in Computer Science from the University of Cincinnati. When not thinking about distributed computing, Tim is enjoying his family and farm in Cold Spring, Kentucky.

SOA-Based Enterprise Integration:

A Step-by-Step Guide to Services-Based Application Integration

Waseem Roshen

New York   Chicago   San Francisco   Lisbon   London   Madrid
Mexico City   Milan   New Delhi   San Juan   Seoul
Singapore   Sydney   Toronto

The McGraw·Hill Companies

Cataloging-in-Publication Data is on file with the Library of Congress

McGraw-Hill books are available at special quantity discounts to use as premiums and sales promotions, or for use in corporate training programs. To contact a special sales representative, please visit the Contact Us page at www.mhprofessional.com.

SOA-Based Enterprise Integration: A Step-by-Step Guide to Services-Based Application Integration

1234567890 FGR FGR 019

ISBN   978-0-07-160552-6
MHID   0-07-160552-5

Sponsoring Editor
Wendy Rinaldi

Editorial Supervisor
Patty Mon

Project Manager
Anupriya Tyagi,
International Typesetting
and Composition

Acquisitions Coordinator
Joya Anthony

Technical Editor
Timothy Frommeyer

Copy Editor
Bart Reed

Proofreader
Marian Selig

Indexer
Jack Lewis

Production Supervisor
George Anderson

Composition
International Typesetting
and Composition

Illustration
International Typesetting
and Composition

Art Director, Cover
Jeff Weeks

Cover Designer
Pattie Lee

*To my wonderful wife, Uzma, to my late mother, Khusnuda,
and to my daughters Sana and Saher*

Contents at a Glance

Contents

Foreword

Almost everyone is familiar with the popular phrases "In today's world, change is the only constant" and the need for the "alignment of business and IT." But when one looks beyond these phrases, it is possible to see that in today's world, with enterprises having to deal with changing market forces and industry imperatives that are truly global in nature, responsiveness to the demands of these changes separates the leaders from others. This responsiveness or agility is more often than not enabled by increased alignment between business and IT. There is a general misconception that I see exists within the industry concerning business and IT alignment—that this alignment does *not* exist. I believe that, given the current level of dependency of business on IT capabilities, the alignment between business and IT clearly exists in almost all enterprises today. The million dollar question is, How can this alignment be improved or enhanced?

Service orientation, at the business and IT architecture levels, is one of the best ways by which this alignment becomes more robust. Enterprises have become increasingly global in their operations, whether it is their own operations expanding across the globe or their dealings with customers, partners, and suppliers who are distributed across the globe. Componentization within the business operations, a trend that we see gaining traction, acts as an enabler for the adoption of service orientation at the business level. Componentization as a means to achieve service orientation leads to the "separation of concerns" between the business function or service and its implementation. Complementing this is the service orientation of the IT systems. Now that the business function and its implementation are separated, Service-Oriented Architecture (or SOA) becomes a natural means of realizing the IT implementation of these functions. Naturally, this increases the alignment between business and IT.

Service-Oriented Architecture is not a piece of technology that is sold as a standalone black-box capability to be purchased and deployed. It is a paradigm that is an integral part of the fabric of how business solutions are built using IT systems. SOA is not a *what,* it is a *how.* In addition, successful adoption of Service-Oriented Architecture is best accomplished when started from the business level down, not from the IT level up. Adoption of SOA is gradual and achieved over a period of time that varies for each enterprise. Invariably, when one looks at the fundamental reason for adopting SOA, one finds that improved agility, increased reuse of capabilities or services, and accelerated time to market are among the top reasons. Several factors are usually taken into consideration when developing a roadmap for the adoption of SOA. Such factors include, but are not limited to, expected return of investment, maturity of the organization (both business and IT), and complexity of existing legacy systems. Therefore, adoption of SOA has significant business value, but has to be carefully planned and executed given the significance of some of these factors.

If agility, flexibility, and increased levels of reuse are critical to achieving SOA adoption, then naturally the IT systems being developed should exhibit the same characteristics. When one develops new applications or systems from scratch—in a green-field environment—adopting these architecture and design principles and developing to them is relatively easy. However, rarely does one find green-field development opportunities. Enterprises usually have a rich set of complex and mission-critical legacy applications that support the business. In such brown-field environments, the role of legacy applications becomes very critical. When adopting and implementing a Service-Oriented Architecture–based solution, it becomes necessary to leverage or reuse functionality that is supported by these legacy applications. Such applications can be package applications from vendors such as SAP, Oracle, and J.D. Edwards, or custom applications developed over time within the enterprise that are currently deployed on platforms such as CICS, J2EE, and .NET. Regardless of which type of applications they are, capabilities or functionalities from within these applications need to be accessed as part of deploying Service-Oriented Architecture–based applications. In other words, in architecting, designing and deploying a service-oriented application requires integration with existing enterprise legacy applications.

This area of enterprise integration within the scope of an SOA-based application is very critical to its successful deployment, but this is also an often-overlooked area. Technical architects, designers, developers, and project managers need to understand the underlying technology of how these legacy applications are constructed and what technologies are used in their deployment so that they can design optimal techniques and patterns on how to integrate with these applications. Short of this, the approaches adopted and the patterns implemented prove to be problematic and suboptimal—clearly not a desired outcome in achieving the overall goals of adopting SOA. More often than not, these integration-related challenges are incorrectly interpreted and misconstrued as a failure of SOA itself. When I conduct technical reviews of large Service-Oriented Architecture deployments, I find that quite often the enterprise integration approaches and techniques adopted have been less than optimal, resulting in lower-than-expected performance characteristics. Addressing this aspect, therefore, is very critical.

Waseem Roshen has addressed this specific area very well through this book. Readers gain an excellent understanding of what the underlying legacy technologies are from an integration perspective. They can use this understanding to learn what the various integration techniques and patterns are and, most importantly, when and where they need to be applied. In my opinion, simple, easy-to-understand examples with descriptive code fragments that illustrate the techniques are the highlight of this book. The practical experience Waseem Roshen has gained through his interaction with clients and the project situations he has been exposed to are at the core of what he has eloquently articulated in this book. The various sections in this book present just enough theory, substantiated by illustrative and easy-to-understand examples supported by code fragments that demonstrate the implementation. This book is a must-read for any technical manager, architect, designer, developer, or quality assurance practitioner who is engaged in or about to be engaged in a project that is adopting Service-Oriented Architecture and needs to integrate with legacy or package applications.

Ray Harishankar
IBM Fellow
Columbus Ohio
March 2009

Preface

Making all the applications in an enterprise work in an integrated manner, so as to provide unified and consistent data and functionality, is a difficult task because it involves integrating applications of various kinds, such as custom-built applications (C++/C#, Java/J2EE), packaged applications (CRM or ERP applications), and legacy applications (mainframe CICS or IMS). Furthermore, these applications may be dispersed geographically and run on various platforms. In addition, there may be a need for integrating applications that are outside the enterprise. SOA-based integration provides a comprehensive solution to the problem of application integration in an enterprise.

According to the author's point of view, Service-Oriented Architecture (SOA) is much more than the Web Services and encompasses many earlier technologies. According to this definition, a service is simply a functionality or data that is offered by one application to the other applications in the enterprise. As long as the interface offered by the service provider application can be described externally, we call this a "service."

The primary goal of this book is to provide a comprehensive description of the SOA-based integration patterns in an easy-to-understand manner so that a reader with no previous knowledge of applications' integration or SOA can benefit from reading the book. For this purpose, a step-by-step approach is adopted by first tracing the evolution of the basic concepts and features involved in SOA-based integration. The description starts with the simplest of the integration patterns. The book also takes a practical approach by providing code samples that can be used as a starting point by developers/programmers and IT architects to develop practical integration solutions.

Another central goal of this book is to fill in important gaps that exist in the current literature. These gaps include the following:

- A unified description of the integration issues and SOA
- A detailed and practical description of the Enterprise Service Bus

- A detailed description of the options for integrating mainframe applications

- A description of the methods of integrating a package application

This book is organized in several parts. The first part of the book provides a general introduction to the field of services-based integration. This part explains the various basic terms and concepts used throughout the remainder of the book. This part also includes summaries of all the chapters in the book as an overview of the book's material.

The second part of the book introduces the integration patterns and technologies, starting with the most simple of these patterns. The patterns and technologies described in this part include sockets, RPC, distributed objects (ORBs), and messaging. In the third part of this book, an overview of the standards (XML, WSDL, SOAP, and UDDI) is provided. These standards help ensure that the patterns and technologies introduced in Part II of this book can interoperate. In addition, to complete the interoperability solution, a detailed description of the Enterprise Service Bus (ESB) is provided. The primary purpose of the ESB is to ensure the interoperability of services, even when the service provider and service consumer are not completely matched.

The fourth part of this book describes different options for integrating mainframe applications, with the primary focus on IMS and CICS applications. Both point-to-point integration options and ESB-based integration options are described. Comparison of the various options is shown in an easy-to-understand tabular format. Next, the integration of package applications is discussed, taking SAP applications as an example. This includes integration through the use of adapters and JCA.

The last part of this book contains detailed descriptions of Web Services and how to expose newer applications (Java/J2EE and .NET) as Web Services. Both the top-down approach and bottom-up approach for developing Web Services are described. Lastly, we describe BPEL (Business Process Execution Language), which is used to compose new services and business processes from the existing services.

As mentioned previously, this book does not assume any prior knowledge of integration issues or SOA. However, some familiarity with programming languages such as Java/J2EE and C/C++ would be very helpful in understanding the sample code provided in this book. The book is intended for a wide variety of IT-related people, including architects, developers and programmers, technical managers, and project managers.

The book contains a fair amount of detail on the software and tools commercially available for use in the enterprise integrations. Most of the tools and software described in this book naturally are IBM tools and software. This is for two reasons: First, the author is most familiar with IBM tools. Second, in the author's opinion, IBM tools and software are usually the best tools and software available in the market.

Acknowledgments

The author acknowledges Professor William F. Saam of Ohio State University for his support and encouragement throughout his career. It was due to the urging of Professor Saam that the author work in the field of IT that this book has become possible.

The origin of this book lies in a series of papers the author wrote for IBM's DeveloperWorks website. These papers explained, in a brief manner, the evolution of the services-based integration patterns. Part of the reason these papers were well received and won several awards was due to the excellent editing by the DeveloperWorks editors Patrick Flanders and Ashleigh Brothers. The work by these two editors helped crystallize many of the ideas presented in this book.

The person most directly related to make the idea of this book into a reality is Wendy Rinaldi, an editorial director at McGraw-Hill. She pushed the idea of this book internally at McGraw-Hill and kept the project on track throughout the writing, editing, and production of the book. Thanks are also due to Joya Anthony for assisting Wendy in gathering various materials for the book.

The person who is most directly related to the technical material of this book is Timothy (Tim) Frommeyer. Tim was the technical editor for this book. He ensured the material in the book was accurate, and he made numerous suggestions for improving the book's material. Many of his suggestions have been incorporated into the book.

Acknowledgements are also due to the production staff, including Anupriya Tyagi and Bart Reed. Anupriya acted as the project manger for the book's production while Bart corrected the English as well as the presentation style. Because of the corrections made by these two people, the book has been rendered more readable.

Lastly, thanks are due to Ray Harishankar, who wrote the foreword for this book. Ray Harishankar is an IBM Fellow. The author thanks Ray for taking time from his busy schedule to read the material of the book and then to write the foreword. In addition, the author is thankful to Sue Miller-Sylvia and Sandra (Sandy) Carter for reviewing some of the book's material and writing the endorsements.

Introduction

Introduction to the Book

A fair number of books that discuss Service-Oriented Architecture (SOA) are currently available on the market. So the logical question to ask is, Why there is a need for another book on SOA? The reason for writing this book is that the books currently on the shelves do not cover a number of very important aspects of enterprise integration, which are described in the following list:

- Although enterprise integration and SOA are very intimately connected, a typical, currently available book does not presents a unified view of SOA-based patterns of integration. There are books that describe older patterns of integration. Separately, there are books that attempt to describe SOA. Some of these SOA books mostly describe how to develop Web Services by building new applications and ignore existing or legacy applications. Other books on SOA are too theoretical and therefore are of little help in building a SOA-based integrated structure. In other words, these books have lots of text and pictures but provide little practical guidance and code on how to build SOA.

- Presently, no book is available that describes the rationale for choosing the SOA-based integration method over other integration methods in an easy-to-understand, step-by-step manner.

- Legacy mainframe applications form the backbone of the IT systems of most large enterprises, including insurance companies, banks, airlines, governments, and so on. For such organizations, these mainframe applications perform all the mission-critical work. Examples include applications based on CICS and IMS transaction management systems. Currently, no book is available that describes how to integrate these mainframe applications using SOA.

- Enterprise Service Bus is an important element of SOA-based enterprise integration, through which applications communicate with each other in a scalable manner so that a large number of applications can be integrated. At present, books available on SOA do not describe Enterprise Service Bus in enough detail to be of practical value.

- Packaged applications are a common occurrence in large enterprises. Examples of such applications include Enterprise Resource Planning (ERP) and Customer Relationship Management (CRM) from vendors such as SAP, Oracle, Siebel, and PeopleSoft. Currently, no book explicitly addresses the problem of integrating these packaged applications with the other applications in an enterprise.

Book Objectives

The primary purpose of this book is to explain SOA-based applications integration in a large enterprise in an easy-to-understand manner. For this purpose, a practical approach is employed, starting with the most simple integration patterns and introducing the various concepts of SOA-based integration in a step-by-step manner.

The second objective of the book is to clarify the relationship of SOA with other integration technologies and patterns for distributed computing systems. As previously mentioned, SOA is very closely intertwined with integration technologies. In particular, for the first time, by tracing the evolution of integration patterns, we show that SOA is mostly an integration technique that is built on and embraces many of the other integration technologies for distributed computing systems. Some of the distributed computing technologies we discuss in relation to SOA are socket programming, remote procedure call (RPC), Object Request Broker (ORB), and asynchronous messaging. We show how these technologies have contributed to the various concepts involved in SOA-based integration. In this regard, we discuss the evolution of the following concepts: loose coupling, code reuse, layering, service providers, service consumers, language and platform independence, language independent interface, discovery of remote services, invocation of remote synchronous and asynchronous services, and more.

Another distinguishing feature of this book is that it is heavy on substance so that the material presented can actually be used to build an integrated system of applications. For this purpose, the book contains extensive examples of computer code for each integration technique we discuss. The examples start with simple file-based data sharing among applications and end with computer code for Web Services.

Many books on SOA discuss Enterprise Service Bus (ESB), because it is considered part of SOA. However, almost all of the descriptions of ESB in these books is very high level and is of little use to technical persons, including IT architects, technical managers, and software developers. This book provides a much more detailed description of the Enterprise Service Bus. Developers, technologists, and technical managers will find our description of the ESB much more useful in their day-to-day work. Our description of ESB includes an explanation of various functional and nonfunctional capabilities supported by an ESB, various types of ESBs, various components of the ESB, and a discussion of deployment issues.

As mentioned previously, mainframe applications form the backbone of most large organizations. However, currently it is difficult to find any book that deals with the subject of integrating these applications with the rest of the enterprise in an explicit manner. A major aim of this book is to provide explicit descriptions of the various options available for integrating mainframe applications with the remaining applications in an enterprise. A large part of this book is devoted to these types of applications. In a similar manner, we explicitly discuss the integration of packaged applications from vendors such as SAP, Siebel, Oracle, and PeopleSoft.

Intended Audience

The material in this book broadly covers the integration of a large enterprise and SOA, and therefore would be of interest to a broad range of IT professionals. This book provides the following three major benefits to the reader:

- No prior knowledge of SOA is assumed.
- No prior knowledge of applications integration issues is required.
- All the concepts and features are introduced and explained in an easy-to-understand, step-by-step manner.

Here's a list of some of the professionals who will benefit greatly from reading this book:

- Enterprise architects
- Enterprise developers/engineers/practitioners
- Integration architects
- Integration developers/engineers/practitioners
- Application architects
- Application developers/engineers/practitioners
- Technical managers
- Project managers

Organization of the Book

The book is organized into six sections. Each of these sections contains multiple chapters. The last section has the references followed by the glossary. Each section of the book deals with one subject matter. Following are brief descriptions of contents of the various sections of the book and the chapters that they contain.

Part I: Introduction

This section contains two chapters.

Chapter 1: Introduction to the Book   This chapter provides a brief description of the reasons for writing this book and as well points out the distinguishing features of the book. In addition, this chapter provides a summary of the various sections of the book.

Chapter 2: Basic Concepts and Overview   The second chapter of Part I provides an overview of SOA-based enterprise integration. In this chapter, we describe the various terms and concepts used in the book. These terms and concepts include service, distributed computing, integration, enterprise, enterprise software, loose coupling and code reuse, as well as service provider and service consumer. We also provide brief descriptions of all the technologies of distributed computing that contribute to and are embraced by SOA. In addition, we point out the evolutionary contributions to SOA made by different programming languages.

Part II: Evolution of SOA-Based Integration

In this section of the book, we trace the evolution of the various concepts that are basic to the SOA-based integration approach by studying some of the technologies that preceded SOA but are now part of SOA.

Chapter 3: Sockets and Data Sharing   In this chapter, we study the various methods of data sharing between applications. These methods include data sharing through reading and writing to a file system, data sharing through a common database, and real-time data sharing through sockets. Sockets in particular introduced the idea of real-time connectivity between applications, which is fundamental to the working of almost all technologies that constitute SOA-based integration. However, raw sockets themselves do not allow functionality sharing between applications.

Chapter 4: Remote Procedure Call (RPC)   In Chapter 4, we describe the remote procedure call (RPC). RPC was an important step in the progress toward enterprise integration because it allowed, for the first time, functionality sharing between applications and specified all the basic steps for the sharing of functionality. In addition, RPC introduced the following new concepts and features:

- The concept of interface declaration through the use of a specification file. The RPC specification file may be considered the "first step" in the development of the services interface in today's world, such as a WSDL file.

- The concept of a service provider application (called the *server)* and the concept of a service consumer application (called the *client)*. The server provides the implementation of one or more functions that can be used or invoked by the client application.

- The concept of the marshalling of arguments for transmission over the network. This refers to the packaging of arguments into one or more messages to be transmitted over the network.

- The encapsulation of all system- and network-related functionality in a library. This encapsulation led to future systems in which this functionality was separated out as a program of its own for the purpose of code reuse.

- The introduction of client and server stubs that shield the programmer from the system and network calls.

- The concept of platform independence via the use of external data representation (XDR), which encodes the data in a machine-independent form.

Chapter 5: Object Request Broker (ORB)   In Chapter 5, we describe the Object Request Broker (ORB) technologies that form the backbone for all modern application servers, such as WebSphere Application Server and JBoss Application Server. In this chapter we start by moving away from procedural languages such as C and Fortran and into the realm of object-oriented programming using computer languages such as C++ and Java. We generalize the concepts of objects in object-oriented programming to distributed objects in which case the objects can reside on different computers connected by a network. Furthermore, we describe the CORBA method, which allows remote objects to interact with one another.

In Chapter 5 we take a big step forward in application integration, by encapsulating the code for parameter marshalling and unmarshalling and the code for networking into a separate software component (or application). We call this component the Object Request Broker (ORB). This remediates the problem of the lack of code reuse in the case of RPC. Various implementations of ORB form the backbone of all the modern commercial application servers, which are needed to support distributed objects. In addition, ORB allows us to move away from point-to-point integration, which is important if a large number of applications need to be integrated. Also, this move away from point-to-point integration leads to the concept of Enterprise Service Bus (ESB), as discussed in later chapters.

In addition, ORB introduces the concept of language independence by the use of an interface definition language (IDL). The interfaces declared through IDL can be mapped to any programming language and can allow, in principle, the client and server to be implemented in two different languages. Another important concept introduced in this chapter is that of a *registry,* which is used by the server objects to register themselves so that they can be located by the client.

Chapter 6: Asynchronous Messaging   This chapter deals with asynchronous messaging, where the sender sends a message but does not wait for a response from the receiving end to continue its work. This increases the scalability of the solution of applications integration in an enterprise, which makes this method of applications integration very desirable when large volumes of messages are involved.

Asynchronous messaging also separates out the code for marshalling and unmarshalling as well as the networking code as a separate application, thus resulting in code reuse because the same communication code can be used by many different applications for communicating among them. Asynchronous messaging also results in loose coupling because the interaction between applications is indirect through message queues.

Another important advantage of messaging is that this method of communication between applications is much more reliable than either the RPC method or the Distributed Objects method of sharing data and functionality. This reliability is achieved by persisting the data being exchanged on both sides of the network. In other words, the data being exchanged is saved on the disks of the two computers involved in the exchange.

As discussed in a later chapter, we can add a few components to the messaging system to turn it into a messaging bus, which is also known as an *Enterprise Service Bus (ESB).* The most notable component that needs to be added to a messaging system for converting it into an ESB is the *router* or a *message broker.* The main function of the message broker is to route the message based on the message content or message context. In this way, a further decoupling between the sending and receiving applications is achieved because the sending application does not need to know the address of the final destination. An ESB based on a messaging system provides a much more scalable solution than an ESB based on an application server.

Part III: SOA-Based Integration

In this section we discuss the technologies that are more commonly known as SOA-based integration technologies. These technologies were mainly the result of the realization that the technologies discussed in

Part II lead to the problem of technological heterogeneity in large enterprises. This problem refers to the fact that, in a large enterprise or an inter-enterprise system consisting of an enterprise and its partners, one usually finds more than one technology used to integrate applications, and it is literally impossible to impose enterprisewide standards in this respect.

Generally, a number of different kinds of technological heterogeneity exist in a large enterprise, including the following:

- **Middleware heterogeneity**   Generally in a large enterprise, more than one type of middleware is being used. The two most common types are application servers and message-oriented middleware (MOM). In addition there is brand heterogeneity, which requires support for different brands of application servers and MOMs.

- **Protocol heterogeneity**   This heterogeneity refers to the different transport protocols being used to access the services offered by various applications. Examples of such protocols include IIOP, JRMP, HTTP, and HTTPS. Related to the heterogeneity of communication protocols is the problem that different applications want to communicate with each other using incompatible protocols. For example, Application A might want to communicate with Application B using HTTP. However, for Application B the suitable protocol might be IIOP. In such cases, protocol transformation is needed so that Application A can communicate with Application B.

- **Synchrony heterogeneity**   There is almost always a need to support both synchronous and asynchronous interactions between applications. In addition, there is sometimes a need for callback methods as well as publish and subscribe. Therefore, many times a situation arises in which the types of interaction supported by the two applications that wish to interact do not match. Hence, these applications cannot interact with one another.

- **Diversity of data formats**   Sometimes the data format being exchanged varies. Most of the time the data is dependent on the middleware being used. This diversity of data can cause a problem if two applications that wish to interact support different data formats.

- **Diversity of interface declarations**   Sometimes there are large differences in the way service interfaces are declared and used to invoke a service. For example, the way interfaces are declared in CORBA and Java RMI are different.

- **No common place for service lookup**   Sometimes there's no common place to look up services to deal with the diversity of services in a large enterprise.

Another common problem is that as soon as a new version of provider software becomes available, the consumer applications must be modified to account for the change in the provider application. The solution to this problem requires that methods be found that allow the services to be extended (for example, by adding more parameters) without breaking the previous versions of the consumer application.

This diversity and extendibility have been partly dealt with by developing standards and partly by further technological development. We provide an overview of these standards in Chapter 7. The further development in technology is discussed next in Chapter 8.

Chapter 7: Web Services   In Chapter 7 we provide an overview of the various standards that have been developed to partly deal with heterogeneity problems. These standards are composed of a collection of specifications, rules, and guidelines formulated and accepted by the leading market participants and are independent of implementation details. Some of the standards we review are

- **XML**   XML is a common data communication language that is independent of different middleware technologies.

- **SOAP**   SOAP defines a common format for messages between applications.

- **WSDL**   WSDL is language- and platform-independent standard that defines the interface for a service offered by a given application.

- **UDDI**   UDDI provides a common way to publish and discover a service.

All these standards are further explained in Chapters 11–15.

Chapter 8: Enterprise Service Bus   In this chapter we deal with the remaining heterogeneity problems as well as provide a scalable applications-integration solution in terms of the number of applications. The two most important remaining heterogeneity problems we discuss in this chapter are

- **Communication protocol mismatch**   This problem refers cases where the service consumer is set up to use one communication protocol while the proper communication protocol for the service provider is another protocol.

- **Data or message format mismatch**   This problem relates to situations where the message or data format required by the service provider is different from the format used for data/messages employed by the service consumer.

The solution to these two (and other) heterogeneity problems is the Enterprise Service Bus (ESB), which provides a large number of facilities and functionalities, including protocol transformation and data/message transformation. We discuss the functionalities provided by the Enterprise Service Bus in much more detail than can be found in any other book. These details include Quality of Service (QoS) and location transparency. Location transparency means that the service consumer does not need to know who the service provider is or where they are located. Similarly, the service provider does not need to know where the service request is coming from.

In addition to a detailed discussion of the various functionalities offered by the ESB, we show how it provides a much more scalable solution in terms of the number and kinds of applications being integrated. We also discuss the structure and the various components essential for an ESB to work. Furthermore, we discuss the various ESB deployment patterns and the various kinds of ESBs available in the market. We compare and contrast three kinds of ESBs, which are based, respectively, on the application server technology, the messaging system technology, and the hardware. Additionally, we provide practical examples involving the use of ESBs for integrating applications in a large enterprise.

Part IV: Integrating Existing Applications

In this part of the book we describe how to integrate existing applications. These existing applications fall into two categories: applications that run on the mainframe and packaged applications (such ERP and CRM applications) from various software providers, including SAP, Oracle, PeopleSoft, and JD Edwards. Integration of mainframe applications is discussed in Chapter 9, whereas integration of package applications is discussed in Chapter 10.

Chapter 9: Integrating Mainframe Applications   We start this chapter by describing the two major types of mainframe applications, including the reasons why these applications are so important in most large enterprises. The two types of mainframe applications we discuss are applications based on CICS and IMS transaction management. For each of these applications types, we describe four different methods of integration using a point-to-point integration approach. We also provide an easy-to-read tabular comparison of the four approaches because none of the four integration approaches is suitable in every situation. For each integration approach, we discuss a large number of factors that must be considered when choosing a given approach. Some of the factors discussed for each integration approach include the work required, technology constraints, real-time access, guaranteed delivery of messages, operating system requirements, additional hardware requirements, security, and tools required. In addition to the point-to-point integration approaches, we describe approaches based on the different types of ESBs. These ESB-based approaches are suitable when the mainframe applications are to be integrated with a large number of other applications in the enterprise. We also provide an easy-to-read tabular comparison of the integration approaches based on the different types of ESBs.

Chapter 10: Integrating Packaged Applications   In this chapter, we describe the integration of package applications, sometimes referred to as *enterprise information systems (EISs)*, with other application types in the enterprise. We focus on the use of adapters, which can be used along with brokers (application servers or ESBs), to integrate these types of applications. We start out with the general description of the adapters and then we discuss the J2EE Connector Architecture (JCA), which reduces the number of different adapters needed for a given package application. Compliance of both the broker and the adapter with the JCA specification greatly simplifies the integration of packaged applications.

Next, we illustrate the use of adapters for integration by considering a specific package application system, namely SAP. For this we first discuss the SAP application and the various interfaces used to connect to the application. Then we describe the WebSphere adapter for SAP applications, which provides a very compressive way to access the functionality and data embedded in an SAP application.

Lastly, we discuss how to indirectly expose the functionality and data pertaining to a package application as a Web Service. This indirect method involves first integrating the package application with J2EE/Java components in an application server via the use of an adapter. Then the Java/J2EE component is exposed as a Web Service using the methods described in Chapter 15.

Part V: Understanding and Developing Web Services

In this part of the book we take a detailed look at what Web Services are and how they are developed. In particular, we discuss in detail the four standards that are typically known as the Web Services, namely XML, SOAP, WSDL, and UDDI. We also describe methods for developing Java/J2EE-based Web Services and how services can be composed using BPEL.

Chapter 11: XML   XML is a standard data description language that can be used for exchanging messages between the service provider and the service consumer. XML is middleware as well as programming language independent. In this chapter we describe the concepts and techniques for XML use that are important in implementing Web Services and their clients. We start with an overview of the XML language. This overview subsection includes the basic concepts as well as a description of the basic structure of an XML document. Next, we discuss namespaces, which are used to avoid the collision of names in different spaces and to extend the use of the vocabulary defined in one specific domain to other domains. Schemas, which define the structure and grammar for a particular type of XML document, are discussed next. Finally, we describe the various models used for parsing, processing, creating, and editing an XML document.

Chapter 12: SOAP   Simple Object Access Protocol (SOAP) is an XML-based messaging specification. It describes a message format and a set of serialization rules for data types, including structured types and arrays. This XML-based information can be used for exchanging structured and typed information between peers in a decentralized, distributed environment. In addition, SOAP describes the ways in which SOAP messages may be transported in various usage scenarios. In particular, it describes how to use the Hypertext Transfer Protocol (HTTP) as a transport for such messages. SOAP messages are essentially service requests sent to some endpoint on a network. The endpoint may be implemented in a number of different ways. In this chapter, we describe in detail the structure of a SOAP message, SOAP attributes, and the associated processing model and its binding with HTTP.

Chapter 13: WSDL   In order for a service consumer (application) to use the service provided by a service provider application, a formal description of the service is required that contains the description of the interface exposed by the service and information on where that service can be found on the network. Such a formal specification is provided by the Web Services Description Language (WSDL). A WSDL document is an XML-based document that describes a formal contract between the service provider and the service consumer.

A WSDL document describes two aspects of a service: the abstract interface exposed by the service, and the description of the concrete implementation. The abstract interface describes the general interface structure, which includes the operations (that is, methods) included in the service, the operations parameters, and the abstract data types. This description of the interface does not depend in any way on a concrete implementation, such as a concrete network address, concrete data structures, and the communication protocol. An abstract interface can have many corresponding implementations, giving the service consumer an implementation choice and allowing it to pick the implementation that best suits its technical capabilities. The concrete implementation description binds the abstract interface description to a concrete network address, communication protocol, and concrete data structures. The concrete implementation description is used to bind to the service and invoke its various operations (methods).

In this chapter, we provide an overview of the WSDL document by considering the simple example of a weather service. Then we describe in more detail the general structure of the WSDL document, including the parts of a WSDL document that correspond to the abstract interface and the parts that correspond to the concrete implementation. We also provide a description of the logical relationships among the different elements of the WSDL document as well as provide a description of some of the SOAP extensibility elements.

Chapter 14: UDDI and Registry Concepts In addition to the WSDL description of a service and the SOAP message format, a central place is needed where the service provider can advertise the services they offer and the service consumers can find the services they require. Such a central place is called a *service registry*. The Universal Description, Discovery, and Integration (UDDI) specification defines a standard way for the registering, deregistering, and looking up of Web Services. First, a service provider registers a service with the UDDI Registry. Then the service provider looks up the service in the UDDI registry. Lastly, the service consumer binds to the service provider and uses the service.

In this chapter, we describe in detail the basic data model of a UDDI registry. This basic model consists of five entities: businessEntity, businessService, bindingTemplate, publisherAssertion, and tModel. A businessEntity is used to store information about a service provider, such as its name and address. Nontechnical information about a service is stored in the businessService structure. Technical information related to a service and its endpoint is stored in the bindingTemplate entity. Perhaps the most important entity is the tModel, which serves the dual purpose of providing the technical fingerprint of a service and an abstract namespace. In this chapter, you will learn how to store categorization and identification information in a tModel using categoryBags and identifierBags. In addition, you will learn how to author or partition a WSDL document related to a service so that it can be easily referenced in a bindingTemplate and in a tModel. Finally, we briefly discuss the two APIs offered by the UDDI specification for publishing and inquiring about an exiting service.

Chapter 15: Web Services Implementation In this chapter we address the core subject of Part V of the book, which is how to develop new Web Services. We describe two approaches for the development of new Web Services in the Java/J2EE environment. The first approach is the top-down approach, which is the recommended approach. In this approach, a WSDL document is either constructed or acquired first. Then automated tools are used to create skeleton code both for the server side and the client side. The server code is then completed according to the given requirements. The second approach is the bottom-up approach of developing Web Services. In the bottom-up approach, either a Java class or Enterprise Java Bean (EJB) is developed first and then automated tools are used to expose the class or EJB as a Web Service. The automated tools also generate the required WSDL document, which is used to generate the service clients through the use of automated tools. Because all the messages in the Web Services are exchanged through SOAP messages, we start this chapter with a discussion of the two major choices for a SOAP engine, which is simply a framework for constructing SOAP processors such as clients, servers, and gateways.

Chapter 16: Integration Through Service Composition (BPEL) Web Services clients' construction is suitable if the interaction of the client application with the service provider is isolated and simple. Such activities are simple and stateless. However, in many scenarios the interaction of the services' clients with the service providers is not so simple. Such is the case of business processes. A business process is a collection of related, structured activities. Such complex structured activities require a stateful environment for the invocation of a chain of Web Services. BPEL (Business Process Execution Language) is a language to describe such long running, stateful interactions. We describe BPEL in some detail in Chapter 16.

In Chapter 16, we start by providing a brief overview of BPEL. The overview is followed by a detailed description of the various elements and structure of BPEL. Then we describe a practical example of a business process to demonstrate how various elements are used together. The last section of this chapter summarizes the contents of the chapter.

Part VI: Appendixes

This section contains the references and the glossary of terms used in the book.

Conclusion

In this chapter we described the rationale for writing this book by pointing out some of the gaps in the existing books on the market and describing how this book covers those gaps. We also identified the people who would be interested in the subject of this book, which would include practically anyone who is interested in enterprise integration through the use of services. We pointed out that no prior knowledge of either SOA or applications integration is required. This chapter ends with brief summaries of each of the 16 chapters of this book.

Chapter 2

Overview and Basic Concepts

We start this chapter with a brief history of the evolution of the idea of service in software and the associated Service-Oriented Architecture (SOA). Whereas the development of various programming styles has contributed only indirectly to the development of the idea of service in software, the major contribution to the present notion of service in software has come from distributed computing. It is important to note that distributed computing almost always requires a computer network.

Next, we outline the business case for the use of services-based integration. In other words, we explain why it is important for large enterprises to use this method of integration. We go on to provide brief descriptions of some terms that are commonly used in this book. These concrete definitions will help to avoid confusion later in the book. Finally, we explain some key concepts, including loose coupling, reusability, and interface and payload semantics.

Services in Software

The word *service* ordinarily refers to one person performing some work or task for somebody else. A slightly more general definition of service is a person or an organization performing some work for another person or organization. A common example is the U.S. Post Office, which delivers letters or mail on behalf of some person or organization.

So the question to ask is, What are the advantages of a service? In the case of a letter being delivered by the post office, it is easy to see that it saves time, money, and effort for the person needing the letter to be delivered. What's more, in the absence of the service provided by the post office, the task of delivering the letter may never be completed because the person needing the service may not have the resources to take the letter to its destination and deliver it. Furthermore, it is also easily concluded that because the post office specializes in the task of delivering letters and mail, it does so in a very efficient manner making the whole system—including the post office organization itself as well as the people and organizations using the mailing service—very efficient and cost effective. This efficiency and cost effectiveness are the result of the reusability of the mail-delivery service offered by the post office. *Reusability* means that the same service can be used by many different persons and organizations. Another advantage of the U.S. postal service is that very loose coupling exists between the service requester and the service provider. In other words, how the post office delivers the letter or package is transparent to the service requester. The post office is free to change the implementation of the service—that is, the post office can change the means by which the letter or package is delivered without the service requester ever knowing about the change.

The notions of reusability and service in the software field are similar to their meanings in real life. In the case of software, the current simplest definition of *service* is one application or computer program performing some work for another application or computer program. This work may include some functionality or data sharing. Most frequently, the applications run in a distributed manner, which means that the service provider application and the service consumer application run on different computers or machines connected by a network. Sometimes these two applications may run on the same machine. However, when the consumer and server applications are running on the same machine, the method that the two applications use to communicate is the same as (or similar to) the method employed if the two applications were distributed across a network. This idea of service in software has evolved over several decades. The major contribution to this evolution has naturally come from distributed computing, but progress in programming languages has also contributed indirectly.

Before the advent of procedural languages such as FORTRAN, C, COBOL, and BASIC, there were sequential languages. These languages offered no reuse at all because they were designed to process instructions in sequence. Thus, if a set of code had to be executed in the program a number of times, the programmer had to type in that code that many times at the right places within the program's code. This was a very inefficient and somewhat risky method of coding because it made the code difficult to maintain. If a certain change needed to be made to the code repeatedly, it had to be made in all the places where the code appeared. This method of programming was also inefficient in the use of computer memory because the repeating code had to be stored a number of times in the address space of the computer's memory.

With the advent of the procedural languages such as FORTRAN, C, COBOL, and BASIC, the most rudimentary form of service notion took hold. The code that needed to be repeated was separated out as a simple procedure, such as a method, function, or subroutine. This method/function/subroutine could then be called by the computer code at different places to perform some "service" for the calling code. This increased the reusability of this portion of the code. Furthermore, the code could be easily maintained because the changes needed to be made only in one place instead of in several different places. It also increased the execution efficiency because the repeatable code exists only in one place in the address space of the computer's memory. An equally important benefit of this separation of repeating code in a method/function/subroutine was that the repeating code became more accurate because it was tested over and over when called by the different portions of the computer program.

After the procedural languages came object-oriented languages such as C++ and Java. Such programming languages introduced the concept of *classes,* which are encapsulated behavior and data. These classes can be used anywhere in the program. Because all the code is encapsulated in classes, which can be used anywhere in the program code, code reuse increased quite substantially.

Although the introduction of procedural and object-oriented languages increased the reuse of code, the reuse was limited to individual computer programs or executables. In other words, the procedure (meaning the method, function, or subroutine) could not be used outside of the program that contained it. Because, as you will see in this book, services and Service-Oriented Architecture are mostly about application integrations—which require the sharing of functionality and data across applications or computer programs—these developments in programming languages did not directly contribute to the development of services and SOA as they are known today. Instead, the major and the most fundamental contribution to the development of the idea of a service and SOA came from distributed computing, which requires interapplication communications.

Distributed computing started with the development of socket programming, which allowed applications to establish live connections and share data in real time. This establishment of connectivity through sockets was fundamental to the development of the idea of services and SOA. Because most, if not all, of the further development in services and SOA came on the top of sockets, it is hard to imagine that the current ideas of services and SOA would have evolved without the advent of sockets.

Sockets only allowed data sharing—they did not allow functionality sharing directly. Therefore, further developments were needed to allow applications to share functionality. This development came in the form of remote procedure call (RPC), which is also known as client/server programming. RPC is built on top of sockets and hides the low-level network programming that is required from the developer or programmer. In addition, concerning the sharing of functionality between applications, RPC also introduced a rudimentary way of declaring a service interface and the idea of platform independence through the use of XDR (see Chapter 4 for a description of XDR).

After RPC came the Object Request Broker (ORB) technology, which introduced object-oriented programming ideas into the realm of distributed computing. In particular, ORB technology extended the idea of objects in object-oriented programming to remote objects, where the objects can reside in different applications running on different computers. ORB technology provided for these remote objects to communicate with each other. These remote objects were able to share functionality and data in much the same way as applications were able to share functionality and data in the case of RPC. The most well-known examples of ORB technologies are CORBA and Java RMI. CORBA, in particular, introduced a number of new ideas related to services and SOA, such as a language-independent service interface, the initial concept of a registry, and the separating into different applications of network-related functionality and the code for marshalling and unmarshalling, which enormously improved code reuse because the same code could be used by a number of different applications. Most of the current application servers, such as WebSphere Application Server and JBoss, are based on the ORB technology.

In parallel with the development of ORB technology, asynchronous messaging was also developed. This technology also relied on sockets in the background but provided some advantages in terms of the scalability of application integration. This scalability primarily resulted from the asynchronous nature of the messaging, which allowed sending applications to continue their work without waiting for a response from the receiving application. What's more, this method of exchanging messages between applications used queues for sending and receiving messages. This indirect method of exchanging messages provided loose coupling between the sending and receiving applications. Yet another advantage is that the delivery of messages can be guaranteed by persisting them on both side of the network. Furthermore, synchronous messaging can be simulated by using correlation IDs to compare the request message to the response message. A closely related development was the development of message routers/brokers, which can route messages based on their content or context.

Then came Web Services, which introduced standards in order to reduce the heterogeneity caused by the use of multiple technologies (such as RPC, ORBs, and messaging). Specifically, they introduced a standard, middleware-independent data format called the Extensible Markup Language, or simply XML. In addition, the previous services interface definitions were refined by introduction of WSDL (Web Services Description Language), which allowed the services interface to be declared in a language-, platform-, and middleware-independent form. Similarly, the previous ideas of service registry were refined by the introduction of Universal Description, Discovery, and Integration (UDDI) interface. Finally, a standard format for message exchange was introduced in the form of SOAP.

In many cases, it was soon discovered that Web Services alone were not enough to deal with all the heterogeneity problems. In particular, Web Services were not able to handle the situation of a communication protocol mismatch between the service provider and the service consumer. Similarly, Web Services were unable to provide a satisfactory solution for a mismatch of the data/message format between the service provider and service consumer. Enterprise Service Bus (ESB) came to the rescue. An ESB provides many functions, including protocol and message transformation, message routing based on content and context, location transparency, Quality of Service (QoS), data enrichment, and other functions. We will discuss these functions in detail in Chapter 8.

In addition to Web Services, which employ new applications and the Enterprise Service Bus, SOA must provide a means of integrating existing applications (such as legacy mainframe applications and package applications) in order to offer a complete integration solution for an enterprise. Many times this requires wrapping existing applications into Web Services or using adapters, which allow these existing applications to communicate with other, more modern applications. We discuss in detail the integration of mainframe and packaged applications in Chapters 9 and 10 of this book.

Web Services standards are discussed in detail in Chapters 11–14, whereas the creation of new Web Services is described in Chapter 15.

To conclude this section, refer to Figure 2.1 for a summary of the development of services and SOA. This figure shows the contributions made by different distributed technologies to the development of SOA. It also shows the many earlier technologies SOA has embraced, starting from sockets.

Business Problem Addressed by SOA

SOA addresses a very common and specific business problem. In the past, business requirements did not change very fast. The product line offered by a company and the methods of marketing and selling those products were fixed. Therefore, IT requirements were also more or less fixed.

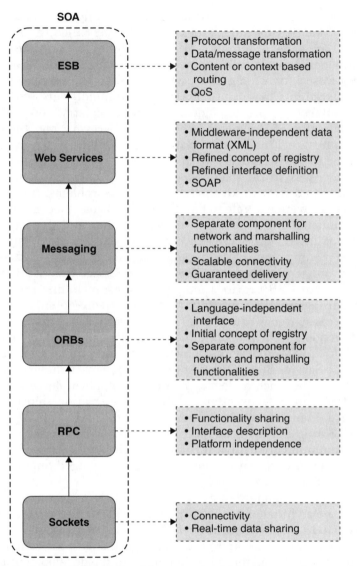

Figure 2.1 Evolution of services-based integration and SOA. The contributions of various distributed technologies are shown in yellow boxes.

However, in the 1990s this situation changed. The lifetime of a product became shorter and the organization started to change very quickly. There are five main reasons for these changes:

■ **Mergers** This refers to two or more companies or organizations joining to form a single, new company.

- **Acquisitions**   This refers to a company increasing its size substantially by buying or acquiring another company.

- **Changing market conditions**   In particular, this involves the fast introduction of new products and the repackaging of existing products in order to survive in a highly competitive market.

- **New technological advances**   Advances such as the Internet and voice response systems provided new opportunities for marketing, sales, and procurements.

- **The nature of business relationships**   A large organization typically has many relationships with external business entities such as business partners and suppliers. These relationships are fluid in nature and frequently change.

These fast-changing business conditions meant that the requirements for the IT systems that supported these business operations also started to change very quickly. In the past, applications were developed to address a specific business need. This required developers to make assumptions related to the problem being solved, the data being used, and the hardware on which the software was supposed to run. New problems required the development of new programs. However, the fast-changing IT requirements meant that the old methods of developing and deploying software systems were no longer sufficient due to the difficulty in developing a large number of computer programs in a short period of time. A new approach was needed to provide flexible, agile IT systems that could meet the fast-changing business needs of the time.

As an answer to this problem, SOA emphasizes agile IT systems through the use of reusable components. In this architecture, computer programs or components are not developed to solve a specific business problem. Instead, they provide some generic functionality. Then, these components can be threaded, linked, or integrated in a specific order or configuration to meet a specific business need. If the business requirement changes, there's no need to develop a new computer program. Instead, the system can be reconfigured to meet the new business requirement.

This is illustrated in Figures 2.2 and 2.3. Figure 2.2 shows a particular configuration of reusable software components that meets a specific

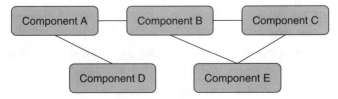

Figure 2.2   A loosely coupled arrangement of reusable components

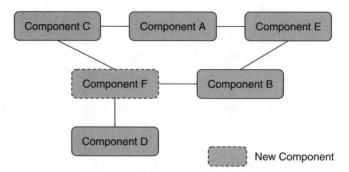

Figure 2.3   A reconfiguration of reusable components for changing requirements

business need for a given time period. Figure 2.3 shows that the same components can be reused in a different configuration to meet the changing business needs. Perhaps an analogy will help to make this point clear. In this analogy, the old approach of developing a new application whenever the business requirements change corresponds to neon sign technology, which can advertise only a fixed commercial product. If the product changes, the old neon sign must be discarded and a new neon sign designed and built. On the other hand, the new SOA approach can be compared to a changeable letter board, which employs reusable letters. These letters can be configured to advertise one product today, and if the product changes tomorrow, the letters can be easily rearranged to advertise the new product.

This analogy also helps to explain another important aspect of SOA: reusability. This aspect relates to the concept of loose coupling. Using the preceding example, notice that we cannot reuse the letters in the neon sign technology because they are strongly linked or coupled. In other words, we cannot easily separate the letters in a neon sign. On the other hand, in the case of the changeable letter board, there is very little (or "loose") coupling between the letters. That is the reason we can separate the letters easily and then reconfigure them to meet changing requirements on a short notice.

In addition to providing agility to IT systems to meet changing business needs, reusable components offer the following advantages:

- They save development and testing time and resources because few, if any, new components need to be developed if the requirements change.
- They provide more consistent functionality and data to the internal and external consumers by eliminating redundant code.
- The code is easy to maintain because changes can be localized to one place in a component.

- The code is well tested because it is used many times in different arrangements and situations.

Definitions

A number of terms are important in discussing the subjects of services and SOA. However, some variations in the use of these terms exist. In other words, these terms have been used with slightly different meanings in the past. Therefore, in order to avoid confusion, this section provides concrete definitions of these important terms to give you a more consistent picture of services and SOA. The second reason for discussing these terms this early in the book is that you might not be familiar with these terms. If this is the case, you will find these descriptions helpful as a way of introduction to the ideas these terms represent. We'll start with the most simple of these terms (but still very important): application.

Application

The term *application* has different meanings in different contexts. Some define an application as a single computer program, which means a single executable. Others define an application as a collection of more than one computer program that work together to provide some functionality. Such is the case for many Internet-based applications. However, in this book we will use the term in the more restricted sense to mean only a single executable or computer program. This will help avoid any confusion concerning its usage.

Distributed Computing

By *distributed computing*, we always mean more than one application (or executable). These programs or applications typically run on separate hardware or machines, but they work together to achieve some function. The different applications running on different computers use some method of communicating among themselves over a computer network. Some of these communication methods include sockets, RPC, ORBs, and asynchronous messaging. We will discuss these methods of communication in detail later in this book.

Enterprise

Among other definitions, the Merriam-Webster online dictionary provides two meanings of *enterprise* that are relevant for our discussion. The first is "a business entity," and the second is "a project or undertaking that is especially difficult, complicated, or risky." These two definitions taken together give a good sense of the entities we are interested in. To be more specific, by *enterprise* we mean any large and complex organization that has an equally large and complex IT system. The large organization comes in many different forms:

- **Large businesses or commercial organizations**   Prime examples of such organizations are IBM, General Electric, and large financial institutions such as banks. Each of these organizations has multiple lines of business, which makes their organization and the supporting IT systems very complex. For example, here are some of the lines of business for IBM:
  - Hardware (including mainframe and midrange servers)
  - Software (including all the WebSphere, System z, and Tivoli products)
  - Global business services (which provide IT consulting services)

  Some of the lines of business for General Electric are listed next:
  - GE Aircraft Engines (makes and sells engines for aircrafts)
  - GE Home Appliances (makes and sells appliances such as washers, dryers, refrigerators, and so on)
  - GE Medical (makes and sells medical equipment such as X-ray and MRI machines)
  - GE Financial Services (provides financial products such as departmental credit cards)
  - GE Lighting (sells light bulbs and other lighting products)

  Similarly, a large bank might offer the following lines of business:
  - Retail banking (including checking and saving accounts)
  - Mortgages
  - Other loans (such as loans for buying cars, appliances, and so on)
  - Individual retirement accounts
  - Investment accounts
  - Credit cards
- **Departments of the federal government**   These include the Department of Defense, Department of Energy, Department of Commerce, and so on. In the same category are the departments run by the various state (or provincial) government agencies. In addition, city governments are sometimes very large and complex.
- **Nonprofit organizations**   These include the Institute of Electrical and Electronics Engineers (IEEE), the American Physical Society (APS), the American Chemical Society (ACS), and so on. All these nonprofit organizations have large and complex IT systems.

In addition to the internal lines of business, usually a large enterprise has many working relationships with external business entities, such as business partners and suppliers. These are commonly known as business-to-business (B2B) relationships and add a new dimension to the workings of the company's IT systems because these relationships are fluid in nature and frequently change. Therefore, the IT systems of these organizations need to be very flexible and agile.

Most of our discussions are centered on enterprise integration, and much of what is discussed also applies to medium-size organizations, which also have a need to provide consistent data and functionality to their internal and external customers.

Enterprise Software

Enterprise software is designed for a large organization that typically has its own internal organization, processes, and business model. The software must take into account both cross-departmental dependencies and external business relationships, such as business partners and external vendors. Therefore, enterprise software must meet a large number of different types of requirements. Many of these requirements are incomplete, unclear, or otherwise conflicting. Furthermore, the requirements keep changing due to the market conditions and organizational changes. Because of these reasons, enterprise software is typically very complex.

One thing that makes the lives of enterprise software developers somewhat easier is that the coding of the business logic is usually not very complicated compared to other types of software, such as software for embedded systems. Similarly, the data structure for enterprise software is also not very complicated compared to other software, such as software for geographic information systems.

Here are some of the distinguishing features of enterprise software:

- The business data and other contents will have a very long lifecycle compared to data for other types of applications.
- A diverse set of technologies will be involved, including different middleware and many different applications.
- Functional requirements will be in a constant state of flux.
- The number of users of enterprise software could potentially be very large. Numbers in the order of tens of thousands of users are not uncommon.
- The number of stakeholders for such software could be large and may include different IT projects, IT maintenance, operations, and different business units.

On the other hand, consider a desktop application such as word processor. The technologies involved in developing such applications are limited in number, and as a result the application will be developed by a more homogeneous team of developers. The application logic is not pervasive but is confined to the application itself. The data involved is more transitory in nature.

Integration

With separate applications that operate in their individual silos, it becomes difficult to provide a consistent and unified view of the functionality and data in an organization. Of course, large organizations usually have a large number of applications, and the problem becomes even harder for these large organizations. In order to solve these problems, the applications must be able to communicate with each other and be able to share functionality and data with each other. This sharing of data and functionality helps avoid duplicating data and functionality and hence provides more consistent and unified data and functionality to the end user. Designing new applications or modifying existing applications so that they are able to share data and functionalities is called *software integration*.

Software Architecture

Usually only a few computer programs are sufficient to service a small company or organization. These small programs are easy to manage, and there is no need for an overall design. However, as we consider bigger and bigger organizations, the number of computer programs grows, and there is greater need for an overall design or design strategy in order to avoid chaos. This overall design or design strategy is called *software architecture*.

Software architecture is similar in nature to building architecture. Both types of architecture require planning according to some principles. For example, in building architecture the steel structure must be designed to support the current floor as well as future additions. In a similar manner, software architecture must be designed for both the current requirements and any upcoming requirements that can be foreseen.

In the past a business application or a computer program was developed whenever a specific need arose. These applications of the past era catered to the specific requirements of the problem being solved, the data being employed, and even the specific hardware on which the application would run. Thus, these applications more or less ran independently of each other in separate silos. There was no need for these commuter programs to talk to each other. However, as the number of applications grew, it became difficult to provide a consistent view of the functionality and data, and the management of these applications, each with its own silo, became very difficult.

It is at this stage that a need arose for an architecture that not only could easily meet the current requirements of a software system involving a large number of applications but could also meet the needs of tomorrow via (mostly) simple reconfigurations of the IT or software system. Service-Oriented Architecture is an architecture that meets the requirements of an agile, large IT system. SOA emphasizes agility and reuse of software assets through the use of software components that can be rethreaded or relinked easily in different configurations.

Some Basic Concepts

In this section we describe two fundamental concepts that are essential for a proper understanding of services and SOA. We start with loose coupling.

Loose Coupling

Of all the concepts, the idea of loose coupling is the major driving principle of the march toward SOA-type integration patterns. This drive for loose coupling has occurred because the number and kinds of applications being integrated have progressively become very large. This requires integration patterns to minimize the effect on other applications due to the changes made to one application. However, the most important business reason for requiring loose coupling is that businesses require agility to meet today's changing business needs. Thus, the integration schemes must allow for this agility and must be flexible.

In software, especially in distributed computing, coupling can occur at many different levels. For distributed systems, the way the remote applications are connected is possibly the most obvious technical factor when examining the problem of coupling. A direct network connection (for example, through sockets) can be thought of as tight coupling, whereas a physical intermediary enables loose coupling. Therefore, use of a messaging system (also called a MOM) results in loose coupling on the physical level because message queues are used as the intermediary. RPC-type applications, on the other hand, are tightly coupled because they rely on direct connections among themselves through sockets. This requires both the application that makes the request and the application that receives the request to be running and accessible at the same time.

Related closely to the issue of physical connection is the subject of synchronous versus asynchronous communications, as indicated in the last paragraph. Asynchronous generally results in loose coupling. However, this assumes that the underlying middleware, such as a MOM, is able to support the asynchronous messaging in a loosely coupled manner. Another way one can simulate an asynchronous call is through a one-way RPC call, in which the client does not wait for the reply from the server. However, this asynchronous call still results in tight coupling between the client and the server because the client and the server have to be running at the same time with a direct physical connection between them.

At the next level of coupling, the stronger the type of system, the stronger the coupling between the different components of the system. For example, in the case of interface semantics, tight coupling exists between different components of the system because interface semantics provide an explicit interface with operation names and strongly typed arguments. This tight coupling means that if the interface changes, a ripple effect occurs throughout the system of applications.

Another important factor that can affect the coupling between components is the interaction patterns of the distributed components. For example, an object-oriented (OO) distributed system will require OO-style navigation of complex object trees. The client would have to understand how to navigate across objects, which results in a fairly tight coupling between the client and the server. On the other hand, RPC-style interfaces do not require such complex navigation, thus resulting in much looser coupling between the server and the client.

Yet another factor that has an effect on the degree of coupling between the components of a system is the control of process logic. A central control of the processes will result in tight coupling between the different subprocesses and transactions. For example, database mechanisms might be used to enforce the referential integrity and general consistency of data owned by different subprocesses. This is often the case with large monolithic applications such as an Enterprise Resource Planning (ERP) or Customer Relationship Management (CRM) system. On the other hand, if the business processes are highly distributed, this results in much looser coupling between different components of the system. An example might be the B2B environments.

The last factor to consider is the method that is used by the client to locate a service. Statically bound services result in tight coupling, whereas dynamically bound services yield loose coupling. Looking up services in a directory or naming server reduces the coupling between components.

The different factors we have discussed and how they affect coupling between components of a system are summarized in Table 2.1.

Interface and Payload Semantics

The interaction between a client application and a server application usually results in the execution of a transaction or activity on the server side. The client must specify the activity that needs to be performed on

TABLE 2.1   Loose Versus Tight Coupling

Factor	Loose Coupling	Tight Coupling
Physical connection	Indirect connection through an intermediary	Direct connection
Communication style	Asynchronous	Synchronous
System type	Weakly typed system	Strongly typed system
Interaction pattern	Distributed logic	Centralized logic
Service binding	Dynamic binding	Static binding

the server side. This specification usually is done in two different ways. The requested transaction or activity can be encoded in the operation signature of the server component's interface, or it can be embedded in the message itself. In the first case, the requested transaction or activity is specified by using a self-descriptive function/method name such as updateBalance() or retrieveBalance(). This is referred to as *interface semantics* and is common in RPC-style interfaces. Figure 2.4 shows this kind of semantics in a schematic manner.

In the second case, the transaction or activity to be performed is embedded directly in the message. This is usually done in two ways. The name of the operation/activity can be included in the header of the message, if the underlying MOM provides such a field as part of the message header. Alternatively, the name of the activity/operation can be part of the application-specific payload. This we refer to as *payload semantics*. Payload semantics is common when MOMs are employed. These MOMs provide a generic API with functions such as MQGET() and MQPUT(). The semantics of these functions is purely technical. Payload semantics is shown schematically in Figure 2.5.

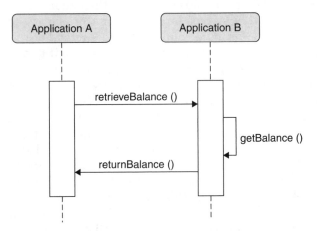

Figure 2.4   Interface semantics with meaningful names for each function

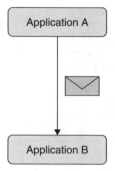

Figure 2.5 Payload semantics in which the remote functionality required is encoded in the message that is sent

Conclusion

We started this chapter with overview of the development of services and SOA. We pointed out that although the development of programming languages indirectly contributed to the evolution of services and SOA, the major and most direct contribution came from the development of various distributed computing technologies. This development of distributed computing started with sockets. The contribution also came from the development of RPC, ORBs, and asynchronous messaging. The most recent advancement in the area of services came from the development of Web Services standards and Enterprise Service Bus. Once again, we'll point out that SOA is based on and embraces all these different distributed computing technologies.

Next, we defined various terms common in the area of SOA and SOA-based integration, including *application, distributed computing, enterprise, enterprise software, integration,* and *software architecture.*

Finally, we discussed some of the key concepts related to SOA and SOA-based integration. Of all the concepts, the major driving principle of the march toward SOA-type integration patterns is the idea of loose coupling. This drive for loose coupling has occurred both for technical reasons and for business reasons, which demand agility and flexibility from the IT systems. We pointed out that coupling can occur at different levels, including the physical connection (network connection), communication style (RPC versus asynchronous messaging), system type (weak versus strong type), interaction pattern (distributed versus centralized logic), and service binding (static versus dynamic binding).

In Part II of this book, we start to discuss the various distributed technologies that have contributed to the evolution of services and services-based integration. We start out in Chapter 3 with the simplest concept of data sharing by applications. In this context, we discuss sockets, which not only allow data sharing among applications in real time but also provide connectivity between applications. This connectivity is a fundamental concept and lays the foundation of all services-based integration schemes.

2

Evolution of Integration Patterns

3

Sockets and Data Sharing

We start out in this chapter by describing the different methods of sharing data between applications. In later chapters we will discuss how applications can share functionality as well. Data sharing is discussed first for two reasons: The first reason is historical in that applications started sharing data long before they started sharing functionalities. The second, and more important reason is that a discussion of data sharing introduces the concept of connectivity between applications. Connectivity is required not only for sharing data in real time but also for sharing functionality.

The three significant methods of sharing data between applications are file-based data sharing, the use of a common database, and sockets. The file-based method of sharing data is the oldest and will be discussed first. Next we will look at the common database method of sharing data. Both of these methods are suitable if the applications are not required to share data in real time. However, if there is a need to share data in real time, we must use the third method (sockets), which provides a real-time connection between applications. The discussion of sockets will lead us into the area of sharing functionalities between applications, which will be covered in the next chapter.

File-Based Data Sharing

The first method of sharing data is through files. This is perhaps the most common method of sharing data because storing data in files is universal. This type of storage is allowed by all hardware systems and operating systems. In this method of data sharing, one application writes data to a file while the other application reads data from the same file. If the two applications are running on the same machine, they can use the machine's disk to read and write. This is shown in Figure 3.1.

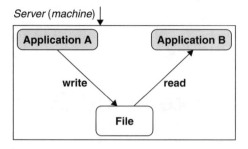

Figure 3.1   Schematic representation of two applications running on the same computer, exchanging data through a file on the computer's disk.

In the case that the two applications are running on two different machines or servers, a file-transfer mechanism between the machines' two disks must be used. One common method of file transfer is the File Transfer Protocol (FTP). The data sharing between two applications running on two different machines is shown in Figure 3.2.

The most common types of file-based data sharing use text files. The reason for using text-based data transfer is that a character is represented by one byte in almost all the important operating systems and languages, unlike numeric quantities such as integers and floating-point numbers. For numeric quantities, different operating systems and languages may use a different number of bytes and a different order of bytes to represent the same numeric quantities. Thus, for example, one system may use two bytes to represent an integer whereas another system might use four bytes to represent the same quantity.

Examples of common types of text files include flat files and XML files. Flat files come in two varieties: fixed-length record files and variable-length record files. Fixed-length files contain data in which the

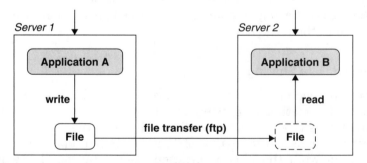

Figure 3.2   Schematic representation of two applications running on two different computers, exchanging data through a file. The file is transferred from one computer to the other by the use of the File Transfer Protocol.

length of each field is fixed and the order in which different fields appear is also fixed. While writing such files, the developer must ensure that all field data has the required length by inserting some filler, such as blanks or zeros, if required. An example of such a file, which describes the color, length, and width of a paper, is shown in Listing 3-1. In this small file, data for three fields is being used. The first field must have a length of six, the second field must have a length of four, and the third field must also have a length of four. For the second field, fillers (zeros) are used to ensure the field has the required length of four.

Listing 3-1

```
/* An example of fixed length flat file, which describes the color,
length, and width of a sheet of paper. */
Yellow01452456
```

The second type of flat file contains variable-length records, and consequently the files themselves have variable lengths, even though they contain the same type of records. Such files use a delimiter such as comma or semicolon to separate various fields in the record. Each field can be of any length, but fields must occur in a predetermined order. An example of a variable-length record flat file is shown in Listing 3-2, which describes the same paper as Listing 3-1. Note in this case that there's no need to use fillers and that the delimiter is a comma.

Listing 3-2

```
/* An example of variable length flat file which describes the color,
length, and width of a sheet of paper */
Yellow,145,2456
```

Recent types of text files use XML. XML uses tags to describe different fields in a record. The advantages of using XML are that the tags are self-describing and the file is human readable. A portion of an XML file, which describes the same sheet of paper, is shown in Listing 3-3.

Listing 3-3

```
/* A portion of an XML file, which describes the color, length,
and width of a sheet of paper. */
<paper>
     <color>Yellow</color>
     <length>145</length>
     <width>2456</width>
</paper>
```

An important thing to note from these listings is that even the numeric quantities, such as length and width, are written and read from the file as character strings. Therefore, the software developer for the application, who is writing to the file, must first convert the numeric quantities into a character string and then write to the file. In a similar manner, the software developer for the application who is reading from the file must convert the character string to the appropriate numeric quantities, such as integer or floating-point number. This could be considered a disadvantage of using the file-based data-sharing approach.

However, writing and reading text from a file are usually simple tasks, and most programming languages provide good facilities to perform these tasks. This is illustrated in Listings 3-4 and 3-5. These two Java code snippets show how to write text to and read text from the files, respectively. Note that the file is named "testFile" and the data that is being written and read is "This is a test for writing to a file."

Listing 3-4

```
/* Java code for writing text to a file */
try
{
      FileOutputStream  fos = new FileOutputStream  ( "testFile");
      DataOutputStream dos = new DataOutputStream (fos);
      dos.writeUTF ("This is a test for writing to a file");
      dos.close();
      fos.close();
}
catch (IOException ex)
{
      System.out.println(ex.getMessage());
}
```

Listing 3-5

```
/* Java code for reading text from a file */
try
{
      FileInputStream  fis = new FileInputStream  ( "testFile");
      DataIntputStream dis = new DataIntputStream (fos);
      dos.readUTF ("This is a test for writing to a file");
      dis.close();
      fis.close();
}
catch (IOException ex)
{
      System.out.println(ex.getMessage());
}
```

Although data sharing through files may be the most common method of sharing data between applications, this method has a number of disadvantages.

The most important disadvantage of this method is that the data is not shared in real time. Generally a substantial lag exists between the time that one application writes to a file and the time the second application reads from the file. This lag in time is usually determined by a business cycle, which may be a few hours, a day, or a week. Many times this lag in reading is not a problem, in which case it is proper to rely on this method of data sharing. However, in many other cases the lag in time is a serious problem, which makes this method of sharing data unsuitable in such circumstances. Consider the situation where a business client has changed their address and reports that change to the business through Application A, which then writes this change of address to a file for Application B to read. However, Application B reads such files only once a week. In the meantime, Application B sends a bill to the wrong address. Thus, the bill might not get paid in time or even paid at all. In such situations, the staleness of data is a serious problem.

Another serious problem with file-based data transfer between applications is that this method is unreliable if a large number of files are involved. File-based data transfer requires a substantial amount of bookkeeping, including when and how to delete files, and a locking mechanism so that a given file is not read from and written to at the same time. These and other issues are discussed further in the next paragraph.

The bookkeeping tasks that need to be performed for file-based data sharing significantly increase the workload for the software developers. These tasks include the following:

- The software developers for both the application writing to the file and the application reading from the file must agree on the format of the file.

- The software developers for both the application writing to the file and the application reading from the file must agree on a file-naming convention.

- The software developers must agree on the directory in which the file must be created and/or transferred if need be.

- Software developers for data-sharing applications must agree on the application responsible for deleting the file when it is no longer needed.

- Software developers must implement a locking mechanism that disallows other applications from reading from the file when one application is writing to the file.

■ If the two applications sharing data through files are running on two different servers (machines), the software developers must decide on which application will be responsible for transferring files from one server to the other.

Sharing data using files is straightforward when the data is in text form. However, if the data is numerical, you must account for the two systems used: big endian and little endian. For example, SPARC is big endian whereas Intel is little endian. In this case, you must explicitly program to account for this difference, which is commonly known as the "big endian versus little endian" issue.

Another serious problem with this type of data integration is that the method is not suitable when a large number of applications need to be integrated because this type of integration is "point to point." The number of point-to-point integrations basically increases as follows:

$$N(N-1)/2$$

In this calculation, N is the number of applications involved in the integration.

Common Database

This method of sharing data between applications is similar to the previous file-based data-sharing method. In this case, one application writes data to a common database, and other applications read the data from that database. This is shown schematically in Figure 3.3. An important difference from file-based data sharing to note from this figure is that the database almost always runs on its own separate machine. This means the data transfer between applications always occurs via a network, even though the applications sharing the data might be running on the same machine. Therefore, this method of sharing data is generally slower than the file-based method. An advantage of this method of data sharing is that the connection between applications in not "point to point," as is the case for file-based data sharing. Any number of applications can share data once it is written to the database. Thus, the data is always consistent across any number of applications.

The use of a common database for application integration is popular due to the widespread use of SQL-based relational databases. Almost all development platforms support SQL, so you don't need to worry about multiple file formats. Therefore, once you learn SQL, you can use it on all different platforms.

Some sample code for reading from a database in Java is shown in Listing 3-6. In this sample code, an application reads the names and phone numbers of employees from a database and displays them on

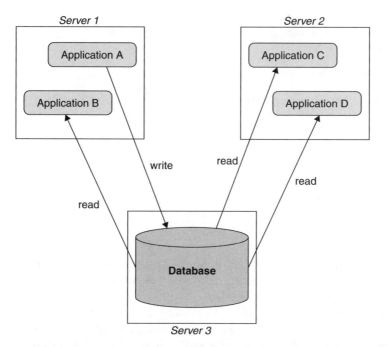

Figure 3.3 Schematic representation of multiple applications-sharing data through a common database. Note that communications always occur over the network. The applications sharing the data could be running on the same computer or separate computers.

the console. The names and phone numbers are stored as two columns in a table named "employee." The code for writing to the database is similar.

Listing 3-6

```java
/* Sample Java code for reading from the database */
import java.io.*;
import java.sql.*;
public class TestClass {
      public void getEmployees (){
      Connection con = null;
      Statement stmt = null;
      ResultSet rs = null;
      try
      {
            Class.forName ("sun.jdbc.odbc.JdbcOdbcDriver");
            con= DriverManager.getConnection ("jdbc:odbc.somedb", "user",
"password");
            stmt = con.getStatement ();
            rs = stmt.executeQuery ("SELECT NAME, PHONE FROM EMPLOYEES");
            while (rs.next ())
```

```
        {
           System.out.println (rs.getString("name") + "   "
+rs.getString("phone");
        }
    catch ( ClassNotFoundException e)
    {
       System.out.println ( e.getMessage());
    }
    catch (SQLException e )
    {
       System.out.println (e.getMessage () );
    }
    finally
    {
       con.close();
    }
}
```

Although data sharing via a common database is an improvement over file-based data sharing in some respects, there are still some disadvantages to this method.

The greatest disadvantage of the common database approach is, just as in the case of file-based data sharing, the data is not shared in real time. This is because when an application writes data to the database, other applications are not informed of the changes. Thus, even though the data is available to other applications for reading, right after an application writes to the database, other applications are not aware of the changes and therefore cannot take advantage of the updates in real time.

Another serious problem of the common database approach is that it is very difficult, and sometime impossible, to come up with a suitable design for the common database. Defining a unified database schema that can meet the needs of multiple applications is very difficult. Furthermore, for the application programmers, the resulting database schema is difficult to work with. There are also severe political difficulties in designing a unified schema. If a critical application is likely to suffer delays due to working with a unified schema, often there is pressure to separate the databases.

The problem of designing a unified database schema is exacerbated if externally packaged applications are part of the system of applications that need to be integrated. Most packaged applications have their own database schema, and these schemas will not work with any other schema. Even if there is room for changing the database schema of a given packaged application, it is likely to be limited to an extent that is not suitable for general integration. In addition, software vendors reserve the right to change the schema with every new release of the software. When vendors change the schema of their packaged applications, interfacing applications encounter a ripple effect that causes development and maintenance issues—or worse, production issues—if schema changes are not advertised properly.

The use of a common database is also not suitable when a number of applications need to be integrated and is therefore not a scalable solution to the problem of application integration. This is because if a fair amount of applications frequently read and write to the common database, the database can be a bottleneck as each application locks others out of the database.

This integration method is also not a suitable solution if the applications are distributed across multiple locations. This is because accessing a single, common database across a wide area network (WAN) is typically too slow to be practical.

Sockets

In order to avoid the problem of stale data, a real-time connection between applications is needed. This is called *connectivity*. The most rudimentary way to establish a connection between two applications is through sockets. A *socket* is a communications connection point (endpoint) that you can name and address in a network. The processes that use a socket can reside on the same system or on different systems on different networks. Sockets are useful for both standalone and network applications. Socket APIs are the network standard for TCP/IP. A wide range of operating systems support socket APIs.

Sockets allow one application to listen at a given port on a given machine for the incoming data, while another application can write to the same socket using the IP address and port address of the first application. The listening application can read the data as soon as the second application writes the data. Thus, the data is shared in real time and the problem of stale data is eliminated. The listening application is usually called a server whereas the other application is called a client.

Because the overhead associated with applications that communicate through sockets is very low, direct socket programming leads to a very efficient way of communication. It is also interesting to note that most of the modern methods of communications (such as MOM/messages) as well as other methods (such as distributed objects) rely on socket programming under the hood.

Listing 3-7 illustrates typical C language code on the server side. Note that the code listing contains the system header files (<sys/socket.h>, <sys/types.h>, and <netinet/in.h>) as the include files. This inclusion allows all the systems-related files to be compiled along with the code shown in Listing 3-7, and it allows the code to make system-level calls related to the sockets.

Listing 3-7

```
/* Typical code for sockets on the server side in C language */
#include <stdio.h>
/* for EXIT_FAILURE and EXIT_SUCCESS */
#include <stdlib.h>
/* network functions */
#include <sys/types.h>
#include <sys/socket.h>
#include <netinet/in.h>
int main()
{
  int socket_desc;
  struct sockaddr_in address;
  int addrlen;
  int new_socket;
/* create the master socket and check it worked */
  if ((socket_desc=socket(AF_INET,SOCK_STREAM,0))==0)
  {
/* if socket failed then display error and exit */
    perror("Create socket");
    exit(EXIT_FAILURE);
  }
/* type of socket created */
  address.sin_family = AF_INET;
  address.sin_addr.s_addr = INADDR_ANY;
/* 7000 is the port to use for connections */
  address.sin_port = htons(7000);
/* bind the socket to port 7000 */
  if (bind(socket_desc,(struct sockaddr *)&address,sizeof(address))<0)
  {
/* if bind failed then display error message and exit */
    perror("bind");
    exit(EXIT_FAILURE);
  }
/* try to specify maximum of 3 pending connections for the master socket */
  if (listen(socket_desc,3)<0)
  {
/* if listen failed then display error and exit */
    perror("listen");
    exit(EXIT_FAILURE);
  }
/* accept one connection, wait if no connection pending */
  addrlen=sizeof(address);
  if ((new_socket=accept(socket_desc,(struct sockaddr *) &address,
&addrlen))<0)
  {
/* if accept failed to return a socket descriptor, display error and exit */
    perror("accept");
    exit(EXIT_FAILURE);
  }
/* inform user of socket number - used in send and receive commands */
  printf("New socket is %d\n",new_socket);
```

```
   sleep(10);
/* shutdown master socket properly */
   close(socket_desc);
}
```

The flow of code is summarized in Figure 3.4. The basic sequence is that first a socket is created by invoking the socket() method. The type of socket address family needs to be specified. In our case, the address family is AF_INET, which is suitable if TCP is used. This address family provides interprocess communications between processes that run on the same system or on different systems. Addresses for AF_INET sockets are IP addresses and a port number. In the code listing, the port number is 4000. This is the port where the server side will listen for incoming requests. We also specify that the incoming call could be from any machine on the network. Next, we bind the listener to the port by using the bind method. The next step is to accept the connection request from the client. Now both the client and the server can read and write from the socket. After exchanging data, the server finally closes the socket using the close method.

The client-side code is similar to the server-side code and is shown in Listing 3-8. The flow of the code is summarized in Figure 3.5. First, a socket is created. Then the IP address and the port of the server are specified. The next step is to make the connection by using the connect() method. Now the client is ready to read from and write to the socket and thus exchange data with the server.

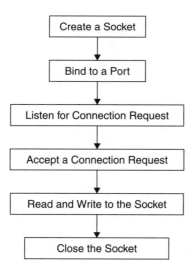

Figure 3.4 Server-side code flow for sharing data in real time between applications using sockets

Listing 3-8

```
/* Typical client side code for the sockets in C language */
include <stdio.h>
#include <sys/types.h>
#include <sys/socket.h>
#include <netinet/in.h>
#include <netdb.h>
void error(char *msg)
{
    perror(msg);
    exit(0);
}
int main(int argc, char *argv[])
{
    int sockfd, portno, n;
    struct sockaddr_in serv_addr;
    struct hostent *server;
    char buffer[256];
    if (argc < 3) {
       fprintf(stderr,"usage %s hostname port\n", argv[0]);
       exit(0);
    }
    portno = atoi(argv[2]);
    sockfd = socket(AF_INET, SOCK_STREAM, 0);
    if (sockfd < 0)
        error("ERROR opening socket");
    server = gethostbyname(argv[1]);
    if (server == NULL) {
        fprintf(stderr,"ERROR, no such host\n");
        exit(0);
    }
    bzero((char *) &serv_addr, sizeof(serv_addr));
    serv_addr.sin_family = AF_INET;
    bcopy((char *)server->h_addr,
          (char *)&serv_addr.sin_addr.s_addr,
          server->h_length);
    serv_addr.sin_port = htons(portno);
    if (connect(sockfd,&serv_addr,sizeof(serv_addr)) < 0)
        error("ERROR connecting");
    printf("Please enter the message: ");
    bzero(buffer,256);
    fgets(buffer,255,stdin);
    n = write(sockfd,buffer,strlen(buffer));
    if (n < 0)
        error("ERROR writing to socket");
    bzero(buffer,256);
    n = read(sockfd,buffer,255);
    if (n < 0)
        error("ERROR reading from socket");
    printf("%s\n",buffer);
    return 0;
}
```

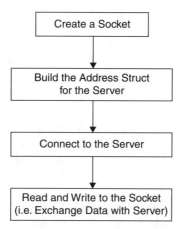

Figure 3.5   Client-side code flow for sharing data in real time between applications using sockets

There are a number of shortcomings of the socket programming approach, including the following:

- The major problem with socket programming is that only data can be shared directly, not the functionality.

- The API for socket programming is rather low level and is therefore difficult to use.

- Because the API is low level, socket programming is not suitable for dealing with complex data types.

- The connectivity code is buried in the applications and cannot be easily reused.

- Socket programming is not platform independent if numeric quantities are involved. This is because applications on both ends must explicitly account for the byte ordering differences (little endian versus big endian) on different platforms such as mainframe and UNIX.

- Tight coupling exists between the two applications because the socket connection is "point to point."

In spite of these shortcomings, sockets are the most essential element of many other integration schemes that allow applications to share functionality in addition to data. As you will see in the next chapter, the remote procedure call (RPC) method of sharing functionality is built on top of sockets. Furthermore, distributed objects and asynchronous messages also rely on sockets. These two methods of sharing functionality are discussed in Chapters 5 and 6.

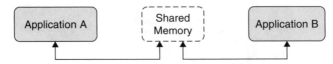

Figure 3.6   Two applications exchanging data by using a common area in memory (RAM)

Note that if the applications are running on the same machine and using the same operating system, there are three other ways of sharing data—especially if the operating system being used is some form of UNIX/Linux. These three methods are shared memory, pipes, and name pipes (or FIFO).

Shared memory may be simultaneously accessed by multiple programs, with the intent to provide communication among them. One process or application will create an area in RAM that the other applications can access. This is shown schematically in Figure 3.6. Shared memory is probably the fastest way to share data in real time. Shared memory remains in existence until the system reboots. Pipes and FIFO are similar but they remain in existence only until the last application that is holding the object open finally closes it. It should be noted that the use of shared memory requires both applications to be running on the same server.

Conclusion

In this chapter we discussed three methods of sharing data between applications: the file-based method, the use of a common database, and sockets. The first two methods do not allow for sharing data in real time, but the third method (sockets) does. While discussing sockets, we introduced the important concept of connectivity between applications.

The major drawback of these three methods is that they do not allow the applications to share functionalities. In the next chapter, we will further develop the concept of connectivity between applications to allow applications to share functionalities—as well as data—among themselves in real time. We have discussed a number of other disadvantages of the three methods of sharing data. In later chapters, we cover other methods of integrations, which progressively remedy these shortcomings.

4

Remote Procedure Call (RPC)

In Chapter 3, we discussed techniques for sharing data between applications. The first two techniques—the file-based data transfer and the use of a common database—are suitable for sharing data when there's no requirement for sharing data in real time. The third technique—using sockets—is employed when data needs to be shared by applications in real time. Sockets can be used when the applications are running on the same machine or on different machines connected by a network. In Chapter 3, we also briefly mentioned pipes and FIFO, which can be used by applications running on the same machine for sharing data in real time.

All these techniques are restricted to sharing data only and do not allow applications to share functionality. However, our discussion of sockets introduced the concept of connectivity between applications, which is required for sharing functionality. Therefore, sockets are almost always involved in the background when applications are sharing functionality, regardless of the method of integration.

In this chapter we begin to address the core subject of this book: how to integrate enterprise applications so that they can share functionality. We start by describing techniques that allow functions defined in one application to be called by other applications in an enterprise. Note that the terms *methods* and *procedures* have the same meaning as the term *functions* in this book. Remember that enterprise applications integration is a difficult process because it involves many different types of applications written in many different languages and running on many different types of platforms, which may be distributed geographically. To understand the underlying problems and their solutions, a step-by-step approach is the best approach. Therefore, the methods described in this chapter should be considered a first step in the study of enterprise integration. Later chapters will build on the material covered in this chapter.

The main topic of this chapter is remote procedure call (RPC). RPC is also known as "client/server" and "two-tier architecture" and is a rung above socket programming. It eliminates the need for network programming. RPC provides a function-oriented interface. The developer defines a function—much like those in functional languages such as C—and generates code that makes the function look like a normal function to the caller. RPC is powerful enough to be the basis of client/server applications. The client/server model has become one of the central ideas of network computing. Most business applications being written today use the client/server model. So does the Internet's main application protocols, including HTTP, SMTP, telnet, and DNS. The most common example is the interaction between a web browser and a web server, where the browser acts as a client and the web server fills the role of a server in the client/server architecture.

RPC was an important step in the progress toward enterprise integration because it introduced some important concepts and features and specified the basic steps necessary for sharing functionality. Recall that Web Services and enterprise integration are mostly about sharing functionality between applications or software components. The new concepts and features introduced by RPC are listed here:

- The concept of interface declaration through the use of a specification file. The RPC specification file may be considered the "first step" in the development of the services interface in today's world, such as a WSDL file.

- The concept of a service provider application (server) and the concept of a service consumer application (client). The server provides the implementation of one or more functions that can be used or invoked by the client application.

- The concept of marshalling of arguments for transmission over the network. This refers to packaging of arguments into one or more messages to be transmitted over the network.

- The encapsulation of all system- and network-related functionality in a library. This encapsulation led to future systems in which this functionality could be separated out as a program of its own, thus leading to code reuse.

- The introduction of client and server stubs, which shield the programmer from system and network calls.

- The concept of platform independence via the use of external data representation (XDR), which encodes data in a machine-independent format.

We start our discussion of RPC by first clarifying the differences between the three possible types of function calls: local function calls, restricted remote function calls (restricted RPC) involving two applications running on the same computer, and more general remote procedure calls between two applications that may be running on two different computers connected by a network. Then we describe how restricted RPC works. Restricted RPC does not involve any network connections and is therefore the simpler of the two kinds of RPC. Next, we discuss more general remote procedure calls. This second type of RPC is the most common, and it includes two applications running on two different computers.

Three Types of Function Calls

Functions can be synchronous or asynchronous. In the case of synchronous functions, the calling code is blocked from doing further work until after the function returns. In the case of asynchronous calls, the calling code can continue to perform other work, without waiting for a return (because there is no return). In this chapter, we restrict our discussion to synchronous functions because RPC involves only synchronous calls. Asynchronous calls are discussed in detail in Chapter 6.

Synchronous functions come in three different types. The first type is the local function call. In this case, the code calling the function and the function being called are part of the same application. This is shown schematically in Figure 4.1. This type of function call is the most familiar because most programming languages allow for this feature. Typically some machine instruction is executed that transfers control to the new function, and the called function saves machine registers and allocates space on the stack for the local variables.

The second type of function call is the restricted RPC type. In this case, the code calling the function and the function code being called reside in two different applications running on the same machine. This second type of function call is shown schematically in Figure 4.2.

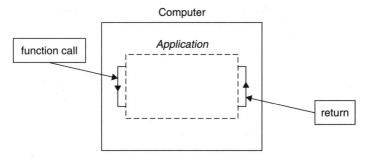

Figure 4.1   Local function call

Computer

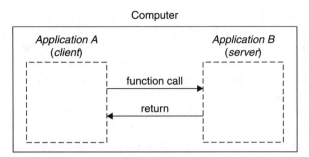

Figure 4.2   Remote procedure call on a single host

This type of function call is similar to the remote function call described in the next paragraph. However, this type of function call does not involve any network routines because both applications are running on the same machine and may be considered a type of interprocess communication (IPC). The particular implementation of this type of call we discuss is called Doors. We discuss Doors later in this chapter.

The third type of functional call generally involves a client application on one host calling a function in another application running on another host, as long as the two hosts are connected by some form of network. This type of function call is depicted in Figure 4.3. We refer to this type of function call as *RPC*. We discuss this type of function call in detail later in this chapter. This type of call relies on sockets under the hood.

Historically, the RPC type shown in Figure 4.3 was developed before the type shown in Figure 4.2. However, we will discuss the second type of call first because it is simpler to understand because there are no network routines.

Normally, with Doors and RPC, the application calling the function is referred to as the *client* and the application in which the function resides

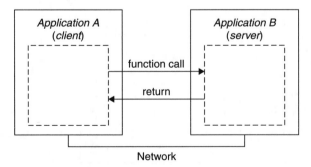

Figure 4.3   Remote procedure call between different hosts

Types of Functions

Local function calls involve one piece of code in one application invoking another piece of code in the same application. Restricted remote procedure calls (restricted RPC or Doors) involve a piece of code in one application calling a piece of code in another application. The two applications must be running on the same host. RPC calls are similar to the restricted RPC, with the difference being that the two applications may be running on separate hosts connected by a network.

is called the *server*. In other words, the application calling the function is the service consumer whereas the application where the function resides is the service provider. Thus, both RPC and Doors involve the concept of services, and we may consider this to be the beginning of the services-based integration pattern.

Doors: Restricted Remote Procedure Calls (Restricted RPC)

In this section we discuss the case where one application (the server) makes a function available to the other applications (clients) running on the same computer, as shown in Figure 4.2. The particular implementation of this type of functionality exchange we discuss here is called *Doors*. Doors is restricted to Solaris systems and cannot be used on other systems. In addition, there are no other RPC systems of this type that can run on other platforms.

When applications are running on a common host, they all share the same operating system, so it is natural to use the kernel of the operating system to provide communication between the applications. Thus in Doors, the kernel of the operating system is used to provide communication between the applications, which make system calls into the kernel. This is shown in Figure 4.4.

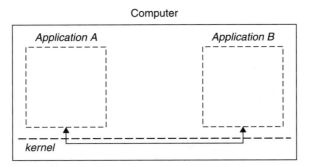

Figure 4.4 Applications running on the same system using the kernel to communicate. A network is not involved.

The major contribution of Doors is that all the systems calls are encapsulated in a library with a header file called <door.h>. Therefore, the programmer doesn't need to know any system-level programming. The Doors library consists of a few functions, a couple of data structures, and a simple protocol to implement this restricted type of remote procedure call. It is a very intuitive and the most efficient way to share functionality if the applications are running on the same host. In fact, Doors can be considered a type of interprocess communication.

In order to understand how Doors works, we start by looking at a simple example. In this example, one application (the server) provides a function to another application (the client) to invoke. The function provided by the server takes a long integer as an input and returns the cube of the input. The server-side code for this example is discussed next.

Server-Side Code for Doors

The server program, server1.c, is shown in Listing 4-1. It consists of server function called cube_proc and a main function. Following this listing is a brief description of the various pieces of code.

Listing 4-1

```
Listing 4.1: Example server side code for Doors - File: server1.c
1   #include <unistd.h>
2   #include <sys/types.h>
3   #include <sys/stat.h>
4   #include <fcntl.h>
5   #include <door.h>
6   #include "ssp.h" //Solaris stuff

7   static void cube_proc(void * pcookie,
8             char * dataptr,
9             size_t argsz,
10            door_desc_t *dp,
11             uint_t ndesc);
12    (
13       long arg, result;
14       arg = *((long *) dataptr) ;

15       result = arg * arg * arg ;

16       Door_return ((char *) &result, sizeof(result), NULL, 0);

17    }

18   int main(int argc, char * argv[])
19   {
20      int fd;
21      int tempfd;
```

```
22      /* get descriptor and bind cube_proc to it */
23      fd=door_create(serv_proc, NULL, 0);
24      unlink(argv[1]) ; /* delete this file if it already exists from a
25      previous run  */
26      tempfd=creat(argv[1], FILE _PERMS); /* create the file associated
27      with the door  */
28      close (tempfd); /* close the file before attaching it to fd */
29      fattach(fd, argv[1]); /* associate door descriptor with an

30      existing file  */
31      while(1)
32      pause(); /* do nothing; the real work is implemented in the server

33              threads  */
34  }
```

Header Files   The listing starts with some header files that include the main library header file <door.h> (see lines 1–6). Header files include only the declaration of various functions. The actual implementations of these functions appear in separate files, which are used when the code is compiled and linked.

Server Function cube_proc()   In lines 7–17, a server function named cube-proc() is defined. This server function takes five arguments as input, but the only one we use is dataptr, which points to the first byte of the argument. The long argument is obtained through this pointer and cubed. Control is passed back to the client, along with the result, by invoking the Door_return function. The first argument to this function points to the result, the second argument is the size of this result, and the remaining two arguments deal with the returning descriptors.

Create a Door Descriptor and Attach It to a Pathname   Lines 18–29 describe a main function that takes a pathname as input. This pathname is supplied at the time the server is started. In this function, first a door descriptor is created for the function cube_proc() by calling the function Door-create(). The first argument to this function is a pointer that's called for this door, namely cube-proc(). Next, the door descriptor is associated with a pathname in the file system, because this pathname is how the client identifies the door. This association is performed by creating a regular file in the file system. After this, we call the function fattach(), which associates a descriptor with a pathname.

Main Server Thread Pauses   In lines 31–34, the main server thread blocks by calling the pause() function. Now, cube_proc() is ready to do its work on the client request. All the work is done by the server function cube_proc(), which executes in a separate thread in the server process each time a client makes a request.

Next, the code is compiled and linked to create an executable called server1. To run the server we use the following command which starts the server in a separate window:

```
Solaris % server1 /tmp/server1
```

Client-Side Code

A sample client program, called client1.c, is shown in Listing 4-2. The program has a main function that takes in two arguments. The first argument, argv[1], is the pathname that specifies the door and is supplied at the time the client is started. The second input on the command line is the number (a long type), which will be cubed by calling the server function. The program starts with a number of header files, including the most important library, <door.h>, which encapsulates all the system-level calls. The client1.c program involves the steps detailed in the following subsections.

Listing 4-2

```
Listing 4.2: Doors' sample client side code: File: cleint1.c
1   #include <unistd.h>
2   #include <sys/types.h>
3   #include <sys/stat.h>
4   #include <fcntl.h>
5   #include <door.h>
6   #include "ssp.h"

7   int main (int argc, char **argv )

8   {
9        int          fd;
10       long         input, output;

11       door_arg_t arg;

12       fd = Open (argv[1], O_RDWR);  /* open the door */

13        /* set up input arguments and pointer to the result */

13       input = atol (argv[2]);

14       arg.data_ptr = (char *) &input; /* pointer to input */

15       arg.data_size = sizeof(long);   /* size of data argument */

16       arg.desc_ptr = NULL;

17       arg.desc_num = 0;
```

```
18    arg.rbuf = (char *) &output;  /* pointer to the output */

19    arg.rsize = sizeof (long)     /* number of bytes for the result */

20       /* call the server function and print result  */

21    Door_call (fd, &arg);

22    printf ( "The result is : %1d\n", output);

23    exit (0);

24  }
```

Open the Door   In line 12, the door is opened by calling the library function Open(). It takes as an argument the pathname specified at the command line when the client program is started. It returns a door descriptor.

Set Up the Input Parameters and a Pointer to the Output   In lines 13–19, the arg structure contains a pointer to the inputs and a pointer to the result. The member data_ptr of the structure arg points to the first byte of input data, and data_size specifies the number bytes in the input data. The two members—desc_ptr and desc_num—deal with passing descriptors. These two members are not very important for our discussion here. rbuf points to the first byte of the result buffer, and rsize is its size.

Call the Server Function and Print the Result   In lines 22–24, the server function is called by invoking the Door_call () function, specifying as arguments the door descriptor and the pointer to the arguments structure. When the function returns, an output variable will have the result, which we print using a printf statement.

After the client program is compiled and linked to produce an executable called client1, the client program is started in a separate window using the following command line with the same pathname argument we passed to the server:

```
solaris % client1 /tmp/server1 3
```

The result is 27.

Doors Process

In Doors, one application makes a function available to other applications running on the same machine by creating a door. The application providing the function is considered a service provider and is called a *server*. The other applications using the function are considered service consumers and are called *clients*. Inside the server, each door is identified by a descriptor. Inside the clients, doors are identified by paths—much like ordinary files. A server creates a door by calling the door_create() function. The first argument of this function is an address of a callback function associated with that door. The return value of door_create() is the descriptor of the new door. Next, the server calls fattach() to associate a door with a pathname. The client opens a door by calling open() with the door's pathname as the argument. The return value of the open() call is a descriptor that the client uses locally as the door's descriptor. Finally, the client invokes the server function by using the door_call() function.

Door calls are synchronous. Therefore, when the client calls door_call(), this function doesn't return until the server procedure returns. Whenever a client calls a server function, a new thread in the server process handles that request. A door-based server can handle multiple requests simultaneously. Such a server is known as a *concurrent server*. The thread allocation and deallocation are transparent to the client because the Door library manages its thread allocation automatically.

Doors Summary

In summary, Doors provides an efficient way for applications to share functionality if the applications are running on the same host machine. In the process of discussing Doors, we introduced the concepts of *service provider* and *service consumer,* as well as the concept of encapsulating all system-level calls in a library.

However, Doors has two major disadvantages: First, Doors is specific to Solaris and is not platform independent. Second, applications running on separate hosts cannot share functionality. In the next section we discuss the full-blown remote procedure call, which allows applications to share functionality even when they are running on different hosts. RPC is also platform independent.

Restricted RPC, or Doors

Restricted RPC (of which Doors is an example) is the most intuitive and efficient way for two applications to share functionality. The communication between the two applications is through systems calls to the kernel, and these calls are encapsulated in a library. There are two important restrictions on the use of Doors: First, applications sharing functionality must be running on the same host. Second, Doors is not platform independent and can only be used on Solaris systems.

Remote Procedure Call (RPC)

We'll now discuss the third type of function call—most commonly known as remote procedure call (RPC) or client/server architecture. RPC further developed the concepts introduced in the last section to enable calls to be made to applications running on separate hosts and connected by a network. RPC introduced for the first time, although in a rudimentary way, the declaration of the service interface. RPC also introduced the concept of marshalling and unmarshalling of parameters, which is required for communication over the network. In addition, RPC further developed the idea of a runtime library so as to include calls to the kernel that involve network routines.

We describe how RPC works with a view toward these new concepts. Therefore, we will consider an example similar to the one discussed in the last section on Doors. The server will expose a function for the client applications to call, which will take as an input a long integer and return the cube of the input to the caller.

Interface Declaration and Use

We begin with the discussion of interface declaration. RPC introduced a rudimentary way of defining an interface between the client and the server through the use of a specification file. The RPC specification file may be considered the "first step" in the development of the services interface (for example, WSDL files) in today's world. A configuration file (cube.x) for the example covered here is provided in Listing 4-3. This file is used to generate the skeleton code for both the server and the client using a tool such as rpcgen. Note that the specification is written in a specific language, such as C, and therefore requires both the server and the client to be written in the same language.

Listing 4-3

```
Listing 4.3 : File: cube.x
1    struct cube_in {              /* input (argument) type */
2            long input;
3    };
4
5    struct cube_out {             /* output (result) type  */
6            long result;
7    };
8
9    program CUBE_PROGRAM {
10               CUBE_VERS  {
11                    cube_out  CUBEPROC ( cube_in)    = 1;  /*func. No.*/
12               }  = 1;              /* version number */
13   }   =   0x312;          /* program number  */
```

Note that the specification file's name ends in .x. The specification file defines the input and output arguments and a single server function, which is exposed to the client. The following subsections provide a brief description of the contents of the sample file shown in Listing 4-3.

This description illustrates the basic steps involved in declaring an interface.

Declare the Input and Output Arguments Lines 1–3 define a structure for the input, which is of the type "long." Lines 5–7 define an output structure that is also of type long.

Define the Program, the Version, and the Function In lines 9–13, we declare an RPC program called CUBE_PROG that consists of one version (CUBE_VERS), and in that version is a single function named CUBEPROC. The input argument to this function is a cube_in structure, and its return value is a cube_out structure. A number 1 is assigned to this function. We assign the version number a value of 1, and we assign the program number a hexadecimal value.

This specification is used to generate four files when it is compiled with the tool rpcgen, as shown in Figure 4.5. One of those files, cube_clnt.c, produces (when compiled by a C compiler) a client stub that is used to marshal and unmarshal the arguments on the client side. Similarly, a file called cube_svc.c produces a server stub that does the same marshalling and unmarshalling of the arguments to the function on the server side. *Marshalling* refers to the packaging of arguments into one or more network messages. The third file produced by compiling cube.x is a header file called cube.h. It must be included in a number of files that are used to compile both the client and the server code. The fourth file, cube_xdr.c, is also very important and is included while the client and server code is being compiled. The inclusion of this file in the client and server code ensures that byte-ordering differences on different platforms are handled automatically by the runtime library, using a standard called XDR (external data representation). Thus, it makes RPC platform independent.

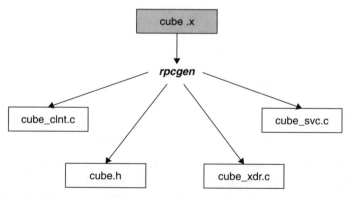

Figure 4.5 Use of a specification file

Next, we briefly discuss the server-side and client-side code for the current example.

RPC Server-Side Code and Compilation

Unlike the server-side code for Doors, the server-side code for RPC is very simple. All we have to do is write the implementation of the server function that's called by the client. The main() function is automatically generated by rpcgen in the file cube_svc.c. The server implementation code for this example is shown in Listing 4-4. We briefly explain the content of this listing in the following subsections.

Listing 4-4

```
Listing 4.4 : file - server.c
1   #include        "unpipc.h"
2   #include        "cube.h"
3
4   cube_out  *   cubeproc_1_svc ( cube_in * in, struct svc_req  *rqstp )
5   {
6           static cube_out out;
7
8           out.output = in->input  *  in->input  *  in->input;
9           return (&out);
10  }
```

Function Name and Arguments   In lines 4-5, you can see that the version number and '_svc' are appended to the named of the function. This allows for two overloaded function prototypes in the header file cube.h. One of these two functions is called by the client and will be discussed later. The second of these two functions is the actual server function. These two functions have different arguments. When the actual server function is called, the first argument is a pointer to the input structure, and the second argument is a pointer to a structure passed by the RPC runtime that contains information about this invocation. We ignore this information about the invocation for this simple example.

Execution and Return Value   After the input argument is obtained, the argument is cubed and the result is stored in a static structure. The address of this static structure is the return value. Note that we cannot use an automatic variable for the result because the automatic variables exist only during the execution of the function.

This server program is compiled along with the three other files and runtime library files. The three files are generated by the rpcgen tool

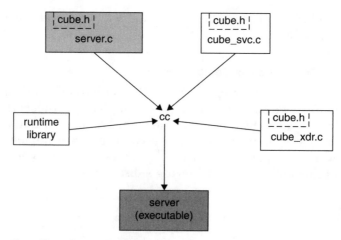

Figure 4.6 Compiling server side code

with the specification file as the input (refer to Figure 4.5). This compilation of the server program is shown schematically in Figure 4.6.

Client-Side Code and Compilation

The client-side code for this example is shown in Listing 4-5. It contains the main() function that calls the remote function defined in the server-side code (Listing 4-4). The following subsections provide a brief explanation of the code.

Listing 4-5

```
Listing 4.5: file - client.c
1    #include            "unpipc.h"
2    #include            "cube.h"
3
4    int main (int argc, char *argv[] )
5    {
6         CLIENT        *cl;
7         cube_input     in;
8         cube_output    out;
9
10        cl = Clnt_create ( argv[1],  CUBE_PROGRAM, CUBE_VERSIONS,  "tcp" );
11
12        in.input = atol (argv[2]);
13        out =cubeproc_1 (&in, cl);
14
15        printf ( "The result is : " %ld\n", out->output);
16        exit (0);
17   }
```

Include the Files In lines 1–2, two header files are included. The file cube.h is generated by rpcgen.

Declare the Variables In lines 6–8, we declare three variables, including the client handle (named cl). Client handles are like standard I/O file pointers. We also declare two other structure variables to hold the input and the output.

Obtain the Client Handle In line 10, we obtain the client handle by calling the function clnt_create(). The first argument is the IP address of the host running our server. The second argument is the program name, and the third argument is the version number, both from the specification file. The final argument is our choice of network protocol. The protocol is normally TCP or UDP. Note that the IP address does not include the port number where the server would be listening for the incoming requests. How the client obtains this port number for the server is explained in the upcoming section "RPC Process."

Call the Remote Function and Print the Result In lines 12–13, we call the remote function, passing two arguments as inputs. The first argument is a pointer to an input structure, and the second argument is the client handle. The return value is a pointer to the output structure declared in the specification file cube.x. We finally print the result.

The client code is compiled along with three other files generated by rpcgen and the runtime library, as shown schematically in Figure 4.7. (Note that in this figure, "cc" is the C compiler.)

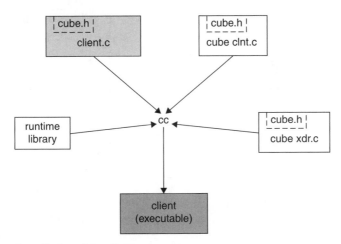

Figure 4.7 Compilation of the client code

RPC Process

Having discussed briefly the code and its compilation, we will now outline the basic steps involved in a remote function call. Figure 4.8 summarizes the steps that take place. The steps are numbered in the order in which they occur.

The very first steps are not shown in this figure. To begin, the server is started and registers a temporary port with what is called the *port mapper*. The server listens for the incoming call at this port on the host on which the server is running. Next, the client is started. When the client invokes the function clnt_create, it contacts the port mapper to find the temporary port of the server. Then the client establishes a TCP connection with the server at this port. These steps are not shown in the Figure 4.8 for the sake of brevity.

One of the important components introduced in Figure 4.8 is the client stub. To the client, the client stub appears to be the actual procedure it calls. The purpose of the stub is to package up the arguments to the remote procedure (possibly), put them into a standard format, and then build

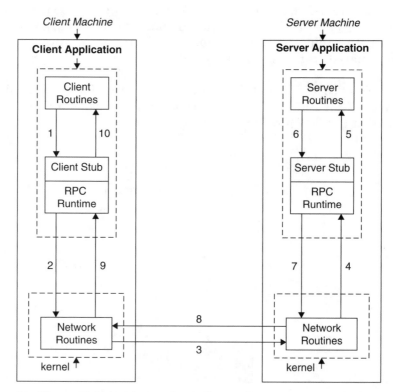

Figure 4.8 The complete remote procedure call process

Port Mapper

The port mapper is a software component that must be started before any RPC server is invoked. When an RPC server is started, it will tell the port mapper what port number it is listening to, and what RPC program numbers it is prepared to serve. When a client wishes to make an RPC call to a given program number, it will first contact the port mapper on the server machine to determine the port number where RPC packets should be sent.

one or more network messages. This packaging of arguments is called *marshalling*. An important aspect of this marshalling is that the byte-ordering differences among the different platforms are handled automatically using a standard XDR, thus making RPC platform independent.

Another important component RPC has introduced is the RPC runtime library. The client stub uses the functions provided in the RPC runtime library to make a systems call into the local kernel in order to send the packaged message over the network to the server machine using a protocol such as TCP. In other words, the RPC runtime encapsulates all the systems calls necessary for the connectivity (that is, to send the packaged arguments over the network). Therefore, the programmer doesn't need to know any systems programming.

On the server side, as the network message is received by the network routines in the kernel, it is sent to the server stub via the RPC runtime. The server stub unmarshals the input parameters and invokes the requested local procedure in the server routines. After the local procedure is completed, the server stub marshals the return value into one or more network messages and sends the packaged return value to the server kernel via the RPC runtime. The server kernel sends the message over to the client machines using a network protocol such as TCP. The client stub reads the network messages from the kernel through the use of RPC runtime routines. After possibly converting the return values, the client stub finally returns to the client function. This step appears to be a normal procedure returned to the client.

RPC

RPC was an important step in the development of an integration pattern because it outlined (for the first time) all the steps necessary for applications to share functionality. RPC can be used between any two applications to share functionality. The applications may be running on separate machines connected by a network. Many of the concepts and components introduced by RPC continue to be used in more modern methods of sharing functionality, as discussed in later chapters. Some of these concepts include the marshalling and unmarshalling of arguments, client and server stubs, and the encapsulation of all system and network calls within a library or a separate software component.

RPC Summary

RPC has further extended the concepts introduced with Doors by including applications running on separate machines. The machines are connected by a network. We further consolidated the concept of encapsulating all system-level calls in a library. This library now includes network-associated calls as well. The discussion of RPC also introduced the concept of marshalling of arguments, which packages the arguments in a system-independent manner for transmission over the network. We also introduced client and server stubs. The client stub acts as a proxy for the server-side code and makes it transparent for the client-side programmer to call the exposed server function. In summary, RPC for the first time outlined all the steps necessary for sharing functionality between applications that may be running on different hosts.

Conclusion

RPC—and the associated Doors—allowed for the first time real distributed computing by allowing applications to share functionality. A number of new concepts were introduced in this chapter (including service provider (server) and service consumer (client), platform independence, interface definition, the marshalling of input and output parameters, and the encapsulation of systems calls in a library) that are necessary for communication over the network.

However, RPC has a number of shortcomings, including the following:

- There is little room for code reuse because the code for marshalling and unmarshalling and the code for network communication are buried in the client and server applications.

- RPC is not language independent, and the client and the server must employ the same programming language.

- Tight temporal coupling exists between the applications. Because the calls are synchronous, the client application must wait for the server to complete the procedure before it can proceed further.

- The integration of the client and server is "point to point" and therefore not suitable when a number of applications need to be integrated.

- RPC is not suitable if a large number of remote calls are involved. Because of the synchronous nature of the call, the client cannot proceed further before the server completes its work. (Note that this problem can be overcome by using multithreading programming. However, this increases the complexity level of the programming and introduces some risks.)

To improve on RPC, two paths have been taken. The first method involves distributed objects, also known as *Object Request Broker (ORB),* and the second method involves asynchronous messaging. The distributed objects approach focuses on code reuse and language independence, whereas asynchronous messaging addresses the problem of tight coupling between applications.

We discuss the distributed objects (or ORBs) approach in the next chapter because it is more closely aligned with RPC. ORB essentially takes the encapsulation of all system-level calls into a library a step further by making this a separate software component (or executable). Today, most of the application servers such as WebSphere, WebLogic, and JBoss are based on ORB technology.

Chapter 5

Distributed Objects and Application Servers

In Chapter 3 we discussed the methods that allow sharing data only. In Chapter 4 we discussed remote procedure call (RPC), which for the first time allowed two applications to share functionality (in addition to sharing data). RPC is powerful enough to be the basis of client/ server architecture, which is commonly used for Internet and network applications.

However, RPC has a number of shortcomings that prevent it from being a complete and satisfactory solution for integrating all applications in a large enterprise. In this chapter, we will begin to address some of these shortcomings, including the following:

- There is little room for code reuse because the code for marshalling and unmarshalling and the code for network communication are buried inside the client and server applications.

- RPC is not language independent. In other words, the server and client applications must be written in the same programming language. Servers and clients written in two different programming languages cannot share functionality.

- RPC integrates the client and server applications in a point-to-point manner, which is not appropriate if a large number of applications need to be integrated. The number of integrations you need to perform in a point-to-point approach increases rapidly (roughly N^2, where N is the number of applications in an enterprise that are being integrated).

- On a related note, in RPC the roles of client and server are fixed, and the relationship between the client and the server is not "peer to peer." In other words, the client can access the functionality embedded in the server, but not the other way around.

In addition to addressing these issues, in this chapter we will look at the need for a directory and naming service. This need for a directory eventually led to the SOA Registry and Repository, which is one of the very important components of SOA.

In order to address these issues, we seek a solution that allows code reuse by separating out the code for marshalling and network communication into a standalone component (application). This separation also allows us to move away from the point-to-point approach because many applications can connect to each other using this new component. Furthermore, we will see a peer-to-peer relationship between the applications rather than a client/server relationship. Two other important features of the solution we seek are language independence and platform independence. Language independence is desired because we would like applications written in different programming languages to be able to communicate and share functionality. Thus, a program written in C++ should be able to communicate with a program written in Java. Platform independence is desired because we would like applications running on different platforms to be able to share functionality and data. For example, an application running on a UNIX system should be able to share functionality and data with an application running on a Windows system or a mainframe system.

A class of solutions that begins to address these requirements is *distributed objects*. The distributed objects extend the concepts of classes and objects introduced by object-oriented programming (OOP). Examples of OOP are the C++ and Java languages. Classes are user-defined type constructs that encapsulate data and behavior (functionality) related to a certain entity. The main advantages of encapsulation include more reliable and robust programming. In addition, OOP includes *inheritance*, which leads to code reuse at the programming level. The third pillar of OOP is *polymorphism,* which basically means that functions that perform similar work can have the same name. However, this third characteristic is not very important for our discussion here. An *object* in OOP refers to a particular instance of a given class at runtime. Previous to distributed objects, only objects belonging to the same application could interact with each other at runtime. With distributed objects, objects belonging to different applications can also interact and exchange data and functionality among themselves at runtime.

With distributed objects, three different models are available: Common Object Request Broker Architecture (CORBA), Microsoft's Distributed Component Object Model (DCOM), and Java's Remote Method Invocation (RMI). Out of these three, CORBA is most general. DCOM is mostly limited to one type of platform—namely, the Windows operating system. RMI is not limited to any platform but can only be used with the Java language. Most of this chapter is devoted to discussing CORBA because it is both platform and language independent. Furthermore, most application servers (such as IBM's WebSphere, BEA's WebLogic, and JBoss) derive their core functionalities from various components of CORBA.

We begin with an overview of CORBA, followed by a more detailed description of the various components of CORBA. In order to demonstrate how the various components fit together, we provide a detailed example of the use of CORBA. Toward the end of the chapter, we discuss application servers, which are closely related to the various components of CORBA. We also provide a brief comparison of Java RMI and CORBA.

CORBA Overview

The most import component of CORBA is Object Request Broker (ORB). ORB took the idea of marshalling and network communication one big step forward by encapsulating the marshalling code and the networking calls code into a separate software component (application). This separation allowed the same code to be reused by many applications as well as a certain amount of decoupling between the applications by moving away from point-to-point integration. This move away from point-to-point integration may be considered the first step in the evolution of the concept of Enterprise Service Bus (ESB). This is illustrated in Figure 5.1, which shows that multiple applications on the same machine can use the same ORB to communicate with each other as well as with applications on different machines. ORB has additional features that are discussed later in this chapter.

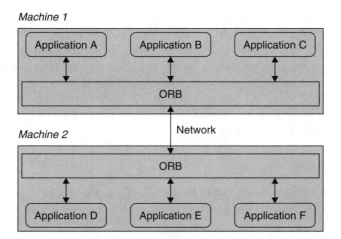

Figure 5.1 ORBs allow applications running on the same machine and on different machines to communicate

The second important contribution of CORBA is a method for declaring interfaces in a language-independent manner. Recall that with RPC, the interface is declared in a specific language such as C. CORBA introduced the interface definition language (IDL), which is not a programming language and can only be used to define interfaces. Because interfaces declared in IDL can be mapped to any programming language, the IDL specification is responsible for ensuring that data is properly exchanged between dissimilar languages. Standard mappings for a number of popular programming languages exist, including mappings for C, C++, Java, COBOL, and Smalltalk. IDL is discussed in greater detail later in this chapter.

CORBA also defined a standard protocol for the ORBs from various vendors to communicate. This protocol is known as the Internet Inter-ORB Protocol (IIOP). IIOP is built on top of TCP/IP and ensures, in principle, true interoperability among products from different vendors, thus enabling CORBA applications to be more vendor independent.

Just like RPC, CORBA includes a client stub. However, the client stub has reduced functionality because the code for marshalling has been taken out of it. It only serves to act as a proxy for the server object and makes the remote calls look like a local call for the client. In addition, CORBA includes a server skeleton, which is a piece of skeleton code that is used to fill in for implementing the server. Of course, the server skeleton is used on the server side.

CORBA maintains the notion of client and server. However, the distinction between the client and server is blurred somewhat. Unlike in RPC, in CORBA a component can simultaneously provide and use various services provided by the other objects. These other objects may have remote locations.

CORBA also has a distinct object model, which we discuss in detail in the next section. In CORBA, all communications between objects is done through object references. These references are known as *interoperable object references (IORs)*. In other words, remote objects in CORBA remain remote, and objects are not passed by value.

Additionally, CORBA provides a number of services, including naming, security, transaction, and persistent object services. We discuss these facilities later in the chapter.

CORBA Model

In this section, we discuss the major components of the CORBA model in detail. The aspects we discuss are

- The Object Request Broker (ORB)
- The Interface Definition Language (IDL)

- The CORBA object model
- The CORBA communication model and IIOP
- The roles of clients and servers in CORBA
- The roles of client stubs and server skeletons in CORBA
- The CORBA services

The Object Request Broker (ORB)

The most important component of CORBA is the Object Request Broker (ORB). ORB is also fundamental to the core functionality of all commercial application servers, including WebSphere, WebLogic, and JBoss. Simply stated, ORB provides all the communication and marshalling (of arguments and return values) needs of the distributed objects. The basic working of an ORB is as follows:

- When an object or component wants to use the services of another object or component, it first obtains a reference for the object providing the service. How this reference is obtained will be discussed later in "The CORBA Object Model" section.
- After this, the ORB locates the corresponding object implementation (that is, the server) on behalf of the client.
- As the server is located, the ORB ensures that the server is ready to receive the request.
- The ORB on the client side accepts the parameters of the method/ function being invoked and marshals the parameters to the network.
- The ORB on the server side unmarshals the parameters and delivers them to the server object.
- The return value is marshaled and unmarshaled at the server side and the client side, respectively, in a similar manner.

Figures 5.2 shows the major steps schematically.

An important point to note about the marshalling/unmarshalling process is that, because parameters are converted upon transmission into a platform-independent format and converted back into a platform-specific format upon reception, the communication between components is platform independent. In addition to platform independence, differences in hardware (such as processor byte ordering) are also made irrelevant because ORB automatically makes these conversions as necessary. Because the process of marshalling and unmarshalling is completely handled by the ORB, developers need not concern themselves with the details of marshalling and unmarshalling.

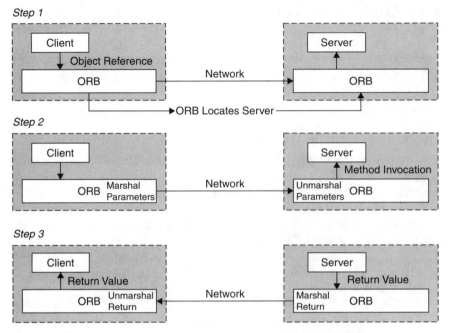

Figure 5.2   The major steps in applications communicating through ORBs

Interface Definition Language (IDL)

The second pillar of CORBA is the Interface Definition Language (IDL). IDL is what makes CORBA, in principle, a language-independent method of integration. Why is language independence important for integration? The main reason is that in a large enterprise, you usually find applications written in a variety of languages, including C/C++, Java, COBOL, VB, and so on. The second reason is related to performance issues in the integrated system. The language independence of CORBA allows developers to choose multiple languages for various components. For example, the client application can be implemented in Java, which ensures that the clients can be run on almost any type of machine. The server component can be written in C++ for high performance. IDL ensures that the data is properly exchanged between dissimilar languages.

IDL is used only to define interfaces. It is not a programming or implementation language. Roughly speaking, it defines method names and method signatures only. Java programmers can think of IDL definitions as equivalent to Java interfaces. Similarly, C++ programmers can think of IDL interfaces as equivalent to header files for classes.

The IDL is independent of any programming language and is a part of the standard CORBA specification. The language independence is achieved through language mappings. Standard mappings exist for many popular languages, such as Java, C, C++, COBOL, and Smalltalk. These mappings "map" IDL language constructs to the constructs of a particular language. For example, in the Java language an IDL interface maps to a Java interface, whereas in the C++ language, an IDL interface maps to a C++ class.

Listing 5-1 shows an example of an interface defined through IDL. This particular listing shows a module containing a single interface named "square." The interface declares one variable of type double that's named arg1. The interface defines one procedure called getSquare(), which takes as input arg1 and returns a double type.

Listing 5-1

```
Listing 5.1: A sample of IDL interface definition
module Test {
      interface square {
            attribute double arg1;
                  double getSquare (in double arg1);
      };
};
```

As with the specification file of RPC, an IDL file is used for generating different files using an automated tool. The automated tool takes the IDL file as input and generates a number of files that are used to develop the client and the server in a given language. For example, a tool called "idl2j" will generate files suitable for developing the client and server in the Java language. More details about these generated files can be found in "Sample CORBA Application" of this chapter.

The CORBA Object Model

Three elements of the CORBA model for objects which may be distributed over multiple machines connected by a network, are:

- Support for the near-transparent distribution of objects
- Object references
- Object adapters (which allow distributed objects to communicate among each other through the use of ORBs)

The distribution of objects is transparent in the sense that the client using the services provided by another object is nearly unaware of the location of the other object. The other object may be located on a remote machine or it may be located locally. In other words, to a CORBA client, a remote method call looks exactly like a local method call.

This transparency is made possible by the use of a client stub. Client stubs are discussed later in this section.

In the case of distributed objects, two methods are possible for one application component to communicate with the object in another application. One method, which CORBA utilizes, is called *passing by reference*. In this method, the object being accessed remains in the remote application while an object reference is passed. Operations on the remote object are processed by the remote object itself. The method of passing by reference is illustrated in Figure 5.3. In this illustration, Application A first

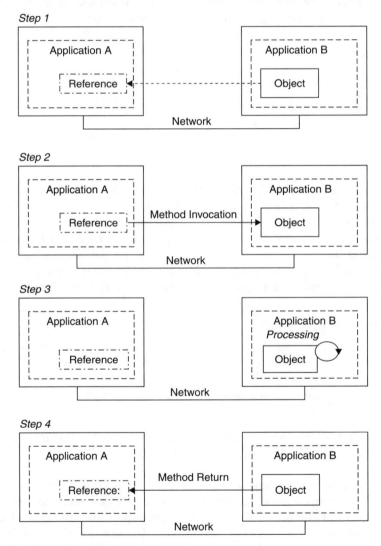

Figure 5.3 Passing by reference

obtains a reference to the remote object in Application B. Then Application A uses the reference to call a remote method on the remote object. Next, Application B processes the method, and finally the remote object sends the response back to Application A.

The second method of object communication is called *passing by value*. In this case, a copy of the object being called is made, which is then sent to the client application by a process called *serialization*. Next, the client application invokes a method on the copy of the object it has received. In this method of communication, the operation performed cannot change the state of the original remote object. The process of passing by value is illustrated in Figure 5.4. First, Application A invokes a method on a remote object in Application B. Application B makes a copy of

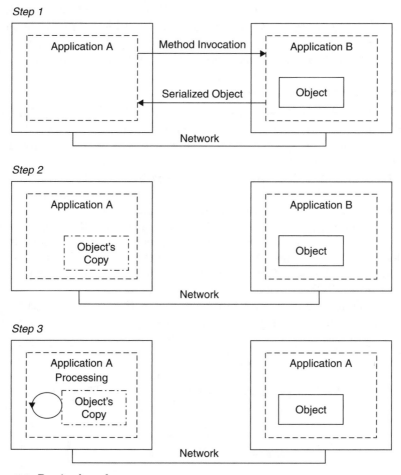

Figure 5.4   Passing by value

the object being called through serialization and sends the serialized copy to Application A. Next, Application A creates a copy of the object locally and invokes a method on this copy of the object. In this way, the original remote object state is not changed by the processing of the request.

As mentioned previously, CORBA uses the passing-by-reference method of communication between object exclusively. However, Java RMI allows passing by value for communication between remote objects. Passing by value requires that the object be re-created at the client application. This, in turn, requires that the client be aware of the implementation details for the methods of the remote object.

The third element of CORBA's object model is the object adapter. The primary purpose of an object adapter is to interface an object's implementation with its ORB. Three types of object adapters are provided by the CORBA specification. We will be mostly concerned with one type: Basic Object Adapter (BOA). BOA provides CORBA objects with a common set of methods for accessing ORB functions. These functions include object activation, authentication, and persistence. Every ORB implementation, which is CORBA-specification compliant, must provide a BOA.

Roles of the Client and Server in CORBA

As in RPC (or client/server architecture), CORBA maintains the basic notion of *client* and *server*. However, the distinction between the two is blurred somewhat, as we discuss in this section, thus moving toward a more peer-to-peer relationship. In CORBA, any application that creates an object and provides other applications with visibility to the object is termed *server* whereas other applications that use the services provided by the server are called *clients*. However, an application can act as a client to some applications while acting as a server to other applications. This is illustrated in Figure 5.5, which shows that Application A acts as a client to Application B. At the same time, Application B also acts as a client to Application C. Thus, Application B is simultaneously a CORBA server and a CORBA client.

The second situation that blurs the distinction between server and client is when the client passes a reference to an object it owns to

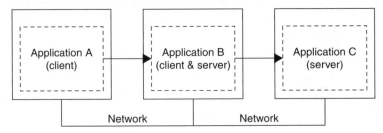

Figure 5.5 Client and server roles in CORBA

the server when it makes a remote procedure call and then the server, in turn, calls a method on the object owned by the client. This is called the *client callback method* and is illustrated in Figure 5.6. In this example, Application A (acting as a client of Application B) first obtains a reference to an object (Object 1) located on the server in Application B. However, when the client uses the object reference to call a remote method, it also passes a reference to an object (Object 2) it owns to Application B on the server. In the process of executing the method, Application B calls a method on the client object (Object 2) using the object references it received from Application A, as shown in Step 3 in Figure 5.6. Again, this calling of the method on the client object is known as the *client callback method*.

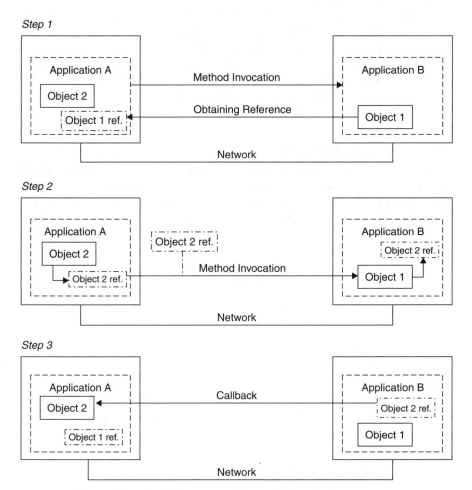

Figure 5.6 Client call method: the server calling a client method

Roles of Client Stubs and Server Skeletons

An IDL file is used with an IDL compiler by developers to generate what are called *client stubs* and *server skeletons*. The IDL compiler is language specific, and the client stubs and server skeleton it creates serve as the glue that connects the language independent IDL interface definition to the language-specific implementation code. Note that, in principle, the server skeleton and client stubs can be generated in two different programming languages by using two different IDL compilers. Client stubs for each interface are used in the client code, and client stubs for a particular interface provide a dummy implementation for each method in that interface. Client stubs do not execute the server functionality but rather communicate with the ORB to marshal and unmarshal parameters.

On the server side, the sever skeleton provides a framework on which the server implementation is built. For each method of the interface, the IDL compiler generates an empty method in the server skeleton, which the developer then uses to provide an implementation. The roles of the client stub and server skeleton are illustrated in Figure 5.7.

The roles of each will become clearer in the next section, where we develop a sample CORBA server and a sample CORBA client.

CORBA Communication Model

In a distributed environment, the application will have to communicate over a network. A network consists of a physical layer at the bottom. In turn, this physical layer may consist of a wired network, such as a telephone line, a fiber-optic cable, a wireless link, or a combination of these

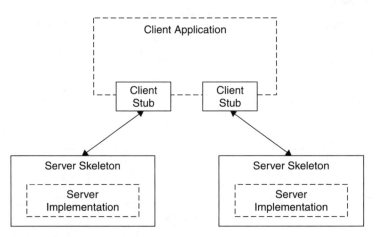

Figure 5.7   The roles of the client stub and server skeleton

networking technologies. Above this physical layer is a transport layer, which is responsible for moving packets of data from one point to another. The most common transport protocol in use is TCP/IP. Another transport protocol is DCE (the Open Software Foundation's Distributed Computing Environment protocol).

CORBA defines a high-level, generalized protocol called the General Inter-ORB Protocol (GIOP). This protocol is not used directly but instead is specialized by a particular protocol that would be used directly. The Internet Inter-ORB Protocol (IIOP) is such a specialized protocol. IIOP is the specialized form of GIOP and is used with TCP/IP transport protocol. An ORB must support IIOP in order for it to be considered CORBA compliant.

CORBA applications are built on top of specialized protocols such as IIOP. Although IIOP is the most common protocol used by CORBA applications, CORBA applications are not limited to using only one of these specialized protocols. An application's architecture can be designed to use a bridge that would interconnect, for example, DCE-based application components with IIOP-based application components. This type of architecture is shown in Figure 5.8.

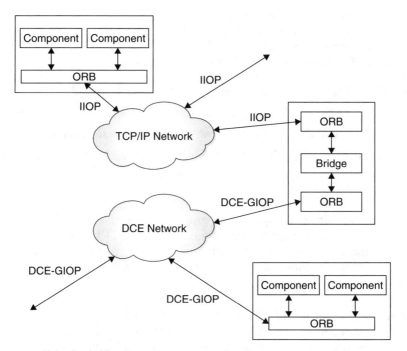

Figure 5.8 Use of a bridge to interconnect applications running on different types of networks

CORBA Services

The Object Management Architecture (OMA), of which CORBA is a part, defines a number of services that are useful for applications being integrated. These services include a naming service, security service, concurrency control service, transaction service, and life cycle service. We briefly discuss some of these services in this section, starting with the naming service, because this service is almost indispensable.

Naming Service   The naming service allows CORBA objects to register and get located by name. It uses the notion of a *naming context,* which consists of a set of unique names. This service also supports a federated architecture in which the named servers can be distributed across the network and work in cooperation with each other. As previously mentioned, this naming service could be considered as containing the seeds of the future development of the SOA registry. It should be noted that as part of the standard binding mechanism, CORBA objects are given names by which other objects can look them up, as you will see later in the sample code. This feature can be thought of as a rudimentary naming service. However, the actual naming service is much more scalable.

Security Service   Security in an integrated environment takes on an added importance because an application, in principle, can be accessed from any other application in the enterprise. The security service provides interfaces for the following security features:

- **Authentication**   Used to verify that the user is who they claim to be
- **Authorization**   Controls the access to various services or objects
- **Security auditing**   Keeps a record of all the user actions
- **Nonrepudiation**   Provides capabilities similar to digital signatures, which means the origin of the data and/or the receipt of the data can be proven irrefutably

Concurrency Control Service   The concurrency control service provides an interface for managing concurrency in shared CORBA objects. The management is done through support for several types of locks. The common types of locks supported are readers-writers locks and intention locks.

Transaction Service   Transaction services are an integral part of any nontrivial application. A transaction requires a set of tasks to be atomic. For example, in the case of a bank application, to coordinate the transfer between two accounts, a transaction should be initiated that causes the accounts involved either to both commit or to both abort the transaction; otherwise, inconsistent data would result.

Life Cycle Service   Life cycle services are responsible for creating, deleting, copying, and moving CORBA objects.

Sample CORBA Applications

In the last section, we described various components of the CORBA architecture. In order to see how these components fit together, we will next develop a simple CORBA client and a simple CORBA server.

This example will be a simple savings account. For this saving account, an object in the CORBA server application will expose three methods, which will allow the account holder to check the balance, deposit an amount, and withdraw an amount from the account using a CORBA client application.

IDL Interface Declaration

The development process starts by defining the account interface using IDL. It is clear that the interface should include three methods that the server exposes. These methods may be named getBalance(), deposit(), and withdraw(). It is also clear that the getBalance() method should have no input parameter and return a floating-point number. On the other hand, the other two methods should both take in a floating-point number as input and return the new balance, which should also be a floating-point number.

It is easy to define the interface using IDL syntax. The resulting IDL file, account.idl, is shown in Listing 5-2. First, we define a module named SavingAccount. Modules are used to group related interfaces. In our case, there is only one interface, named Account. In this interface, we define three methods. The first method is getBalance(). This method does not take any parameters as input but returns the balance as a float type. The second method, withdraw(), takes as input a parameter of the float type; we have named this input withdrawalAmount. This second method returns the new balance as a float type. The third method, deposit(), is defined similarly.

Listing 5-2

```
Listing 5.2
1       // account.idl
2
3       module SavingAccount    {
4
```

```
5                    interface    Account      {
6
7              // define the method for obtaining the balance
8              float   getBalance ();
9
10              // define the method for withdrawing money
11              float    withdraw ( in float withdrawalAmount );
12
13              // define the method for depositing money
14              float    deposit ( in float depositAmount );
15                         };
16           };
```

The next step in the development process is to choose a development language. In the last chapter on RPC we used C as the programming language, so here we will use Java for the sake of diversity.

In a method similar to that used in RPC, the IDL file is compiled using an automated tool such as idl2j, which produces the client stub, the server skeleton, and a few other files, as shown schematically in Figure 5.9. For the file account.idl, the following files are produced upon using the idl2j compiler:

- AccountServer.java
- AccountServerHolder.java
- AccountServerHelper.java
- _AccountServerImplBase.java
- _AccountServerStub.java

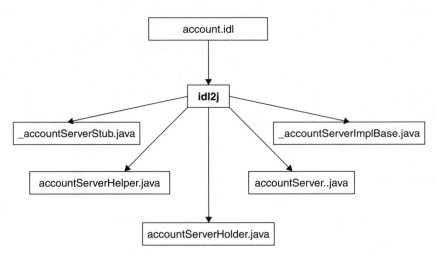

Figure 5.9 Results of compilation of the IDL file

The first four files are used in implementing the server. The file
_AccountImplBase.java is the server skeleton we have talked about.
The file _AccountServerStub is the client stub; this file is used while
implementing the client application. We discuss the server implementation next.

Server Implementation

The Java interface definition of the services provided by the server is
contained in the file AccountServer.java. The contents of the file appear
in Listing 5-3. Notice from this listing that idl2j translated the module
name, SavingAccount, as the Java package name. Furthermore, notice
that the interface extends the org.omg.CORBA.Object interface. All
CORBA object interfaces extend this interface. You can also see that
the interface contains the three methods we declared in the IDL file.
Note that IDL types have been mapped to the corresponding Java types.
The interface declared in this file will be implemented by the server, as
you will see shortly.

The implementation of the server starts from the server skeleton
generated by idl2j and is fairly straightforward. The entire server implementation class, AccountServerImpl.java, is shown in Listing 5-3. Next
we discuss this code, line by line.

Listing 5-3

```
Listing 5.3: AccountServerImpl.java
1       package      SavingAccount;
2
3       import org.omg.CORBA.ORB;
4       import  org.omg.CosNaming.NamingComponent;
5       import org.omg.CosNaming.NamingContext;
6       import org.omg.CosNaming.NamingContextHelper;
7
8       public class AccountServerImpl extends _AccountServerImplBase
implements
9            AccountServer   {
10
11             private float balance;
12
13             public AccountServerImpl ()   {
14                   balance = 0.0;
15             }
16
17             public float getBalance ()   {
18                         return balance;
19             }
20
21             public float withdraw ( float withdrawalAmount)   {
```

```
22                            balance = balance - withdrawalAmount;
23                            return balance;
24              }
25
26        public   float  deposit (float depositAmount )   {
27                            balance = balance + depositAmount;
28                            return balance;
29         }
30
31        public static void main ( String args [] )   {
32
33           try  {
34                     // Initialize the ORB
35                 ORB  orb = ORB.init (args, null );
36
37                     // instantiate an AccountServerImpl object and
register it with the ORB
38                 AccountServerImpl  accountServer = new
AccountServerImpl ();
39                 orb.connect ( accountServer);
40
41                 //Obtain the root naming context
42                 org.omg.OCORBA.Object  obj = orb.
43                     resolve_initial_references ("NameService");
44                 NamingContext namingContext = NamingContextHelper.
narrow (obj);
45
46                 // Bind the accountServer object reference in the
naming context
47                 NameComponent nameComponent = new NameComponent (
48                         "AccountServer", "");
49                 NameComponent  path [] = { nameComponent };
50                 namingContext.rebind (path, accountServer);
51
52                 //wait for method invocation requests from the clients.
53                 java.lang.Object  waitObject = new java.lang.Object ();
54                 synchronized (waitObject)  {  waitObject.wait (); }
55           }
56           catch ( Exception ex )    {
57                 System.out.println ( "Could not bind accountServer:
" + ex.getMessage ());
58           }
59      }
60 }
```

Package Declaration   Because the AccountServer interface is the part of the SavingAccount module, the IDL compiler places the Java class and interface definition into the SavingAccount package (see line 1). For convenience, we place the AccountServerImpl also in the same package.

Imported Classes   Lines 2–5 contain the commonly imported files in a CORBA application. The first file provides the functionality to communicate through the ORB. The other three files are related to the CORBA naming service. The naming service enables CORBA objects to register and be located by name. This service uses the notion of a *naming context*, which contains a set of unique names. The naming service may be considered the first step toward the development of a service registry, which is required in SOA.

Extending the Base Class   In lines 8 and 9, the base implementation class, AccountServerImplBase, and the interface, AccountServer, are generated by the IDL compiler. Our server implementation class extends the base implementation class and implements the generated interface. The base implementation class contains all the functionality the server needs to communicate with its ORB.

Server Class Member   In the example we are considering, we need to track only one quantity, namely the account balance. Therefore, we have defined exactly one class member, named balance, which is of Java type float (see line 11).

Methods Implementation   Lines 13–29 contain the implementation code for the three methods declared in the AccountServer interface. The first method, getBalance(), returns the current balance amount as a Java float type. The second method, withdraw(), takes the withdrawal amount and subtracts it from the balance. The new balance is the return value. Similarly, the third method, deposit(), takes the deposit amount and adds it to the balance. This method also returns the new balance.

Main Method   In the main method, shown in lines 31–60, we create an instance of the AccountServerImpl class, bind the instance to a naming context, and then wait for the clients to make method invocation requests. Some of this code is explained in more detail in the upcoming subsections.

ORB Initialization, Object Instantiation, and Registration   In lines 35–39, we first initialize the ORB and then create an instance of the AccountServerImpl class. The newly created object is then registered with the ORB.

Locating the NamingContext Object   In order for clients to connect to AccountServerImpl, they must have some way of locating the service on the network. One way to do this is through the CORBA naming service. In lines 42–44, a NamingContext object is located by resolving a reference to an object named NameService.

Binding the AccountServer   In lines 47–50, we bind the server with the naming context using the name AccountServer. After this binding, the clients can query the naming service for an object by this name, which will return a reference to this AccountServerImpl object.

Waiting for the Clients to Make Requests   Because the AccountServerImpl object is now registered with the naming service, the only thing left to do is to wait for the clients to invoke methods on this object. The actual handling of these requests for method invocation occurs in a separate thread, so the main() method simply needs to wait indefinitely (see lines 53–55).

Catching Exceptions   Lines 56–58 simply catch any exception thrown by the preceding code and print out an error message.

All that's left to do on the server side is to compile the Java server code using the Java compiler (javac) and then run the server.

Client Implementation

The client implementation is similar but simpler than the server implementation. It was a conscious design decision to put the complexity on the server side in order to keep the client-side programming as simple as possible. Listing 5-4 shows sample code for a client implementation. This client first obtains a reference to the server and then invokes two methods on the server. The following subsections explain some of the client code.

Listing 5-4

```
Listing 5.4: SavingAccountClient.java
1        //   SavingAccountClient.java
2
3        package SavingAccount;
4
5        import   org.omg.CORBA.ORB;
6        import   org.omg.CosNaming.NameComponent;
7        import   org.omg.CosNaming.NamingContext;
8        import   org.omg.CosNaming.NamingContextHelper;
9
10     // simple client of the   AccountServer
11     public class   SavingAccountClient   {
12        // constructor for the client class
13          SavingAccountClient () {
14            }
15
16          public static ORB   ourORB;
17          private AccountServer   ourAccountServer;
18
19          public static void main (String args []))   {
20
```

```
21              // initialize the ORB
22              ourORB = ORB.init (args, null);
23
24              SavingAccountClient  client = new SavingAccountClient ();
25
26           try {
27
28                  ///Obtain the root naming context
29                  org.omg.CORBA.Object obj = ourORB.
30                              resolve_initial_references
("NamingService");
31                  NamingContext  namingContext = NamingContextHelper.
narrow(obj);
32
33                  // Try to locate the Accountserver in
the naming context
34                  NameComponent nameComponent = new NameComponent (
35
 "AccountServer",  ""):
36                  NameComponent  path [] = { nameComponent };
37                  ourAccountServer = AccountServerHelper.narrow
(namingContext,
38
 resolve ( Path ) );
39              }
40           catch (Exception ex )  {
41                  System.out.println ( "Could not locate the server :  "
+ ex.getMessage () );
42                  return;
43              }
44           // check the initial balance
45           System.out.println ( "The balance before deposit was :  " +
46
 ourAccountServer.getBalance () );
47           //deposit $10 and check the balance again
48           System.out.println ( "The balance after the deposit is : $ " +
49                                      ourAccountServer.
deposit (10.0));
50       }
51    }
```

Package, Imports, and Class Name   In lines 3–14, we first declare the package name and list the classes that need to be imported. The package name and the import classes are the same as those in the server class. We can choose any class name for the client class. We have chosen the class name SavingAccountClient and defined a no-argument constructor for the class.

Class Members   In lines 16 and 17, we declare two class variables. The first is the reference to the ORB we are going to use and the second is a reference to the server on which we are going to invoke two methods.

Main Method and Class Instantiation   Every Java program has a main method with standard signature. We declare the main method in the usual way and then initialize our ORB. Next, we instantiate the SavingAccountClient class (see lines 19–24).

Obtaining a Reference to the Server   In lines 26–43, we obtain a reference to the server by using the naming service. This code is similar to the code on the server side, so it will not be explained further. The code is enclosed in a try/catch block in order to deal with any exceptions that may be thrown in the process of obtaining the reference to the server class.

Invoking Methods on the Server   Lines 44–49 are used to invoke two methods on the server. First, we invoke the method getBalance() and print the result. Next we add $10 to the account using the method deposit(). This method returns the new balance, and we print the return value. Note that the method invocation looks like a local method call. This is because the code for marshalling and unmarshalling has been taken out of the client application and incorporated in the ORB.

Application Servers

We now turn our attention to the commercial products that support distributed objects. These commercial products are commonly known as *application servers*. Currently, a large number of products are available, including IBM's WebSphere Application Server, IBM's WebSphere Application Server Enterprise Edition, BEA WebLogic Server, JBoss, VisiBroker for Java, VisiBroker for C++, Orbix for Java, and Orbix for C++. The two most common application servers are IBM's WebSphere Application Server and BEA's WebLogic Server.

The backbone of all these products consists of some implementation of CORBA's ORB. In addition, these products also support a number of other features of CORBA, including security and transaction services. However, most of these products have been specialized to one particular language or a particular type of application.

The most common type of application servers are those that support J2EE applications and the Java development environment. J2EE consists of different types of components, such as Enterprise Java Beans (EJBs), servlets, JSPs, and Java clients. These components, except for the Java client, run in containers that run on top of the underlying ORB. For example, the servlets and JSPs run in a web server, whereas EJBs run in an EJB container. The containers handle system functions for the EJB component and use the underlying ORB to handle the protocols required for client and server interaction. In addition, an EJB can directly access the CORBA ORB, if required for communication with other CORBA applications that may be written in a different language. Figure 5.10 summarizes some of the interactions an EJB component can have with other J2EE components and other CORBA applications that may be written in a language other than Java. However, this kind of interaction is assured only by some implementation vendors. Notable among these vendors is IBM, who ensures interoperability between their various ORB products.

In the context of J2EE-specific application servers, it is interesting to consider the parallels between the CORBA and J2EE programming models. Java has another independent method of distributed objects, called Remote Method Invocation (RMI). The RMI architecture is very similar to the CORBA architecture but is limited to the Java language. In other words, RMI provides functionality and services very similar to CORBA for applications written in Java only. To use services provided by RMI, the client first must obtain a reference to the remote object. To do that, the client must know where to find the remote object, what it is called, and what method call it provides. These location services are provided by an RMI registry, to which the remote object must register first. Java provides an interface called the Java Naming and Discovery Interface (JNDI), which is used to locate and bind to the server object. Table 5.1 summarizes some of the parallels between CORBA and RMI.

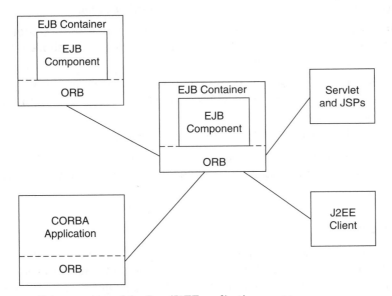

Figure 5.10 Interoperation of the Java/J2EE application server

Table 5.1   Parallels Between the CORBA and RMI Programming Models

	CORBA Programming Model	EJB Programming Model
Interface definition language	IDL	Java EJB home and remote interface or IDL
Object invocation	IDL code	RMI code or IDL code
Communication protocols	IIOP	IIOP and RMI-to-IDL mapping (if required)
Security protocol	CORBA security interface	CORBA security interface
Naming service	CosNaming Service	JNDI or CosNaming Service
Transaction service	Object Transaction Service	Java Transaction Service or Object Transaction Service

The second most common type of application servers are those that cater to C++ applications and components. Notable among this type of application server is IBM's WebSphere Application Server Enterprise Edition and VisiBroker for C++. In general, various products from a given vendor interoperate quite well. For example, IBM's WebSphere Application Server works together with IBM's WebSphere Application Server Enterprise Edition quite well.

In theory, the various ORB products from different vendors should also interoperate quite well. However, in practice, the following factors restrict or limit the full interaction between CORBA applications from different vendors:

- **Proprietary extensions**   Some ORB implementations have added proprietary extensions to the CORBA specifications.

- **Specification levels**   Some ORB implementations conform to different levels of the CORBA specifications, and these different levels are not always compatible with each other.

- **Ambiguities**   Some ORB implementations differ in the way they implement parts of the CORBA specifications because of ambiguities in the specifications.

- **Bugs**   Some CORBA ORBs simply have bugs.

- **Interpretability problems**   Problems with interpretability are more serious if the products are designed to be used with different languages.

Conclusion

In this chapter, we introduced the concept of distributed objects by moving away from procedural languages such as C and into the realm of object-oriented programming (OOP) and object-oriented design (OOD). Examples of object-oriented languages include Java, C++, and Visual Basic (VB). We extended the concept of objects to include distributed objects, where the objects can be distributed over a network. Furthermore, we described the standard CORBA, which allows remote objects to interact with one another.

We took a big step forward in application integration by encapsulating the code for parameter marshalling and unmarshalling and the code for networking into a separate software component (or application). We called this component Object Request Broker (ORB). This remediates the problem of the lack of code reuse in the case of RPC, which was described in the last chapter. Various implementations of ORB form the backbone of all the modern commercial application servers, which are needed to support distributed objects. In addition, ORB has allowed us to move away from point-to-point integration, which is important if a large number of applications need to be integrated. Also, this move away from point-to-point integration leads to the concept of the Enterprise Service Bus (ESB), as you will see later.

In addition, we introduced the concept of language independence via an interface definition language (IDL). The interfaces declared through an IDL can be mapped to any programming language and can allow, in principle, the client and server to be implemented in two different languages. Another important concept introduced in this chapter is the registry, which is used by the server objects to register themselves so they can be located by the client.

The major issue we did not address in this chapter that was mentioned in Chapter 4 as a shortcoming of RPC, is the issue of scalability. This lack of scalability in cases of RPC and distributed objects results from the synchronous nature of the interaction between the server and the client. For synchronous method calls, the client is blocked from performing further work until the server completes its work and returns control to the client. In the next chapter, we discuss asynchronous messaging and address this issue in detail.

6

Messaging

In the last chapter we discussed distributed objects, which have overcome many of the shortcomings of RPC, described in Chapter 4. In particular, distributed objects allowed for code reuse by separating out the code for marshalling and networking into a separate software component. This separation also allowed us to move away from point-to-point integration patterns. In addition, distributed objects introduced the concept of language independence, which is important for large enterprise integration projects. Distributed objects also blurred the distinction between the client (or service consumer) and the server (or the service provider). Thus, a more peer-to-peer type of relationship can be established between applications. Finally, distributed objects allowed us to develop a rudimentary concept of a registry.

Although distributed objects provided a big step forward on many fronts in the battle for enterprise applications integration, they failed to address two very import shortcomings of RPC:

- Both RPC and distributed objects employ synchronous interaction between the applications being integrated. This means that the client application is blocked from doing further work until the server application completes its work and returns control to the client application. This leads to strong coupling between applications and a lack of scalability in the integration solution. In other words, if a large number of applications need to be integrated, neither RPC nor distributed objects is the proper solution.

- RPC- and ORB-based communication is not reliable and there is no guarantee that the messages and return values will be delivered to the intended targets. Thus, the client application may experience a hang-up in its operation under certain circumstances (such as a break in the network connection or when the two applications are not up and running at the same time).

In this chapter, we discuss asynchronous messaging, which overcomes these two major problems with RPC and distributed objects. In addition, asynchronous messaging has other advantages, which are elaborated upon later in this chapter. In asynchronous messaging, the client or client object sends a message to the target application but does not wait for the response to continue its work, thus leading to a certain amount of decoupling between the applications involved. Therefore, asynchronous messaging may be employed as the basis for integration if high transaction volumes are expected.

We start this chapter with an overview of a messaging system. Then we discuss the various components of the messaging system in detail. To demonstrate how these components work together, some sample code is provided. Finally, we conclude by discussing certain disadvantages of the messaging approach to application integration.

Overview

As mentioned, in asynchronous messaging the client (or service consumer) sends a message to the server but does not wait for the response. This allows the client application to perform further work while the server is completing the request from the client. This decoupling between the client and server means that more work can be accomplished in a given timeframe. In other words, it leads to a more scalable solution.

In messaging, the applications do not communicate with each other directly and do not have a dedicated communication link established between them. Instead, they communicate indirectly through queues. A queue—sometimes called a *channel*—behaves like a collection of messages that can be shared across multiple computers. Figure 6.1 shows two

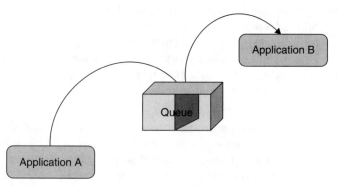

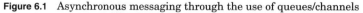

Figure 6.1   Asynchronous messaging through the use of queues/channels

applications exchanging a message through a queue. Application A first sends a message to the queue. Application B then retrieves the message from the queue after it has been delivered by Application A.

As with ORB or distributed objects, in asynchronous messaging the code for the communication and marshalling is separated out as a separate software component, which allows for code reuse (that is, multiple applications can use the same code to communicate with each other and with applications on another machine). This separate software component is often called a *messaging system* or *message-oriented middleware (MOM)*. Figure 6.2 shows the basic steps involved in transmitting a message from Application A to another application (Application B) running on a separate computer. Here are the five steps involved in transmitting the message:

1. Application A creates a message and populates the message with data.

2. Application A sends the message to the queue inside the messaging system (MOM).

3. The messaging system transfers the message from the sender's computer to the receiver's computer, making it available to the receiver.

4. Application B reads the message from the queue.

5. Application B processes the message received in step 4.

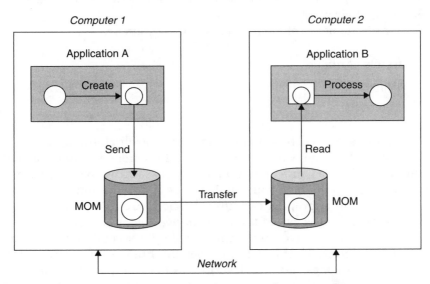

Figure 6.2   Basic steps involved in exchanging an asynchronous message

Another important feature of a messaging system is that it can guarantee delivery of a message to the target application by persisting the message. The messaging system achieves this by trying again and again until the message is delivered (if it is unable to deliver the message to the intended target the first time). The messaging system may not be able to deliver the message in the first few tries for various reasons. For example, the server application may not be running or the network is down.

Yet another important problem that asynchronous messaging solves relates to applications specifically designed to run disconnected from the network, yet synchronize with servers when a network connection is available. Examples include applications deployed on laptop computers and PDAs. Messaging fits in very well for enabling this synchronization. Data to be synchronized is queued as it is created, waiting until the applications connects to the server.

The decoupling between the client and server application achieved through messaging also helps to avoid another serious problem that can occur with RPC and distributed objects. That problem is *throttling,* which refers to the fact that with RPC and distributed objects, a single server can be overloaded with requests from different clients. This can lead to performance degradation and even cause the server to crash. Because the messaging system queues up requests until the server is ready to process them, the server can control the rate at which it operates on the requests so as not to overload itself by too many simultaneous requests. The clients are unaffected by this throttling because communication is asynchronous, so the clients are not blocked from continuing their work.

The three elements of a basic messaging system are

- Channels or queues
- Messages
- End points

Channels are used to transmit data, and each channel acts as a virtual pipe that connects a receiver with the sender. Channels do not come preconfigured in a newly installed messaging system; rather, you must determine how your applications need to communicate and then create the appropriate channels. There are two basic types of channels. The first is called the *point-to-point channel,* in which only one receiver can receive a given message. The second is called *publish-and-subscribe.* In this second type, any number of receivers can get and act on a message. We describe these two types of channels in detail later in this chapter.

Messages encapsulate the data to be transmitted. A message consists of a header and a body. The information contained in the header is primarily for the messaging system to use. The header contains information regarding destination, origin, and more. The body contains the actual data the receiver consumes. The data contained in the body can be of different types. It can be a command message, which is used to invoke a procedure (method) in the receiving application, or it can be a document message, which is used to transfer data from one application to another. It can also be an event message, which is used to inform the receiving application of an event in the sending application.

A messaging system acts like a server, and the application sending or receiving a message acts as a client of the messaging system. The messaging system usually supplies a client API for the client to interact with the messaging system. For example, IBM's WebSphere MQ supplies an API called MQI, which the applications can use to connect to the MQ messaging system and to send and receive messages. The API is not application specific. The client therefore must contain a set of code that uses this API to connect to the messaging system to exchange messages with other applications. This additional set of code is called a *message end point,* which the rest of the application uses to send or receive messages. A messaging end point can be used either to send or receive messages, but not both.

JMS is a standard vendor-neutral API that can be used to access messaging systems. JMS is analogous to JDBC: Whereas JDBC is an API that can be used to access many databases; JMS provides the same vendor-independent access to messaging systems. Many enterprise messaging systems support JMS, including IBM's WebSphere MQ. Software applications that use the JMS API for sending or receiving messages are portable across JMS vendors. Java applications that use JMS are called *JMS clients,* and the messaging system that handles the routing and delivery of messages is called the *JMS provider.* A JMS client that sends a message is called a *producer,* whereas a JMS client that receives a message is called a *consumer.* A single JMS client can be both a producer and a consumer.

In addition to IBM WebSphere MQ, other products in this category include WebMethods, TIBCO, SeeBeyond, Microsoft's BizTalk, and many others. Many application servers, such as the IBM WebSphere Application Server, also offer the basic capability to send and receive asynchronous messages. In many cases, this provides a cheaper alternative to a full-blown messaging system. However, if the number of applications to be integrated is large, as is usually the case in a large enterprise, application server asynchronous messaging capabilities are limited in scalability.

Channels

As mentioned previously, there are two basic types of channels. We discuss these in some detail in this section. In particular, we discuss how point-to-point channels can be used for synchronous messaging between two applications.

Point-to-Point Channel

The point-to-point messaging model allows messaging system clients to send and receive messages asynchronously via virtual channels known as *queues*. The point-to-point messaging model has traditionally been a pull- or polling-based model, where the messages are requested from queues, instead of being pushed to the client automatically. The point-to-point messaging model is intended for one-to-one delivery of messages, as shown in Figure 6.3.

As shown in this figure, a queue may have multiple receivers, but only one receiver may receive each message. The message system (sometimes called the JMS provider) will take care of doling out messages among the receivers, thus ensuring that each message is consumed by only one receiver.

The point-to-point asynchronous messaging model can also used to simulate synchronous messaging or interaction between two applications. This is shown in Figure 6.4, where one queue (the request queue) is used to deliver the request while the return values are obtained through another queue. The request queue is the output queue for the requesting application (Application A), while at the same time it serves as the input queue for the receiving application (Application B). Similarly, the response queue is used as an output queue for Application B and as an input queue for the return value for Application A. In order to correlate the request with the response, a correlation ID is included in the header of the response. The value of this correlation ID is usually the request message ID.

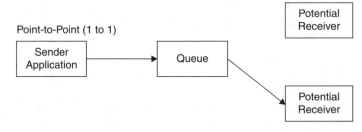

Figure 6.3   Point-to-point messaging

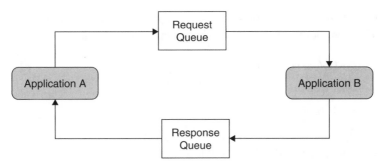

Figure 6.4   Simulating a synchronous exchange using the messaging system

Publish-and-Subscribe

In publish-and-subscribe messaging, one producer can send a message to any number of consumers through a virtual channel called a *topic*. Consumers can choose to subscribe to a topic. Any messages addressed to a topic are delivered to all the subscribers. Every subscriber receives a copy of each message, as shown in Figure 6.5. The publish-and-subscribe messaging model is mostly a push-based model, where messages are automatically broadcast to consumers without the topic being polled for new messages. In the publish-and-subscribe messaging model, the publisher may not care if everybody is listening, or even if nobody is listening. For example, consider a publisher that broadcasts stock quotes. If any particular subscriber is not listening and misses out on a great quote, the publisher is not concerned.

Messages

A message consists of a header and a body. The body contains the data to be processed by the receiving application. The header contains the message identification and control information, intended to be used

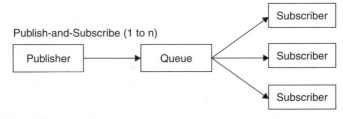

Figure 6.5   Publish-and-subscribe model

mostly by the messaging system. A typical header would have a number of attributes. Some of the commonly occurring attributes are

- Message ID/correlation ID
- Persistent/nonpersistent
- Return address
- Priority
- Segmenting/grouping information
- Date and time
- Lifetime of a message
- Version

The message ID and correlation ID are used to identify a specific request or reply message. As the programmer, you can move a value in one or both fields or have the messaging system create a unique ID for you. Before you put the request message in the queue, you can save the ID(s) and use it in a subsequent "get" operation for the reply message. The program that receives the request message copies this information into the reply message. This allows the originating program (the one that gets the reply) to instruct the messaging system to look for a specific message in the queue instead of getting the first one in the queue.

Persistent messages always arrive at their destination, even when the system fails. They are "hardened" (that is, saved on disk). You can make a specific message persistent or all messages on a particular queue persistent.

You can assign a priority to a message and thus control the order in which it is processed.

The return address is important for request/reply messages. You have to tell the server program where to send the reply message. Clients and server have a one-to-many relationship and usually the server program cannot find out from the user data where the request message came from. Therefore, the client provides the reply-to queue and reply-to queue manager in the message header.

Messages can be segmented or grouped. Message segmenting can be transparent to the application programmer. If permitted, the queue manager segments a large message when it does not fit in a queue. On the receiving end, the application has the option to either receive the entire message in one piece or each segment separately. This may depend on the buffer size available for the application.

A second method of segmenting leaves you as the programmer in control so that you can split a message according to logical boundaries or the buffer size available for the program. The programmer puts each segment as a separate physical message; thus, several physical messages build one logical message. The queue manager ensures that the order of the segments is maintained.

To reduce traffic over the network, you can also group several small messages together and build one larger physical message. This message is then sent to the destination and is disassembled there. Message grouping also guarantees that the order in which the messages are sent is preserved.

You can also specify an expiration date. When this date is reached and a read request is issued, the message will be discarded. There is no "daemon" that checks a queue for expired messages. Expired messages can stay in a queue for weeks, until a program attempts to read it.

As mentioned previously, the body of a message contains the data to be processed by the receiving application. In the case of Web Services, this message may be a SOAP message. An example of a SOAP message is given in Listing 6-1.

Listing 6-1

```
Listing 6.1: A SOAP message
1     <SOAP-ENV:Envelope xmlns:SOAP-ENV="SOAPEnvelopeURI"
2              SOAP-ENV:encodingStyle="SOAPEncodingURI">
3       <SOAP-ENV:Header>
4       </SOAP-ENV:Header>
5       <SOAP-ENV:Body>
6             <m:GetLastTradePrice xmlns:m="ServiceURI">
7                   <tickerSymbol>IBM</tickerSymbol>
8             </m:GetLastPrice>
9       </SOAP-ENV:Body>
10    </SOAP-ENV:Envelope>
```

It is interesting to note that in JMS, a message is represented by the type (class) Message, which has several subtypes. In each subtype the header structure is the same; it is the body that varies by type. Here are the different message types supported by JMS:

- **TextMessage** This is the most common type of message. The body is a string such as literal text or an XML document. A SOAP message is an example of an XML document.

- **BytesMessage** This is the simplest and most universal kind of message. The body is a byte array.

- **Object Message** The body is a single Java object. The Java object must implement the serializable interface.

- **StreamMessage** The body is a stream of Java primitives such as char, int, and long.

- **MapMessage**   The body behaves like a java.util.Map, where the keys are String objects.

In discussing SOAP messages, which are transmitted through the messaging system (such as IBM WebSphere MQ), it is interesting to note the recursive nature of the messages. This means that a messaging system object contains the SOAP message as the body. The messaging system itself employs a transport protocol such as TCP to transmit the data.

End Points

A message end point contains a set of code that is used to connect to the messaging system and to send or receive a message. The rest of the application uses the end points whenever it needs to send or receive a message. Message end points are of two general types. The first type is used to send a message whereas the second type is used to receive messages. Within the first general type are two subtypes: The first subtype is used to send the message in a point-to-point model, whereas the second subtype is used to send a message in a publish-and-subscribe model. In addition to these types of end points, message-driven beans can also serve as consumers of messages. We will discuss examples of these end points using JMS because JMS is a vendor-neutral API. Message-driven beans will be described separately.

Sending a Message (Point-to-Point)

In a point-to-point model, a message is not sent directly to the intended receiver. Instead, the message is sent to a queue, as shown previously in Figure 6.3. As discussed in the "Messages" section, there are different kinds of messages. For the sake of simplicity, we will demonstrate the working of this type of end point by sending a message of the type text: "Hello World". The general flow of the code is shown in Figure 6.6, and the actual code is shown in Listing 6-2.

Listing 6-2

```
Listing 6.2: Code snippet for sending a message to a queue in
a point-to-point model
1    String message = "Hello World";
2    QueueConnectionFactory factory = (QueueConnectionFactory)
3        jndiContext.lookup("java:comp/env/jms/QueueFactory");
4    Queue queue = (Queue)
5        jndiContext.lookup("java:comp/env/jms/MyQueue");
6    QueueConnection connect = factory.createQueueConnection();
7    QueueSession session = connect.createQueueConnection (true, 0);
```

```
8    QueueSender  sender = session.createSendor (Queue);
9     TextMessage  textMsg = session.createTextMessage ():
10   textMsg.setText (message);
11   sender.send (textMsg);
12   connect.close ();
```

We now walk through this code snippet, line by line:

- **Line 1** This line simply defines the data for the message. In this case, the data is a String: "Hello World". This is the message body we want to send to the queue.

- **Lines 2–3** In order to send a JMS message, we need a connection to the JMS provider. The connection to the JMS provider is obtained through a JMS connection factory. This factory is obtained through an environment variable called QueueFactory.

- **Lines 4–5** Next we look up the queue to which we will send the message by name using JNDI. Our queue is named MyQueue. Once again, behind the scenes it looks up the environmental variable for the queue.

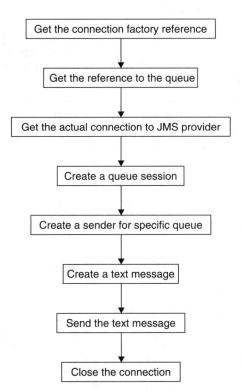

Figure 6.6 Flow of code for sending a message in a point-to-point model

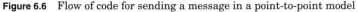

- **Line 6** Next we use the connection factory to obtain a connection to the JMS provider by calling the method createQueueConnection().

- **Line 7** Once a queue connection is obtained, it is used is create a QueueSession, which is used to group the actions of sending and receiving messages.

- **Line 8** Next we use the QueueSession to create a QueueSender for the specific queue we are interested in.

- **Line 9** From the QueueSession we also create a message object. In this case the message is a text message, so we create a message object of type text.

- **Line 10** Next we set the content of the text message object by using the String "Hello World".

- **Line 11** We send the message using the send() function.

- **Line 12** As a last step, we close the connection in order to conserve resources.

Sending a Message in Publish-and-Subscribe Model

In the publish-and-subscribe model, the message is sent to a topic instead of a queue, as was done previously with the point-to-point model. Any number of receivers can subscribe to a given topic, and each of the subscribers will receive a copy of the message to act upon. A snippet of the code that sends a message to a topic is shown in Listing 6-3, and the flow of the code is shown in Figure 6.7. As can be seen from the code listing as well as from the code flow diagram, the code is very similar to the code used in the point-to-point model. Thus we will not explain the code here.

Listing 6-3

```
/Listing 6.3: Code snippet for sending a message to a queue
in a publish-subscribe model
1    String message = "Hello World";
2    TopicConnectionFactory factory = (TopicConnectionFactory)
3         jndiContext.lookup("java:comp/env/jms/TopicFactory");
4    Topic topic = (Topic)
5         jndiContext.lookup("java:comp/env/jms/MyTopic");
6    TopicConnection connect = factory.createTopicConnection();
7    TopicSession session = connect.createTopicConnection (true, 0);
8    TopicPublisher  publisher = session.createPublisherr (topic);
9    TextMessage  textMsg = session.createTextMessage ():
10   textMsg.setText (message);
11   publisher.publish(textMsg);
12   connect.close ();
```

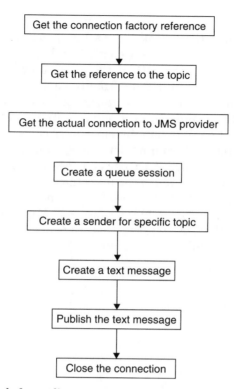

Figure 6.7   Flow of code for sending a message in a publish-and-subscribe model

End Points for Receiving Messages

In this section, we provide the skeleton code for receiving a message. Once again we will employ JMS API because it is vendor neutral. To get a better idea of how JMS is used to receive and process a message, we develop a simple JMS client application. The application just receives text messages and prints the message to the standard output device.

In general, there are three subtypes of message end points for receiving messages. The first type receives messages in a point-to-point scenario; the second type receives messages in a publish-subscribe scenario. These two subtypes contain similar code; therefore, we describe only one of these subtypes—namely, the publish-and-subscribe message receiving end point. The third subtype, which is becoming very common, is the message driven bean. Message driven beans will be described separately in the next section.

The skeleton code for receiving a text message in a publish-and-subscribe scenario is shown in Listing 6-4. In this case, the application takes as input a name for the topic factory and a name for the topic.

These names are used by the application for lookup purposes. Much of this code is similar to the code used for sending messages in the publish-and-subscribe model. Therefore, we only briefly describe the code.

The constructor JmsClient() of the class JmsClient obtains the TopicConnectionFactory and Topic from the JNDI InitialContext. This context is created with vendor-specific properties. After this, the client application creates a TopicConnection and a TopicSession, as you have seen previously. Then a TopicSubscriber is created, which is designed specifically to process incoming messages that are published to its specified Topic. The TopicSubscriber can receive messages directly, or it can delegate the processing of the messages to a MessageListener. We have chosen to implement the MessageListener interface so that the JmsClient class can process messages itself. MessageListener implements a single method, onMessage(), which is invoked every time a new message is sent to a subscriber's topic.

Listing 6-4

```
Listing 6.4: A Java class for receiving a text message in a publish
subscribe scenario
1       import javax.jms.Message;
2       import javax.jms.TextMessage;
3       import javax.jms.TopicConnectionFactory;
4       import javax.jms.TopicConnection;
5       import javax.jms.TopicSession;
6       import javax.jms.Topic;
7       import javax.jms.Session;
8       import javax.jms.TopicSubscriber;
9       import javax.jms.JMSException;
10      import javax.naming.InitialContext ;
11
12      public class JmsClient implements javax.jms.MessageListener  {
13
14        public static void main (String []  args) throws Exception {
15          if ( args.length != 2 )
16             throw new Exception ("Wrong number of arguments");
17               new JmsClient ( args[0], args[1] );
18               while (1)  { Thread.sleep (20000); }
19        }
20
21        public JmsClient ( String factoryName, String topicName )     {
22
23            InitialContext  jndiContext  =  getInitialContext ();
24            TopicConnectionFactory  factory = (TopicConnectionFactory)
25            jndiContext.lookup (factoryName);
26            Topic topic = (Topic) jndiContext.lookup(topicName);
27            TopicConnection connect = factory.createTopicConnection ();
28            TopicSession session =
29              connect.createTopicSession (false,Session.AUTO_
ACKNOWLEDGE);
```

```
30              TopicSubscriber subscriber = session.createSubscriber (topic);
31              subscriber.setMessageListner(this);
32              connect.start();
33      }
34
35      public void onMessage (Message message)   {
36
37          try  {
38                  TextMessage textMessage = (textMessage) message;
39                  String text = textMessage.getText ();
40                  System.out.println ("Message Received : \n" + text);
41              }
42          catch (JMSException ex)  {
43                  System.out.println (" JMS ERROR : " +
ex.getMessage() );
44              }
45          }
46      }
```

Message-Driven Beans

Message-driven beans (MDBs) are stateless, server-side, transaction-aware components for processing asynchronous messages. MDBs are part of J2EE components. MDBs provide significant advantages over traditional JMS clients, such as those described previously. One of the most important advantages is that MDBs can consume and process messages concurrently. The MDB containers manage concurrency automatically, so that the bean developer can focus on the business logic of processing the messages. The MDB can receive hundreds of messages from various applications and process them all at the same time, because a large number of instances of the MDB can execute concurrently in the container. Thus, they represent a very scalable solution for message processing.

Although an MDB is a complete enterprise bean, there are important differences from entity and session beans. In particular, an MDB does not have component interfaces. The component interfaces are absent because a message-driven bean is not accessible via the Java RMI API. An MDB responds only to asynchronous messages.

To provide a concrete example, we consider an MDB that just receives an asynchronous text message and prints it out on the standard output device. The code for this MDB is shown in Listing 6-5. We briefly describe the important parts of this code.

The MDB class implements two interfaces. The javax.jms .MessageDrivenBean interface defines callback methods similar to those in entity and session beans. The two methods this interface contains are ejbRemove() and setMessageDrivenContext(), the latter of which is called at the beginning of the MDB's life cycle and provides the MDB instance with a reference to its MessageDrivenContext. The other method, ejbRemove(), provides the MDB instance with an opportunity to clean up any resources it stores in its instance fields. In our case, we use it to close the JNDI context and set the ejbContext field to null.

The second interface that is implemented is javax.jms.MessageListener. This interface was discussed previously. It defines a single method, onMessage(). This is where all the business logic goes in order to process the message received. In our case, because we are assuming a text type message, we first cast the Message object to a TextMessage object. Then we invoke the method getText() on the text message object in order to get the content of the message. Finally, we print the message on the standard output device.

Listing 6-5

```
Listing 6.5: A simple message-driven bean for consuming text messages
1       import javax.jms.Message;
2       import javax.jms.TextMessage;
3
4       public class MyMDB implements javax.ejb.MessageDrivenBean,
5           javax.jms.MessageListener  {
6
7           MessageDrivenContext ejbContext;
8           Context jndiContext;
9
10          public void setMessageDrivenContext (MessageDrivenContext mdc)
{
11                  ejbContext = mdc;
12              try {
13                      jndiContext = new InitialContext ();
14              } catch (NamingException namingEx)  {
15                      throw new EJBException (namingEx);
16              }
17          public void ejbCreate ();
18          public void onMessage ( Message message )  {
19              try {
20                      TextMessage  textMsg = (TextMessage) message;
21                      String  msg = textMessage.getText ();
22                      System.out.println ( "Received Message : \n" +
msg );
23              } catch (Exception ex )  {
24                      throw new ejbException (ex);
25              }
26          }
27          public void ejbRemove () {
30              try {
31                      jndiContext.close (0;
32                      ejbContext = null;
33              } catch (NamingException ne )  {}
34          }
35      }
```

Conclusion

This chapter described asynchronous messaging, which may provide the most scalable way for applications to share data and functionality. It is also suitable for applications integration when large transaction volumes are involved. This scalability is due to the asynchronous nature of the messaging, which does not require the client application to suspend its work until the server completes its work, as is the case for RPC and distributed objects.

Another important advantage of the messaging described for this method of communication between applications is that it is much more reliable than either the RPC or distributed objects method of sharing data and functionality. This reliability is achieved by persisting the data being exchanged on both sides of the network.

As you will find in a later chapter, we can add a few components to the messaging system to turn it into a messaging bus, which is also known as an Enterprise Service Bus (ESB). The most notable component that needs to be added to a messaging system for converting into an ESB is called a *router* or a *message broker.* The main function of a message broker is to route the message based on the message content or context. In this way, a further decoupling between the sending and receiving applications is achieved because the sending application does not need to know the address of the final destination. The ESB based on a messaging system provides a much more scalable solution than the ESB based on an application server.

It should also be noted that because of the power and popularity of asynchronous messaging, many of the commercial application servers provide some facility to send and receive asynchronous messages. This messaging facility is usually built on top of the systems bus rather than as a standalone messaging system. Therefore, this messaging capability is not very scalable.

In spite of the power of messaging, it is important to realize that messaging is not suitable in all situations, and proper tradeoffs must be made in arriving at an integration solution for a given situation. Here are some of the disadvantages of asynchronous messaging:

- Generally speaking, asynchronous messaging software is costlier in monetary terms than the ORB-based middleware. For example, the cost of an ESB based on the asynchronous messaging middleware is typically more than ten times higher than the cost of an ESB based on an ORB-based middleware.

- A learning curve is associated with the asynchronous messaging environment.

- A certain amount of overhead and bookkeeping is involved in simulating a synchronous interaction between two applications.

Service-Oriented Architecture–Based Integration

Web Services Overview

In this chapter, we begin to discuss the ideas that are usually considered the most important components of the Service-Oriented Architecture (SOA) and related services-based application integration. However, recall that SOA also encompasses all the integration ideas we covered in Chapters 3–6. Therefore, we will start this chapter with a recap of all the important ideas covered so far. Next, we describe the heterogeneity problem caused by the use of the various technologies described in Chapters 3–6. As a solution to the heterogeneity problem, we discuss the Web Services standards and further development of technology—in particular, the Enterprise Service Bus (ESB) pattern. In the remainder of this chapter, we briefly review each of these standards, including XML, SOAP, WSDL, UDDI, and WS-I Basic Profile. The next chapter deals with the Enterprise Service Bus pattern.

Review of Part II (Chapters 3–6)

Part II of this book began by covering the methods applications use to share data only (refer to Chapter 3). We discussed three methods of exchanging data between applications: file-based data sharing, using a common database approach, and sockets. You learned that the first two approaches are suitable when the data need not be shared in real time, whereas the third approach, sockets, allows applications to share data in real time. Perhaps the most important thing you learned is the idea of the connectivity of applications through the use of sockets. Sockets not only allow applications to share data in real time, they are also fundamental to sharing functionality between applications. Sockets are always present in the background regardless of the integration approach being discussed.

In Chapter 4 you learned about the remote procedure call (RPC) method of sharing functionality and data among applications. You learned that

RPC (also known as *client/server architecture*), is built on top of sockets technology. RPC was an important step in the progress toward enterprise integration because it introduced some critical ideas and features, and for the first time outlined the basic steps necessary to share functionality among applications or software components. RPC introduced the following new features and ideas in the realm of enterprise integration:

- The concept of interface declaration through the use of a specification file. The RPC specification file may be considered the first step in the development of the services interface, such as a WSDL file.

- The concept of a service provider application (called the server) and the service consumer application (called the client). The server provides the implementation of one or more functions that can be used or invoked by the client application.

- The concept of marshalling of arguments for transmission over the network. This refers to the packaging of arguments into one or more messages to be transmitted over the network.

- The encapsulation of all system- and network-related functionality in a library. This encapsulation led to future systems in which this functionality was separated out as a program of its own, thus leading to code reuse.

- Client and server stubs, which shield the programmer from the system and network calls. These stubs, in various forms, continue to be used even in a Service-Oriented Architecture.

- The concept of platform independence via the use of XDR (external data representation), which encodes the data in a machine-independent format.

Chapter 5 introduced the concept of distributed objects by moving away from procedural languages such as C and into the realm of object-oriented programming (OOP) and object-oriented design (OOD). In the case of distributed objects, the objects concept is generalized so that the objects can be distributed over a network. These objects are able to interact with each other through the use of a technology called CORBA.

With distributed objects, we took a big step forward in application integration by encapsulating the code for parameter marshalling and unmarshalling and the code for networking into a separate software component (or application). We call this component the Object Request Broker (ORB). This remedies the problem of the lack of code reuse in RPC. Various implementation of ORB form the backbone of all the modern commercial application servers, which are needed to support distributed objects.

In addition, ORB allowed us to move away from point-to-point integration, which is important if a large number of applications need to be integrated. Also, this move away from point-to-point integration leads to the concept of Enterprise Service Bus (ESB), as you will see later.

Chapter 5 introduced the concept of language independence via the use of an interface definition language (IDL). The interfaces declared through IDL can be mapped to any programming language. They allow, in principle, the client and server to be implemented in two different languages. Another important concept introduced in Chapter 5 is the registry, which is used by server objects to register themselves so they can be located by the client.

You also learned that the major drawback of both distributed objects and RPC is the lack of scalability. This lack of scalability results from the synchronous nature of the interaction between the server and the client. For synchronous method calls, the client is blocked from performing further work until the server completes its work and returns the control to the client.

Another disadvantage is that RPC- and ORB-based communication is not reliable and there is no guarantee that the messages and return values will be delivered to the intended targets. Therefore, the client application may experience a hang-up in its operation under certain circumstances, such as when the network connection is down or when the two applications are not up and running at the same time.

Asynchronous messaging is used to overcome these two problems, as discussed in Chapter 6. In addition, asynchronous messaging has other advantages. In asynchronous messaging, the client or client object sends a message to the target application but does not wait for the response to continue its work, thus leading to a certain amount of decoupling between the applications involved. Therefore, asynchronous messaging may be employed as the basis for integration if high transaction volumes are expected. Asynchronous messaging can also guarantee delivery of messages between applications being integrated. As you will see in Chapter 8, an asynchronous messaging system can also form the core of an Enterprise Service Bus.

In the next section we discuss how the introduction of these new and different technologies for enterprise applications integration led to the problem of heterogeneity in large enterprises. The various solutions to this problem are what led to further developments that are most commonly associated with SOA and service-oriented integration.

Heterogeneity Problem

Perhaps the development of SOA and services (for example, Web Services), beyond the ideas discussed in Part II of this book, owes much to the realization that the technologies discussed in Part II lead to the problem of technological heterogeneity in large enterprises. This problem refers to the fact that in a large enterprise or an inter-enterprise system consisting of an enterprise and its partners, more than one technology is generally used to integrate applications. Therefore, it is literally impossible to impose enterprisewide standards in this respect.

Various kinds of technological heterogeneity can exist in a large enterprise, including the following:

- **Middleware heterogeneity** In a large enterprise, more than one type of middleware is generally used. The two most common types are application servers and message-oriented-middleware (MOM). In addition, brand (vendor) heterogeneity requires support for different brands of application servers and MOMs.

- **Protocol heterogeneity** This heterogeneity refers to the different transport protocols being used to access the services offered by various applications. Examples of such protocols include IIOP, JRMP, HTTP, and HTTPS.

- **Synchrony heterogeneity** There is almost always a need to support both synchronous and asynchronous interactions between applications. In addition, there is sometimes a need for callback methods and publish-and-subscribe. Therefore, many times a situation arises where the styles of interaction supported by the two applications that wish to interact do not match. Hence, these applications cannot interact with one another. This situation is shown schematically in Figure 7.1.

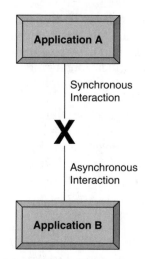

Figure 7.1   Synchrony mismatch problem

- **Protocol mismatch**   Related to the heterogeneity of communication protocols is the problem that arises when different applications want to communicate with each other using incompatible protocols. For example, Application A might want to communicate with Application B using HTTP. However, for Application B the suitable protocol might be IIOP. In such cases, a protocol transformation is needed so that Application A can communicate with Application B. This protocol mismatch problem is shown schematically in Figure 7.2.

- **Diversity of data formats**   A problem arises when there's diversity in the data format being exchanged. Most of the time the data is dependent on the middleware being used. This diversity of data can also cause a problem if two applications that wish to interact support different data formats. This problem is shown schematically in Figure 7.3.

- **Diversity of interface declarations**   A problem arises when there are large differences in the way the service interfaces are being declared and used to invoke the services. For example, the way interfaces are declared in CORBA and Java RMI are different.

- **No common place for service lookup**   A problem arises when there's no common place to look up services to deal with the diversity of the services in a large enterprise.

Another common problem is that as soon as a new version of provider software becomes available, the consumer applications must be modified to account for the change in the provider application. The solution to this problem requires that methods be found that allow the services to be extended—for example, by adding more parameters—without breaking the previous versions of the consumer application.

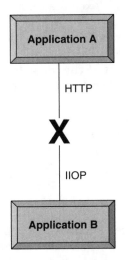

Figure 7.2   Communication protocol mismatch problem

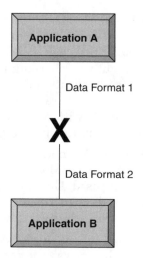

Figure 7.3   Data formats mismatch problem

This diversity and extendibility have been partly dealt with by developing standards and by further development in technology. We discuss these standards in this chapter, whereas the further development in technology is discussed in Chapter 8. Standards are discussed in detail in Chapters 11–14 in this book.

The standards are a collection of specifications, rules, and guidelines formulated and accepted by the leading market participants and are independent of implementation details. Standards establish a base for commonality and enable wide acceptance through interoperability. Examples of standards include a common communication language (XML), a common format for exchanging messages (SOAP), a common service specification format (WSDL), a common means for service lookup (UDDI), and a standard that specifically deals with interoperability issues (WS-I Basic Profile). Examples of technology development include further development of the ideas behind ESB, so as to be able to handle the different protocols for the service provider and service consumer, and the further development of registries for easy registration and discovery of services.

We start our discussion of standards with the Extensible Markup Language (XML) because XML forms the basis on which most of the other standards are built.

XML

To begin with, XML has been adopted as a popular middleware-independent standard format for the exchange of data and documents. XML is basically the lowest common denominator upon which the IT industry can agree. Unlike CORBA, IDL, and Java interfaces, XML is not bound to any particular technology or middleware standard and is often used today as an ad-hoc format for processing data across different, largely incompatible middleware platforms. XML is free and comes with a large number of tools on many different platforms, including different open-source parsing APIs such as SAX, StAX, and DOM. These tools enable the processing and management of XML documents. Another advantage of XML is that it retains the data's structure in transit. In addition, XML is very flexible, and this flexibility positions XML as the most suitable standard for solving middleware and application heterogeneity problems. XML also solves the data format problem mentioned previously.

XML is probably the most important of the standards on which Web Services are built. XML documents are often used as a means for passing information between the service provider and service consumer. XML also forms the basis for WSDL (Web Services Description Language), which is used to declare the interface that a Web Service exposes to the consumer of the service. Additionally, XML underlies the SOAP protocol for accessing a Web Service. Lastly, UDDI (Universal Description, Discovery, and Integration), which is used to publish and discover a Web Service, is also based on XML. The dependence of the data exchange and various other standards on XML is shown schematically in Figure 7.4.

Similar to HTML, XML uses tags. However, unlike HTML, where tags are used to indicate how the data should be presented or displayed, in XML tags are used to describe what the data is. Another difference from HTML is that tags are not fixed but can be invented whenever there is a need for a new one.

The general structure of an XML document is shown in Figure 7.5.

This figure shows that a basic XML document consists of a top element. This top element may consist of data (the payload), an attribute, and any number of other elements in a recursive manner. A sample portion of a simple XML document is shown in Listing 7-1. This document

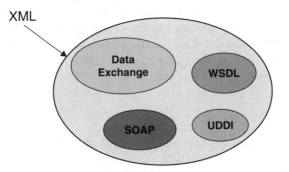

Figure 7.4 Dependence of data exchange, WSDL, SOAP, and UDDI on XML

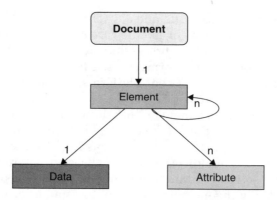

Figure 7.5   The general structure of an XML document

contains a top element named address, which has a single attribute that's used to specify the country. This top element has also four child elements, which provide information on the name of the person, the street address, the city, and the postal code. Each of these child elements has data (that is, a payload) contained in them. For example, the data for the name element is "John Smith".

Listing 7-1

```
Listing 7.1: Basic XML document structure
1    <address country="USA">
2            <name>John Smith</name>
3            <street>43 Walcut St</street>
4            <city>Dublin</city>
5            <state>Ohio</state>
6            <postal-code>45561</postal-code>
7    </address>
```

The grammar and structure of an XML type document is defined in a schema. Another important concept used in XML is namespaces, which are used to avoid the collision of names in different spaces and to extend the use of vocabulary defined in one specific domain to other domains. We will discuss XML in detail in Chapter 11. The discussion will include schemas, namespaces, and various models to use for XML parsing, processing, creating, and editing.

SOAP

Although adoption of XML is an important step forward in dealing with heterogeneity and extensibility requirements, XML by itself it is not sufficient for two parties (the service provider and service consumer applications) to properly communicate. For effective communications, the parties must be able to exchange messages according to an agreed-upon format. Simple Object Access Protocol (SOAP) is such a protocol, providing a common message format for services.

SOAP is a text-based messaging format that uses an XML-based data-encoding format. SOAP is independent of both the programming language and the operational platform, and it does not require any specific technology at the end points, thus making it completely agnostic toward vendors, platforms, and technologies. Its text format also makes SOAP a firewall-friendly protocol. Although SOAP was originally designed to work only with HTTP, any transport protocol or messaging middleware can be used to carry a SOAP message.

The structure of a SOAP message is shown in Figure 7.6. The SOAP message is a complete (or valid) XML document, with the top element being the envelope element. The envelope element contains a body element and an optional header element. The body element usually carries the actual message, which is consumed by the recipient. The header element is generally used for advanced features for intermediate processors. A simple but complete example of a SOAP request for obtaining a stock quote is shown in Listing 7-2. The listing shows how a SOAP message is encoded using XML and illustrates some SOAP elements and attributes.

As the listing shows, the top element in SOAP must be the envelope element, which must contain two namespaces. The namespace

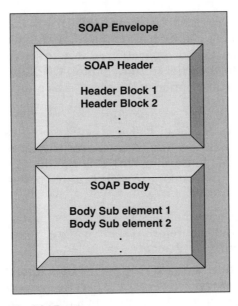

Figure 7.6   Structure of a SOAP message

SOAP:encodingStyle indicates the SOAP encoding, and the other namespace connotes the SOAP envelope. The header element is optional, but when it is present it should be the first immediate child of the envelope element. The body element must be present in all SOAP messages and must follow the header element if it is present. The body usually contains the specification of the actual message. In this example, the message contains the name (GetLastTradePrice) of the method as well as an input parameter value (IBM).

Listing 7-2

```
Listing 7.2: An example of SOAP message
<soap:envelope xmlns:soap="http://schemas.xmlsoap.org/soap/
envelope/"
soap:encodingStyle="http:/schemas.xmlsoap.org/soap/encoding/"/>
      <soap:header>
      </soap:header>
      <soap:body>
          <m:GetLastTradePrice  xmlns:m="http://example.org/
Tradeprice"  >
          <tickerSymbol> IBM </tickerSymbol>
          </m:GetLastTradePrice>
      </soap:body>
</soap:envelope>
```

WSDL

Web Services Description Language (WSDL) is an XML-based language for describing the interface and other characteristics of a Web Service. This is the second application of XML to solve the heterogeneity problems mentioned earlier in this chapter. WSDL offers the following advantages in the description of the services as compared to previously described approaches:

- Unlike CORBA's IDL and RPC's specification files, WSDL is more completely agnostic toward programming languages and middleware technologies. This feature of WSDL is the direct result of it being based on XML, thus making WSDL suitable to describe almost any type of service.

- WSDL provides a method of specifying a communication protocol for invoking a service. Therefore, a service is free to choose any protocol it can conveniently implement.

- WSDL also provides a way to specify a message format for communicating with a given service. Therefore, a service is free to choose any convenient message format. An example of a message format is SOAP.

- WSDL also provides wide latitude for the service provider to specify the type of service operations they offer. In general, four different types of service operations can be specified, including synchronous operations and asynchronous operations.

- Finally, WSDL has a method for specifying a service end point. A *service end point* is the network address at which the service is available for invocation.

It is instructive to look at an example of a WSDL document. A sample WSDL document is shown in Listing 7-3 that declares a service for getting weather information.

Listing 7-3

```
Listing 7.3: A example of WSDL document
<?xml version="1.0" encoding="UTF-8"?>
<definitions name ="WeatherWebService"
          targetNamespace="urn:WeatherWebService"
          xmlns:tns="urn:WeatherWebService"
          xmlns="http:/schemas.xmlsoap.org/wsdl/"
            xmlns:xsd="http://www.w3.org/2001/XMLSchema"
            xmlns:soap="http://schemas.xml.soap.org/wsdl/soap/"
      <types/>
```

[Abstract data type definitions]

```
      <message name="WeatherService_getWeather">
```

[Data that is sent]

```
            <part name="City" type="xsd:string"/>
      </message>
      <message name="WeatherService_getWeatherResponse">
```

[Data that is returned]

```
            <part name="result" type="xsd:string"/>
      </message>
      <portType name="WeatherService">
```

[Port type containing one operation]

```
            <operation name="getWeather" parameterOrder="City">
```

[An operation with input and output messages]

```
                <input message="tns:WeatherService_getWeather"/>
                <output message="WeatherService_
getWeatherResponse/>
            </operation>
      </portType>
      <binding name="WeatherServiceBinding" type="tns:
WeatherService">
```

```
            <operation name="getWeather">
                <input>
                    <soap:body use="literal"  namespace="urn:
WeatherWebService"/>
                </input>
                <output>
                    <soap:body use:literal namespace="urn:
WeatherWebService"/>
                </output>
                <soap:operation soapAction=""/>
            </operation>
            <soap:binding transport="http://schemas.xmlsoap.ord/
soap/http"  style="rpc"/>
```

[Binding to a specific protocol]

```
    </binding>
    <service name="WeatherWebService">
```

[Binding to a specific service]

```
        <port name="WeatherServicePort" binding="tns:
WeatherServiceBinding">
            <soap:address location=http://mycompany.com/
weatherservice"/>
        </port>
    </service>
</definitions>
```

As this listing shows, a complete WSDL document consists of a set of definitions, starting with a root "definitions" element, followed by six individual element definitions—types, message, portType, binding, and service/port—that describe a service. The relationships between these elements and other elements are shown schematically in Figure 7.7. These elements are discussed in detail in Chapter 13, but here is a brief description of the top six elements:

- **types** This element defines the data types contained in messages exchanged as part of the service. Data types can be simple, complex, derived, or array types. Types (either schema definitions or references) that are referred to in a WSDL document's message element are defined in the WSDL document's type element.

- **message** This element defines the messages the service exchanges. A WSDL document has a message element for each message that is exchanged, and the message element contains the data types associated with the message. For example, in the Listing 7-3, the first message contains a single part that is of the string type.

- **portType** This element specifies, in an abstract manner, operations and messages that are part of the service. A WSDL document has one

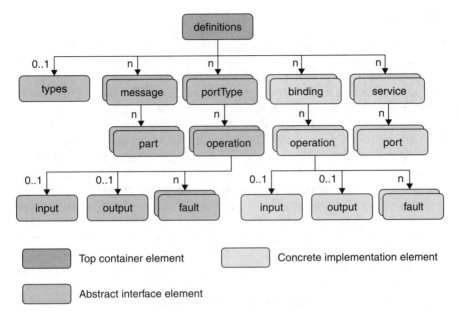

Figure 7.7 Elements of a WSDL document and their relationships

or more portType definitions for each service it defines. In Listing 7-3, only one port type, WeatherService, is defined.

- **binding** This element binds the abstract port type, and its messages and operations, to a transport protocol and to a message format. In Listing 7-3, one operation, getWeather, is defined, which has an input message and an output message. Both of these messages are exchanged in SOAP body formats. The binding transport protocol is HTTP.

- **service and port** These elements together define the name of an actual service and, by providing a single address for binding, assign an individual end point for the service. A port can have only one address. The service element groups related ports together and, through its name attribute, provides a logical name for the service. In Listing 7-3, one service (WeatherWebService) is defined that has a single port (or end point) with the address http://mycompany.com/weatherservice.

In summary, WSDL characterizes the interface, which consists of two parts:

- An abstract interface description containing the supported operations, the operation parameters, and their types.
- A binding and implementation description containing a binding of the abstract description to a concrete transport protocol, message format, and network address.

UDDI Registry

In addition to service interface declaration (WSDL) and the SOAP messaging standard, a large enterprise also needs a central place where the service provider can publish their services using WSDL and the service consumers can discover existing services. This is mainly due to the fact that in a large enterprise, developer resources may be dispersed geographically. In particular, the service providers and service consumers may be located far apart. Such a central place is given the name *registry*. A registry is like a library card catalog used for recording the arrival of new books and other media as well as looking up books and other media. Another common analogy is the telephone system's Yellow Pages, used by service providers to publish their services and by service consumers to find services.

The Universal Description, Discovery, and Integration (UDDI) specification defines a standard way of registering, deregistering, and looking up services. Figure 7.8 shows how UDDI enables the dynamic description, discovery, and integration of services. A service provider first registers a service with the UDDI registry. A service consumer looks up the required service in the UDDI registry. Then, when it finds the required service, the consumer directly binds with the provider to use the service.

Figure 7.9 shows the basic structure of the data model of a UDDI registry. This structure consists of five basic constructs. The meaning, the use, and the relationships among these basic constructs will be explained in Chapter 14.

The role of the UDDI registry in Web Services is similar to the role played by a search engine on the Internet. The power of the search engine comes from the keywords used to classify content. In a similar manner, a fine-grained search for a Web Service is possible only if a service is classified properly. The classification and identification taxonomies present in the UDDI registry provide a starting point for describing Web Services. Equally important is the classification of the businesses and organizations that offer Web Services.

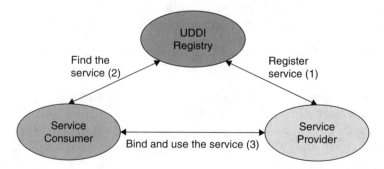

Figure 7.8 Working of a UDDI registry

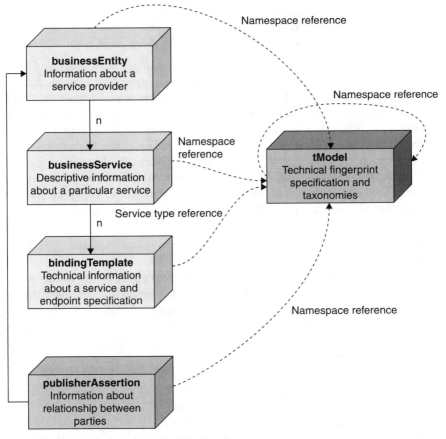

Figure 7.9   Basic constructs of the UDDI registry data model

Here are the three categories of binding to a specific service after the service has been discovered through the use of the registry:

- **Development time binding**   In this case, in addition to the signatures of the service operations and the service (network) protocol, the actual physical location of the service is known at development time. The client logic is developed accordingly. Thus, the binding is hard-coded to use a specific service and is permanent.

- **Partly runtime binding**   As in the previous case, the signatures of the service operations, as well as the network protocol are known at development time. However, the address of the specific service is not known during code development. In this case, the consumer application is enabled to dynamically bind to different service instances by looking up services with a specific name or property in the repository. For example, a consumer application looks up printing services with different names, depending on the printer name selected by the user. Another example is the case where a printer service is selected based on properties such as the floor number and document type.

■ **Runtime binding**   In this case, even the service specification (that is, the operations signatures) and the protocol are not known at development time. The client can still discover a service via properties such as floor number and document type, but with an unknown service interface. In this case, some kind of reflection mechanism must be implemented at the client side that enables the client to dynamically discover the semantics of the service and format of valid requests. This type of service discovery is the most complex and is not used often because it requires very complex client logic to dynamically interpret the semantics of an unknown service interface.

WS-I Basic Profile

The Web Services Interoperability (WS-I) Organization is an open industry effort chartered to promote Web Services interoperability across platforms, applications, and programming languages. The organization brings together a diverse community of Web Services leaders to respond to customer needs by providing guidance, recommended practices, and supporting resources for developing interoperable Web Services.

The WS-I Basic Profile provides constraints and clarifications to those base specifications (XML, SOAP, WSDL, and UDDI) with the intent to promote interoperability. Where the profile is silent, the base specifications are normative. If the profile prescribes a requirement or constraint, it supersedes the underlying base specification. Some of the constraints imposed by the profile are intended to restrict, or require, optional behavior and functionality so as to reduce the potential for interoperability problems. Some of the constraints or requirements are provided to clarify language in the base specification that may be the source of frequent misinterpretation and have been a frequent source of interoperability problems.

Here are some examples of WS-I Basic Profile specifications:

■ The Basic Profile prohibits protocol bindings other than SOAP, because SOAP binding is the most commonly used and well defined. In this case, the WSDL standard is being restrained.

■ The Basic Profile limits the transport protocol to HTTP and HTTPS.

■ The Basic Profile vetoes the use of any encoding, including SOAP encoding.

■ The Basic Profile disallows overloading operation names.

Conclusion

In this chapter, we reviewed the standards that together are commonly referred to as *Web Services*. These standards have been developed to address some of the heterogeneity problems that resulted from the use of different technologies, such as the following:

- No common way to describe the service interface and other characteristics.
- No common place to look up what services are available.
- No common way for a data exchange between applications that is independent of languages and middleware technologies.
- No common message format for exchanging information between applications.
- No way to specify different communication protocols.

The standards we discussed are XML, SOAP, WSDL, UDDI, and WS-I Basic Profile. XML provides a middleware-independent format for the exchange of data and documents. SOAP provides a common message format for application interaction.

WSDL provides a language- and platform-independent way to specify the interface offered by a service. A WSDL document consists of two parts. The first part describes in an abstract manner the operations, input and output parameters, and data types. The second part, which consists of a binding and implementation interface, specifies the transport protocol, message format, and service end point network address. The Universal Description, Discovery, and Integration (UDDI) specification defines a standard way of registering, deregistering, and looking up services. The last standard, WS-I Basic Profile, promotes the interoperability of services operating on different platforms by specifying additional constraints and clarifications on the aforementioned standards. In Part IV of this book (Chapters 11–14), we take a more detailed look at these standards.

Although these standards, known as Web Services, are able to solve some of the heterogeneity problems, they are not able to solve all of these types of problems. Some of the heterogeneity problems not addressed by Web Services standards include the following:

- **Protocol mismatch**   Related to the heterogeneity of communication protocols is the problem that different applications want to communicate with each other using incompatible protocols. For example, Application A might want to communicate with Application B using HTTP. However, for Application B the suitable protocol might be IIOP. In such cases, a protocol transformation is needed so that Application A can communicate with Application B.

■ **Message format mismatch**   Related to protocol mismatch is the problem of a mismatch of message formats between the service provider and the service consumer. This problem refers to the situation where a service provider may be set up to receive messages in one format (such as SOAP), while the service consumer is set up to use another message format (such as Java RMI).

These and other problems have been addressed by further development in the technologies. In particular, the evolution of Enterprise Service Bus patterns solves many of the remaining heterogeneity problems as well as other problems. We discuss these problems and the Enterprise Service Bus in the next chapter.

Chapter 8

Enterprise Service Bus

Chapter 7 provided an overview of the standards generally known as Web Services. The main objective of these standards is to provide a solution to the various heterogeneity problems found in large enterprises. Toward the end of Chapter 7, you learned that Web Services can provide only a part of the solution and that some heterogeneity problems are still left unresolved. In particular, quite often there is a need to provide a mechanism for a communication protocol switch and to provide a mechanism for data transformation in order to match the requirements of a service provider with that of a service client.

In this chapter, we tackle the remaining heterogeneity problems by discussing the Enterprise Service Bus (ESB) pattern. ESB provides a comprehensive, scalable way to connect a large number of applications without the need for each pair of applications to make a direct connection. Such a direct connection between two applications is called a *point-to-point connection*. Note that even in the case of Web Services, the connection between the service consumer application and the service provider application is "point to point." The point-to-point connection approach does not scale well because the number of applications involved in the integration increase; therefore, this integration approach is not suitable for a large enterprise where a large number of applications need to be integrated.

We start this chapter with a brief overview of the scalability problem and how an ESB pattern solves this problem by using content- and context-based routing. We also elaborate on the solutions of the heterogeneity problems that have not been addressed yet. Then, we summarize the core functions supported by an ESB and provide a brief discussion of the optional features that are sometimes available in an ESB. Next, we describe the various logical components of an ESB and how an ESB works. The various abstract ESB deployment patterns are discussed next.

Then, we describe the various types of ESBs available on the market and their characteristics. We also describe some practical scenarios with specific requirements by using a large bank as an example. We also show how different ESB products can be used to address the various requirements of this large bank.

Routing and Scalable Connectivity

In this book, we are mostly concerned with the integration of a large enterprise that has a large number of applications. Although Web Services provide solutions to some of the heterogeneity problems usually found in a large enterprise, they only provide part of the solution of integrating a large enterprise. This is because Web Services integration is still "point to point." In other words, each pair of applications in the enterprise needs to have a separate connection. This approach may be suitable for small organizations consisting of a few applications, but not for a large enterprise.

To understand this problem of scalability for the point-to-point approach, we consider two cases. In the first case, we consider a small company that has only three applications that need to be integrated. The connections required to connect these applications in the point-to-point approach is shown in Figure 8.1. You can see that the number of connections required is three, which incidentally is equal to the number of pairs of applications. Therefore, this approach does not look too bad for this small company and hence could be an acceptable approach.

Next, we consider a slightly bigger company that needs to integrate six applications. The connections required to connect these six applications are shown schematically in Figure 8.2. You can see that the number of required connections in this case is 15. This number is again equal to the number of distinct pairs of applications in the integration scheme. By comparing the number of connections in these two cases, we learn a very important lesson. Although the number of applications

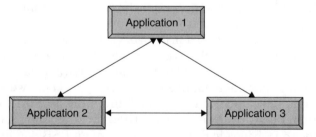

Figure 8.1   The number of connections required for integrating three applications using the point-to-point integration approach

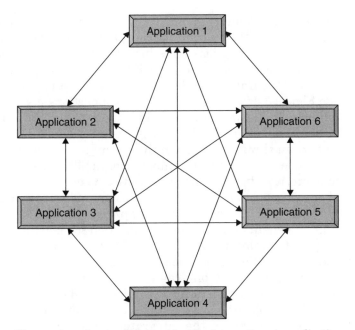

Figure 8.2   The number of connections required for integrating six applications using the point-to-point integration approach

has only increased by a factor of two (from three to six), the number of connections required in this point-to-point approach has jumped by a factor of five. This is termed a *hairball problem* because it can clog any network. In fact, it can be shown that if an enterprise has N applications to be integrated, the number of connections required in the point-to-point approach is

$$N(N-1)/2$$

This is easy to understand because the number of distinct pairs of applications is also $N(N-1)/2$. The use of this formula shows that when the number of applications is ten, the number of connections required is 45 in the point-to-point approach. This rather high number of connections is obviously not a satisfactory solution. Hence, we can conclude that the point-to-point integration scheme is not suitable for integrating a large enterprise and another solution should be found that has better scalability.

Enterprise Service Bus provides an excellent solution to the scalability problem of the point-to-point integration approach and therefore is suitable for medium-to-large enterprises that need to integrate a significant number of applications. In the Enterprise Service Bus interaction style, the applications do not interact directly with each other. Instead, the applications connect to the bus and the bus provides the means for connections among the applications. This indirect interaction is shown in Figure 8.3, which shows six applications interacting among themselves through the use of the Enterprise Service Bus. The most important thing to note from Figure 8.3 is that the number of connections needed is only six. This number is substantially less than the number of connections needed for six applications in the point-to-point scheme (that is, 15). Another important thing to note from this figure is that the number of connections needed is equal to the number of applications being integrated. Therefore, if we had ten applications we only need ten connections. This number of connections is very small compared to the number of connections needed in the point-to-point approach (that is, 45).

Another great benefit of this indirect connection scheme through ESB is that it is easy to maintain and upgrade. In other words, it is easy to add or remove applications from the integrated structure. For example, to add one application, only one connection to the ESB is required. This one connection is sufficient for this added application to interact with all the other applications. No changes are required in the existing applications that are part of the integrated structure. Contrast this situation with the point-to-point integration scheme, where the addition of one single application requires building a connection to each of the remaining applications—which may require changes in all the existing applications. In a similar manner, the removal of an application from the integrated structure is very easy because only one connection to the ESB is required.

Yet another advantage of this indirect connection scheme is that it provides more agility to the integrated structure. This is because this indirect connections scheme allows for the easy replacement of

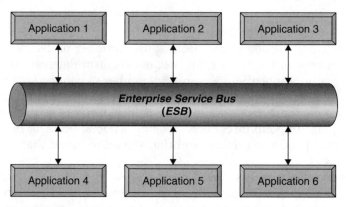

Figure 8.3   Indirect connections between applications using the message routing capability of ESB

the service provider with an equivalent provider if for some reason the original provider is no longer able to offer the service. The basic reason for this ability is that with the service bus structure there is no need to hard-code the network address of the service end point into the client application. The bus provides for looking up the service end point address based on the content and context of the service request it receives from the client application. This routing capability is one of the three core capabilities an Enterprise Service Bus offers. In fact, this capability means that the service client is unaware of who the provider of the service is, and the service provider is unaware of the identity of the application making a service request.

You've learned that ORBs (or application servers) and asynchronous messaging provide some form of routing based on the content and context of the request. Therefore, both these technologies are in a position to form the backbone of the Enterprise Service Bus. Based on which of these two technologies is chosen as the backbone of an Enterprise Service Bus, there can be two types of buses.

The first type of Enterprise Service Bus utilizes ORBs (or application servers) as the backbone. This type of Enterprise Service Bus has the advantage of being easy to set up and is comparatively less expensive. However, the functionality it provides does not scale as well where the rate of transactions is concerned. Therefore, this type of ESB should be used when lower volumes of transactions are expected. This type of ESB is usually designed to deal with Web Services, XML, and Java RMI only. The ESBs in this category also cannot handle a more diverse set of applications.

The second type of ESB is based on the asynchronous messaging systems. It is relatively more expensive and requires a more elaborate setup. This type of Enterprise Service Bus has three main advantages over the first type. The first advantage is that this type of ESB provides a highly scalable solution in terms of the volume of transactions and therefore is able to support a much higher rate of transactions. The second benefit is that this type of ESB can be used to integrate a more diverse set of applications. Probably the most important advantage of this type of ESB is that it can guarantee delivery of the messages between applications. It is important to note that the Web Services themselves do not provide a guarantee of message delivery between applications This guarantee of message delivery may be required for certain transactions due to contractual or legal reasons. Also note that in the absence of this guarantee, the service consumer application may hang if the network connection breaks or if the service provider application is not running at the same time. The asynchronous messaging systems can ensure the delivery of messages by persisting them on both sides (the service consumer side and the service provider side) of the network.

Protocol Transformation

In addition to providing a scalable solution to the problem of enterprise application integration, an Enterprise Service Bus pattern also provides solutions to the two remaining heterogeneity problems mentioned at the end of Chapter 7.

The communication protocol mismatch problem arises because in a large enterprise different applications typically employ different protocols for communications. In other words, in the real world a proliferation of these protocols exists, including HTTP, HTTPS, JRMP, IIOP, and JMS. Because of this proliferation, sometimes a protocol mismatch will occur between the service consumer application and the service provider application. Therefore, without a facility to transform one communication protocol to another, the service consumer application will not be able to invoke the service offered by the service provider application. This inability to invoke the service is shown schematically in Figure 8.4.

Ideally, the communication protocol should be standardized so that every application in the enterprise uses the same protocol. For example, an enterprise could standardize to using only HTTP, which is the standard protocol for Web Services. However, in the real world such a transformation may be difficult and impractical in most situations. The difficulty includes the lack of developer resources and time constraints. Also, the security and quality of service requirements might dictate the use of different protocols.

Therefore, another core functionality that should be included in an ESB is a protocol transformation facility that can translate one protocol into another. With this transformation facility, the applications

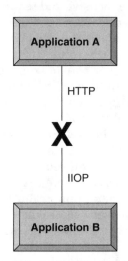

Figure 8.4 Protocol mismatch problem in the absence of an ESB

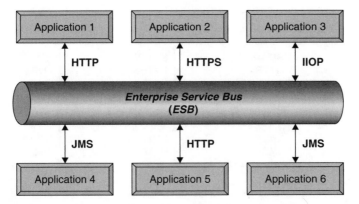

Figure 8.5 Using an ESB, applications with different transport protocols can communicate

using different protocols can interact with each other, as shown in Figure 8.5.

Data/Message Transformation

One more heterogeneity problem is not addressed by Figure 8.5—the problem of data/message format mismatch. This problem refers to the fact that sometimes the data format provided by the service consumer and the data format required by the service provider application do not quite match. This prevents applications from interacting with each other. The problem is depicted in Figure 8.6.

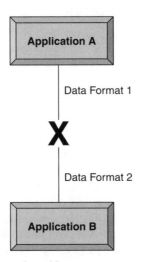

Figure 8.6 Data/message mismatch problem

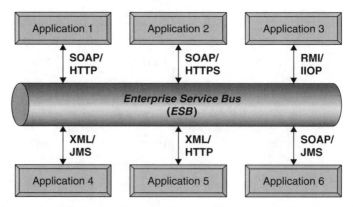

Figure 8.7 Using an ESB, applications can interact even when their data/message formats do not match.

Therefore, another core functionality that needs to be provided by an ESB is data or message transformation. When this functionality is combined with the other two ESB functionalities, the applications are easily able to connect and interact with each other, even when their interfaces and protocols do not match completely. This is shown in Figure 8.7.

Core Functionalities

To summarize, an ESB offers the following key functionalities:

- Content- and context-based routing
- Protocol transformation or switch
- Data or message transformation

These three basic functionalities of an ESB are depicted schematically in Figure 8.8.

With these three functionalities incorporated into an ESB's core, the ESB can offer a number of virtualizations. The three main categories of virtualizations are as follows:

- **Location and identity virtualization** The service consumer application does not need to know the address or location of the service provider application, and the service provider does not need to know the identity of the service consumer application. The service request can be filled by any one of a number of service providers. This allows the service provider to be added or removed from the integrated structure without bringing down the system, thus providing for uninterrupted service to the service consumer.

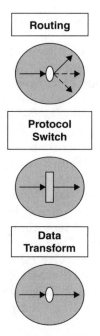

Figure 8.8   The core functions supported by an ESB

- **Interaction protocol**   The service consumer and service provider need not share the same communication protocol or interaction style. For example, a service request coming in as SOAP over HTTP can be serviced by a provider that understands only Java RMI over IIOP.
- **Interface**   The service consumer need not agree on an exact match with the interface offered by the service provider. The ESB reconciles the difference by transforming the request message into the form expected by the service provider.

The virtualization of these aspects allows an ESB to provide a transparent service provider implementation to the service consumer, both at development time and at deployment time. The ESB takes responsibility to deliver a service request to the appropriate service provider, and the service provider responds to the service request without knowing where the service request is coming from.

Additionally, the ESB itself is transparent to both the consumer and the provider of a service. Application logic can consume or provide a service without ever knowing whether the connection is direct or an ESB has been employed. Therefore, whether or not to employ an ESB is a deployment-time decision because no change to the application code is necessary or required.

An ESB supports a number of different types of interactions between the service consumer application and the service provider application. These interaction types include synchronous request-and-response operation, asynchronous interaction, and publish-and-subscribe. Note that an ESB can convert between these types of interactions. For example, a service request coming as a synchronous (request and response) operation can be serviced by an asynchronous service provider. Recall from Chapter 6 that a correlation ID can be used for servicing a synchronous call using an asynchronous provider.

So far we have discussed only the functional requirements that are met by the core functionalities offered by an ESB. However, equally important are the nonfunctional requirements by the applications being integrated. These nonfunctional requirements are generally known as the Quality of (Interaction) Service (QoS) requirements. These QoS requirements are specified by the service participants, and an ESB provides services to implement these requirements for the service participants. Here are some of QoS requirements commonly supported by an ESB:

- **Performance and reliability** Performance requirements may include that the response time of a service not exceed a certain fixed amount of time, such as 50 milliseconds. An example of a reliability (or availability) requirement might be that the service provider is up 99.999% of the time.

- **Security services** Security is an important issue in general for distributed computing, but it is especially important when external third-party services are consumed by your system or when your system provides services to the external third parties. The ESBs that offer security services do not directly provide security themselves. They simply provide a framework for security software to plug into as well as capabilities to help the ESB navigate through the network without getting blocked by firewalls or any other kind of security arrangement. An example of security software that can work with an ESB is Tivoli Suites from IBM. Some security services provided by an ESB include the following:

  - Data encryption to ensure the privacy of the data.

  - Authorization of service requests. Is the user of a service who they say they are?

  - Data integrity. Is the data genuine?

  - Auditing service. Automatic auditing of service interactions for contractual/legal reasons or for billing purposes.

Optional Features

In addition to the core ESB functionalities discussed in the last section, you'll commonly find a number of optional features in a particular implementation of the ESB patterns. These additional features, along with the core functionalities of an ESB, are called *mediation patterns*. Here are some of the optional features included in an ESB:

- **Data enrichment**   This feature allows an ESB to augment the message payload from an external source so as to match the requirements of a service provider. External sources may include a database. This augmentation is shown schematically in Figure 8.9. A sample situation where such an augmentation is needed is an incoming service request that contains an address without a country name. However, the service provider needs the complete address, including the name of the country, for it to process or service the request. In such a case, an ESB can augment the incoming payload message with the name of the country, perhaps a default name, from a data source. It is interesting to note that, in principle, enrichment can occur in the service response as well.

- **Distribution**   This ESB feature allows multiple consumer applications to subscribe to a particular type of message, and the ESB distributes the message to each of those applications. This is shown schematically in Figure 8.10. An example where this might be needed is the request for a stock quote.

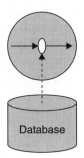

Figure 8.9   Data enrichment

Figure 8.10   Distribution of messages

Figure 8.11   Deriving a complex event from multiple messages or from a stream of events

Figure 8.12   Monitoring of messages being exchanged

- **Correlation**   This feature provides a facility to derive a complex event from multiple messages or from a stream of events. This facility relies on the rules for pattern recognition and the rules for forming the complex output message. The correlation feature is shown schematically in Figure 8.11.

- **Monitoring**   This feature provides the facility to observe messages as they pass through the mediation unchanged. It can be used to monitor service levels, to assist in problem determination or to meter usage for subsequent user billing, or to record business-level events (such as purchases above a certain dollar value). It can also be used to log messages for audit or for subsequent data mining. This monitoring facility is shown schematically in Figure 8.12.

In addition to these optional services, an ESB usually provides technical services such as logging and exception handling.

Logical Components

In order to implement the core and optional functionalities described in the last two sections, a number of components are required in an ESB's construction. In this section, we provide a conceptual or logical view of some of these important components (see Figure 8.13).

Adapters

Adapters are probably the most important components of an ESB. These adapters exist at the peripheries of the ESB. All the requests coming in and going out use these adapters. Adapters allow the ESB to interact

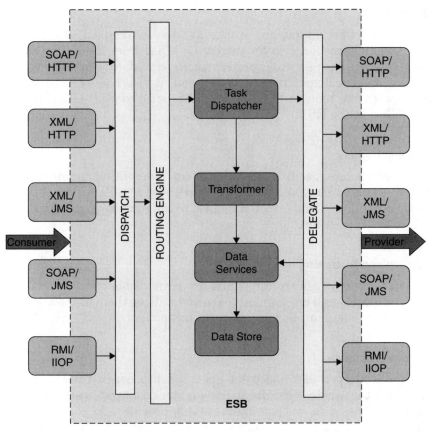

Figure 8.13   Some of the logical components of an ESB

with varied input and output mechanisms. Each adapter caters to the need of a specific service consumer or service provider. These service consumer–specific and service provider–specific adapters understand only certain combinations of communication protocol and message format. For example, you can have an input adapter that takes in all requests that come in as SOAP over HTTP. Similarly, you can have a separate adapter that takes in requests that come in as XML over HTTP. Some of the common combinations include SOAP/HTTP, XML/HTTP, RMI/IIOP, XML/JMS, and SOAP/JMS. Adapters provide a uniform view to ESB components by abstracting the specifics of entry and exit point mechanisms and protocols. This allows the ESB components to receive input from any protocol and send output to any protocol.

Dispatcher

The dispatcher component works as the centralized entry point. Dispatcher is responsible for retrieving input from the adapters and passing it to a task for appropriate routing, transformation, and enrichment work. The dispatcher sends the request to a request handler and, along with the request handler, provides basic content-based routing capability to the ESB.

Request Handler

Each service has specific request handlers. The routing engine receives service-specific parameters from the request handlers and then the request handlers hand over the request to the routing engine for appropriate task execution.

Routing and Rules Engine

The rules engine and routing task are responsible for executing the transformation and enrichment tasks and routing them to the appropriate service delegates. Service delegate components are described next.

Service Delegates

Delegates are provider end point–specific components. They communicate with the service provider using adapters. Delegates are specific to the provider-specific end point because they provide more coarse-grained abstraction about the semantics of communication with the provider end point. Adapters, on the other hand, abstract a more fine-grained protocol mechanism to connect to the end point. Thus, to provide logical operation delegates, use the appropriate adapters for executing the service interface.

Transformation Engine

The transformation engine component transforms the incoming (or source) data/message into a format that's compatible with the format required by the service provider. This is one of the core elements of ESB that facilitates integration between disparate service interfaces.

Enrichment Component

This component allows an ESB to augment the message payload from an external source so as to match the requirements of a service provider. The external source may be a database. A sample situation where such an augmentation is needed is an incoming service request containing an address without containing a country name. However, the service provider needs the complete address, including the name of the country, for it to process or service the request. In such a case, an ESB can augment the incoming payload message with the name of the country (perhaps a default name) from a data source.

Sometimes the functionalities offered by the transformation engine component and enrichment component can be combined in a single component.

Logging Component

This component provides the necessary logging support for the ESB components.

Exception-Handling Component

This component handles all the exceptions generated by the various components of an ESB.

Deployment Configurations

Deployment patterns of Enterprise Service Bus depend on many factors. The main factor determining how ESBs are deployed is the size of the enterprise. For a small enterprise, a single ESB with a single registry attached to it might suffice. However, for larger enterprises, more complex deployment patterns involving several ESBs with a number of registries might be needed. The type of ESBs needed in each of these patterns is determined by the specific connectivity requirements of each of these enterprises. For example, an enterprise needing to connect to third-party partners and vendors may need an ESB specially designed to handle the security situations for connecting to the third parties. Such ESBs are known as *gateways*. Later in the chapter, we discuss some specific usage scenarios and how to design different connectivity solutions for such scenarios.

Note that there are basically four known configurations for deploying ESBs. The patterns and conditions under which each of these configurations should be employed are discussed next.

Global ESB

In this pattern of deployment, there is a single ESB for the entire enterprise. The ESB employs a single registry. This configuration is suitable for a small enterprise or a single line of business. In this case, all the services are available to all the participants. There is no requirement

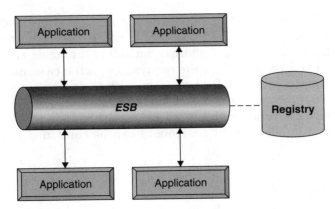

Figure 8.14   Global ESB

to connect to third-party external vendors or partners; therefore, the requirements for security are minimal. This pattern of interaction between participants is shown schematically in Figure 8.14.

Directly Connected ESBs

The second method employs directly connected ESBs. This involves more than one directly connected ESB, as shown in Figure 8.15. This pattern employs a common registry so that the services are visible throughout the enterprise. For example, this pattern can be employed to connect a set of packaged applications (such as SAP applications) to the rest of the enterprise. Such packaged applications usually have

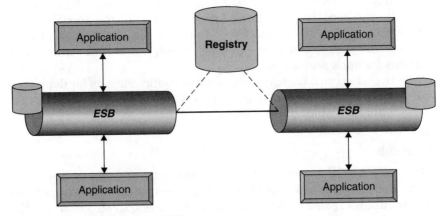

Figure 8.15   Directly connected ESBs

their own ESB, which connects different modules (such as CRM and ERP). For example, the SAP modules are connected by their own ESB called NetWeaver. NetWeaver can be connected to, for example, IBM's WESB to provide connectivity between SAP applications and other applications (Java/J2EE).

Federated ESBs

The third pattern is *federated ESBs* and is similar to the directly connected ESBs pattern in that multiple ESBs are connected, as shown in Figure 8.16. However, one of the participating ESBs has a master/slave relationship with the other ESBs and exerts control over what is accessible to the participants. This third pattern can be used by moderately autonomous departments in an enterprise that want to share their services with other departments.

Brokered ESBs

The fourth deployment pattern is *brokered ESBs*. In this pattern, a broker is employed to mediate between connected ESBs. Each ESB has its own registry and controls what type of interactions are allowed

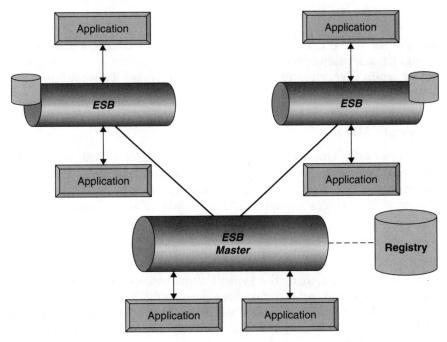

Figure 8.16 Federated ESBs

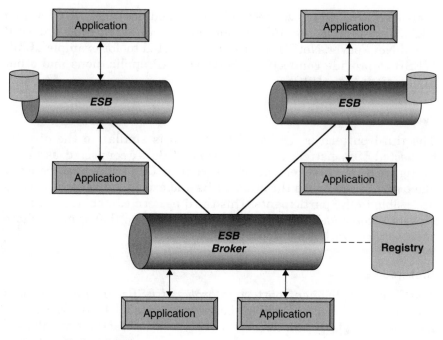

Figure 8.17   Brokered ESBs

outside its domain. This pattern can be used by autonomous departments that develop and deploy their own services but want to expose a
select group of services to the rest of the enterprise. This configuration
is shown in Figure 8.17.

Types of ESBs

Fundamentally, three kinds of ESBs are available on the market. Of
course, IBM has the most complete and comprehensive product line in
the area of connectivity products. We briefly describe each type of ESB
and related products as well as the main advantages of each of them.

Application Server–Based ESBs

This type of Enterprise Service Bus uses application servers as the
backbone. In addition to the typical synchronous function, they also
have some support for asynchronous messaging. For the asynchronous
message, the systems bus is used as the backbone. The main advantage
of these ESBs is that they are comparatively low-cost products. Another
important advantage is that they are easy to set up at deployment time.

These products' strength is in dealing with XML and Java. However, they offer challenges if a more diverse set of applications need to be integrated. In addition, they are typically used to integrate a comparatively small number of applications because this type of ESB is not scalable for a large number of applications.

The prime example of this type of ESB product is IBM's WebSphere Enterprise Service Bus (WESB), which is based on IBM's WebSphere Application Server (WAS). WESB offers the following features and advantages:

- Provides standards-based integration, which allows you to create and deploy interactions between applications and services quickly and easily, with reduced number and complexity of interfaces.

- Offers easy-to-use tools that require minimal programming skills and are simple to install, configure, build, and manage.

- Reconfigures dynamically to meet changing business processing loads. Provides easy interactions with any JMS and HTTP applications.

- Supported on a large number of operating systems, including AIX, HP UNIX, I Family, Linux, Sun Solaris, Windows, and z/OS.

- Increases business agility and flexibility and extends easily to a federated ESB model.

- Supports hundreds of independent software vendors (ISVs) through WebSphere adapters. Adapters are discussed in Chapter 9.

Messaging System–Based ESBs

In this type of ESB, the backbone is a messaging (asynchronous) system such as IBM's WebSphere MQ. These Enterprise Service Buses also support both types of messaging: synchronous and asynchronous. There are three main advantages of this type of ESB over the other two:

- They offer the most scalable solution to the problem of application integration as far as support for high transaction volume is considered.

- They provide for integrating the most diverse set of applications, including Java, C/C++, and COBOL applications.

- They guarantee delivery of messages exchanged between the service consumer and service provider. Note that the two other types of ESBs cannot provide such a guarantee. However, messaging system–based ESBs require substantially more work to set up as compared to the other two types of ESBs. Also, this type of application integration costs substantially more when compared to the two other integration schemes.

The most powerful ESB available today is IBM's WebSphere Message Broker (WMB). WMB has IBM WebSphere MQ as the backbone and provides the most scalable solution in terms of the number of transactions. It has the following salient features:

- Integrates the most diverse set of applications, including modern Java/J2EE applications and C/C++ applications, packaged applications such as CRM applications, and mainframe COBOL applications. These applications can be running on almost any platform.

- Can handle very large volumes of transactions.

- Validates and transforms messages in-flight between any combination of different message formats, including Web Services, other XML, and non-XML formats.

- Routes messages based on (evaluated) business rules to match information content and business processes.

- Provides for dynamically reconfiguring information distribution patterns without reprogramming end point applications.

- Supports a powerful security model to address security concerns.

- Supports virtualization of services through the use of WebSphere Services Registry and Repository (WSRR).

- Mediates (provides routing, transformation, and logging) between Web Services requesters and providers.

- Works with the latest implementations of standards, such as WSDL, SOAP, SOAP with attachments, any JMS, HTTP, HTTPS, MTOM/XOP, and MQ.

- Includes WebSphere MQ transports for Enterprise, Mobile, Real-Time, Multicast and Telemetry end points. Extends the reach, scope, and scale of the Enterprise Integration Bus out to mobile and handheld devices, along with embedded devices such as sensors or actuators.

- Available on IBM z/OS, IBM AIX, Linux (zSeries, Intel, Power), Solaris (x86-64 and SPARC), HP/UX(PA-RISC, Itanium) and Microsoft Windows Server.

Hardware-Based ESBs

This third type of ESB relies on hardware to do most of the processing. These ESB devices are easy to set up, and they offer increased security and efficient processing. IBM has a unique product line of integration devices. They offer a number of products in this category under the umbrella name of WebSphere DataPower Appliances. The most comprehensive of these appliances is WebSphere DataPower

Integration Appliance X150. This product has many of the features of an ESB, including the following:

- Transforms between disparate message formats, including binary, legacy, and XML, and provides message routing and security, MQ/HTTP/FTP connectivity, and transport mediation.
- Provides transport-independent transformations between binary, flat-text, and other non-XML messages, including COBOL Copybook, ISO 8583, ASN.1, and EDI, to offer an innovative solution for security-rich XML enablement, enterprise message buses, and mainframe connectivity.
- Offers standards-based, centralized governance and security for SOA, including support for a broad array of standards such as WS-Security and WS-SecurityPolicy.
- Allows interaction among multiple heterogeneous applications, including native connectivity to registries and repositories, as well as direct-to-database access.

In this section, we covered the three types of ESB products on the market. IBM offers the most complete product lines in this area. These IBM products are superior in many respects to other products available on the market. In the next section, we provide practical examples to illustrate the use of these three types of products in real-life situations.

Practical Usage Scenarios

In this section, we consider some real-life usage examples to demonstrate the use of the three types of devices we discussed in the last section and one of the deployment patterns discussed in an earlier section of this chapter. We will use IBM products as representative of these three classes: WESB represents the class of products based on the application server, WMB represents the messaging system–based products category, and WebSphere DataPower Integration Appliance X150 represents the class of ESB products based on hardware.

As a practical example, we consider a large financial institution such as a major bank. We'll call this financial institution PremierBank. PremierBank has a headquarters and a large number of remote branch offices. PremierBank has five major lines of business:

- **Retail banking** This line of business offers checking accounts, money market accounts, saving accounts, and certificates of deposit.

- **Mortgage and loan**   The bank offers mortgages both for commercial and residential properties. In addition, the bank offers other types of loans, such as short-term loans for buying cars and loans for small businesses.

- **Credit card**   This line of business offers various types of credit cards, both to individuals and to businesses.

- **Investment**   This line of business offers stocks, bonds, and mutual funds for investment purposes.

- **Retirement funds**   This line of business offers the management of retirement funds, with various investment options, such as certificate of deposits, stocks, bonds, and mutual funds.

PremierBank has grown over a number of years through acquisitions and mergers, which have resulted in a heterogeneous and complex IT environment. The IT environment consists of an older back-end system as well as newer, more modern applications such Java/J2EE applications. Some of the functionalities of these applications have been exposed as Web Services. In particular, the Account Open process has been exposed as a SOAP/HTTP Web Service. However, a number of issues still require further development/deployment in the area of connectivity. A careful, detailed analysis has identified four pressing requirements that need new development/deployment solutions. We discuss each of these four requirements and their suggested solutions in the following four subsections.

Multichannel Access for Existing Systems

The current connectivity environment at PremierBank does not allow easy access to a process or application from different channels. We define a *channel* as a particular combination of message type (for example, SOAP) and protocol (for example, HTTP). There is a current requirement to be able to access the Account Open process from a number of different environments, including rich clients, intranet browsers, and Internet browsers, in a manner that is suitable for each consumer application (that is, the consumer application for the Account Open process Web Services) without the need for a different mechanism for each access channel. This requirement results from the PremierBank IT environment, which has browser-based intranet and Internet users, interactive voice-response system users, and Microsoft .NET application platform users.

The solution requires a mechanism that encapsulates different access mechanisms so as to insolate other architecture and development teams from the different access styles used within the IT environment at PremierBank.

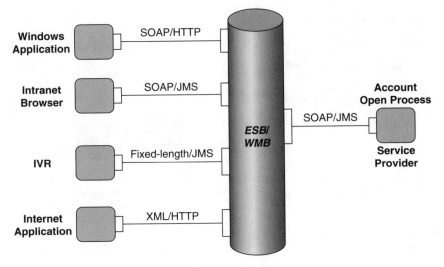

Figure 8.18   Multichannel access to existing services

Because an ESB can interact with multiple channels and can convert the different message types from each channel into a single canonical format that is passed to the Account Open process, deployment of an ESB will clearly address the requirement for multiple-channel access of the Account Open process. This solution is shown in Figure 8.18. The architecture shown in Figure 8.18 will also facilitate the integration of additional channels in the future.

Note that WebSphere Message Broker (WMB) has been chosen as an implementation of the ESB. This choice is driven by the requirement to integrate a diverse set of applications/channels as well as the heavy volume expected in the use of the Account Open process.

Open Standards–Based Internal Access

PremierBank's remote branch offices need to issue a controlled set of service requests to headquarters. Some of these requests are standards based (that is, SOAP based), whereas others are XML-formatted requests that need to be mapped to SOAP-based requests. There is a need to exercise centralized control over these requests. The applications in the remote branch offices are all modern applications that use JMS (Java Message Service) as the transport protocol. However, the headquarters applications that receive these requests all require SOAP over HTTP.

The architecture of the solution is shown in Figure 8.19. This figure shows an ESB employed in each remote branch office that is linked to

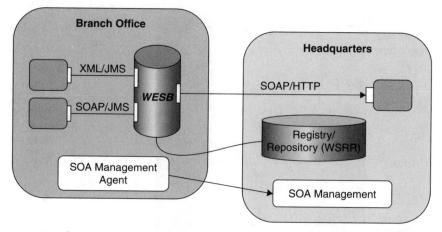

Figure 8.19   Open standards–based internal access

a registry/repository at the headquarters. Because we need support for both Web Services (SOAP over HTTP) and JMS in this scenario, WebSphere Enterprise Service Bus (WESB) is a good fit for deployment as an ESB on the service consumer side. This choice of ESB is also proper in regard to the cost effectiveness of the solution because each branch office will need an ESB—and WESB is a low-cost choice. Another advantage of using WESB is that it is easy to set up. For the registry/repository, IBM WebSphere Service Registry and Repository (WSRR) can be used at the headquarters.

In addition to employing WESB, each branch office also employs an SOA Management agent that sends management data to the headquarters domain for control purposes. At the headquarters, the control data is received and stored. The ability to monitor service calls is provided by IBM Tivoli Composite Application Manager for SOA.

Secure and Reliable Connectivity to Third-Party Providers

PremierBank has a requirement to use third-party services such as credit and address verification for opening new accounts and processing loan applications. However, the connection to the third-party service provider must be secure because of the confidentiality requirement for credit data. In addition, connectivity should not expose the PremierBank IT system to the external system. Controllable/managed connectivity is required to the third-party system.

To meet these requirements concerning connectivity to the third-party vendors/partners, the solution is a gateway pattern, as shown in Figure 8.20.

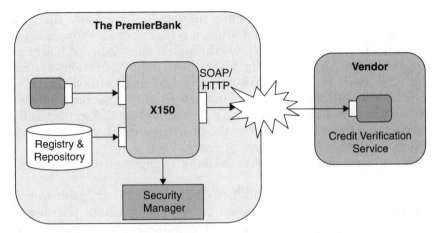

Figure 8.20   Secure and reliable connectivity to third-party vendors/partners

This solution is based on an integration device from IBM called WebSphere DataPower Integration Appliance X150, which provides the required functions related to the security and control of the communication between the PremierBank IT environment and the third-party credit-verification service. Appliance X150 has a service proxy built in. The service proxy performs the following two functions:

- It uses a service registry and repository to ensure that only the services sanctioned by the PremierBank architecture team are accessible from the PremierBank IT system. IBM WebSphere Service Registry and Repository (WSRR) is employed.

- It mediates the service request, so that the service that is actually invoked may be different from the service provider request by the user.

In addition to the proxy services, Appliance X150 also provides a full range of security (for example, data encryption and authentication) as required for secure communication with vendors such as the credit-verification service.

Connectivity Between Domains (Federation)

To demonstrate the use of the ESB deployment patterns discussed earlier, we will consider a situation that requires the use of a federation pattern.

PremierBank, after implementing the aforementioned changes, has a distributed architecture. It consists of various remote branch offices, which work somewhat autonomously and have their own ESBs.

These branch offices want to have the freedom to choose their own implementation of ESBs. In addition, a requirement for future expansion of the PremierBank enterprise through acquisitions and mergers is that these new additions bring in their own implementations of ESBs. Therefore, there is need to join heterogeneous implementations of ESBs used in different domains. The management of PremierBank wants to impose some standards for service interactions but also wants to allow the domains to make changes to the providers and interfaces without impacting the bank customers.

The current situation at PremierBank is depicted schematically in Figure 8.21.

Each PremierBank branch office (BO) makes direct, point-to-point connections with the services running in the headquarters (HQ) domain. For an application running in the remote office to communicate with a service running at HQ, the following interactions take place:

- The remote office application interacts with the ESB in the remote office.

- The remote ESB looks up the service provider in the registry/repository in the HQ office.

- The remote ESB makes a direct connection to the application in the HQ office offering the service.

The solution works fairly well but is somewhat rigid in that it does not allow changes in the HQ applications easily. In particular, if the HQ

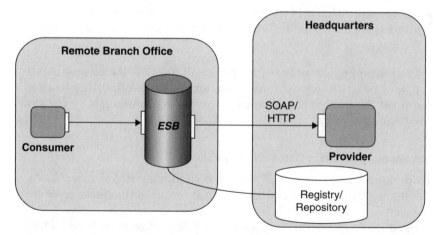

Figure 8.21 Current situation at PremierBank after implementing the previous three solutions

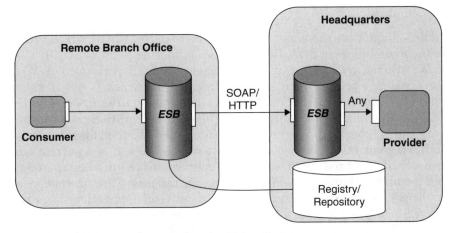

Figure 8.22   Connectivity between domains (federation)

service changes its interface, every remote office ESB would need to be updated to take this change into account.

The solution is to introduce a powerful, central ESB at the HQ domain that can support dynamic, loosely coupled routing in all domains. The solution is shown in Figure 8.22.

An ESB, employing IBM WebSphere Message Broker (WMB), is installed at HQ. The ESBs at the remote branch offices connect through the ESB at HQ instead of directly connecting to applications at HQ. WMB is selected as the ESB at HQ because it maximizes the interfaces and bindings it can work with. Furthermore, WMB is capable of handling the expected large volume of transactions.

The following are the two main advantages of this new federated architecture:

- The HQ can make changes to the services it offers without impacting the branch offices. New and multiple service provider applications can be added, new interfaces or bindings can be defined, and services can be versioned. The ESB in the HQ domain keeps track of all the changes. Therefore, changes in the implementation are not exposed to the branch offices.

- In the previous architecture, if the ESB at the remote office did not support the binding or interface at the HQ service, it could not connect to the service. In this new proposed solution, the HQ ESB acts as an adapter, transforming service bindings and protocols, thus allowing remote office ESBs to connect to the previously inaccessible services.

Conclusion

In this chapter, we discussed Enterprise Service Bus (ESB), which is one of the main pillars of SOA. (Web Services is another pillar of SOA.)

We started by looking at the reasons why ESBs are needed. Web Services only provide point-to-point integration, which is not suitable when a large number of applications need to be integrated. This is because the number of connections required for integration rises sharply with the number of applications being integrated. We then discussed how indirect connections between applications via the use of a service bus can significantly reduce the number of connections required compared to point-to-point connections. We noted in this discussion that the ability of an ESB to provide an indirect connection between applications requires the ESB to provide a facility to route messages based on content and context. To provide this routing facility, the ESB relies on its backbone, which may be a messaging system such as IBM's WebSphere MQ or an application server such as IBM's WebSphere Application Server.

Next, we tackled the remaining two heterogeneity problems not addressed in Chapter 7 while discussing Web Services. The first heterogeneity problem relates to the mismatch of the communication protocols being used between the service consumer and the service provider. This mismatch does not allow the service consumer to invoke the service being offered by the service provider. ESB has solved this problem by providing a facility to convert one communication/transport protocol into any other required protocol. For example, this facility would be able to transform the HTTP protocol into the JMS protocol. With this facility, applications are able to communicate even when the protocols of the service consumer and the service provider do not match.

The second heterogeneity problem relates to the mismatch of message formats being used by the service consumer and service provider. Once again, this mismatch is a major hurdle in the communication between the service consumer and the service provider. This problem is solved by requiring the ESB to provide a facility to transform the message format used by the service requester to the message format required by the service provider. For example, this facility would be able to transform a SOAP message into another XML-based format.

The three facilities of an ESB are known as its *core functionalities*. In summary these core functionalities are as follows:

- Content- and context-based routing
- Protocol transformation or protocol switch
- Data format or message transformation

With these core functionalities, an ESB provides some virtualization to the services. For example, an ESB provides location virtualization in that the service consumer does not need to know the network address of the service provider, and the service does not need to know where the request is coming from.

In addition to these three facilities, an ESB also provides an implementation of the Quality of (Interaction) Service (QoS) requirements by the service consumers. Examples include performance, reliability, and security requirements.

Furthermore, sometimes ESBs offer additional services, which are known as *optional services*. Examples of such optional services are data enrichment (from a data source), distribution, correlation, and monitoring of messages exchanged between the service provider and the service consumers.

Next, we discussed the various logical components needed to implement an ESB. Some of these components are adapters, a service delegate, a routing and rules engine, a transformation engine, a request handler, and an enrichment component.

Next we discussed some of the ESB deployment configurations (or patterns) that may be employed:

- **Global ESB**   This pattern employs a single ESB for the entire enterprise and is suitable for relatively small organizations.

- **Directly connected ESBs**   In this configuration, ESBs are directly connected. This configuration employs a single service registry and is typically used to connect packaged applications (such as SAP applications) with other types of applications (such as Java/J2EE).

- **Federated ESBs**   This configuration employs several ESBs, one of which has a master-slave relationship with the other ESBs. This configuration is suitable for an organization consisting of moderately autonomous departments or domains.

- **Brokered ESBs**   This configuration employs a broker to administer the interactions between autonomous departments. Each of these departments employs its own ESBs. Each of these departments wants to expose only a subset of the services it offers to the other departments.

Next, we discussed the three basic types of ESBs available on the market. The most powerful, versatile, and scalable ESBs are based on an (asynchronous) messaging system, such as IBM's WebSphere MQ. The prime example is the IBM WebSphere Message Broker (WMB). This type of ESB can handle a vast class of applications, protocols, and message types. It can also handle large transaction volumes. The second type of ESB is based on application servers such as IBM's WebSphere Application Server. The prime example is IBM's WebSphere Enterprise Service Bus (WESB). These ESBs are designed for ease of setup and lower cost, but they cater to a more restricted class of applications, protocols, and message types. There also hardware-based devices that can perform some functions of ESBs. IBM is the leader in this class of ESB and offers several products in this area. Most notable among these products is the WebSphere Integration Appliance X150, which offers enhanced security and high performance in XML processing.

We continued our discussion by considering a specific example of a large bank that has various requirements related to connectivity. We demonstrated the use of three types of ESBs as well as the use of one deployment pattern by using several different scenarios.

To complete our discussion of ESBs, we want to mention one issue that may become important in the near future. The issue involves the interoperability of the brand ESBs from different vendors. Sometimes different brands of ESBs are prevented from working together in a smooth fashion. One solution for this problem is the development of industrywide ESB interoperability standards.

As mentioned at the beginning of this section, the ESB is one of the two important pillars of SOA. The other pillar is Web Services. We provided a review of the Web Services in Chapter 7. You can obtain a more thorough understanding of Web Services by reading the chapters in Part V of this book. These chapters discuss how to develop Web Services by building new applications. In the next chapter, we will consider how to expose existing applications as Web Services. For this we will consider mostly mainframe applications because almost all large organizations employ mainframes as their back-end system and usually have made a large investment in such a system. Therefore, they are reluctant to replace these systems with more modern applications.

Integrating Existing Applications

Integrating Mainframe Applications

The last chapter provided an overview of Web Services. From there, a natural progression would be first to describe new applications that can be exposed as Web Services. This would allow the integration of new or modern applications into an SOA-based integrated enterprise. However, we have chosen to describe methods of integrating existing applications—particularly applications that run on a mainframe—first in this chapter and we have postponed the details of integrating new applications until Chapter 11. The reasons for describing mainframe applications integration first will become abundantly clear in this chapter, which describes some of the facts about the two major types of mainframe applications. We have done this mainly because for large corporations, mainframe applications almost always form the backbone of the IT structure. Also, many consider integrating mainframe applications the most difficult task of creating a complete SOA-based integrated IT structure. Therefore, it is imperative that we discuss the integration of these mainframe applications first.

It may be argued that an obvious way to incorporate the functionalities embedded in mainframe applications in an integrated enterprise is to convert them into modern applications such as Java and C++. However, this is made very difficult by the fact that most of these mainframe applications evolved over long periods of time and these applications are not well documented. Furthermore, the persons who wrote the code or are familiar with the code might no longer be available either due to retirement or moving to another job. In addition, the resources and time are not available to extract the functionalities embedded in mainframe applications and then rewrite the applications. Therefore, in most cases, it is not viable to convert these mainframe applications into more modern applications.

Because it is not practical to convert mainframe applications into more modern applications, we must find ways to integrate existing mainframe applications into an integrated IT structure that is also likely to contain more modern applications such as Java/J2EE and C++ applications. In this chapter, we consider two broad categories of mainframe-integration schemes. First, we consider mainframe-integration approaches that employ point-to-point integration, which is the proper technique to use if the mainframe applications need to be integrated with a few other applications. Next, we consider the Enterprise Service Bus–based integration of mainframe applications. This technique is suitable if mainframe applications need to be integrated with a larger number and various types of applications.

In the point-to-point category, we describe four different approaches for each major type of mainframe application. Two of these four approaches expose the mainframe applications' functionalities as Web Services, whereas the other two approaches expose these applications as services based on messaging. The four approaches for one type of mainframe application (that is, IMS applications) are

- MQ Enablement
- MQ Bridge for IMS
- IMS SOAP Gateway
- IMS TM Resource Adapter

Similarly, for the other major type of mainframe application (that is, CICS applications), the four approaches are

- MQ Enablement
- MQ Bridge for CICS
- Web Services support in CICS TS V3.1 and higher
- CICS Transaction Gateway with CICS TS Resource Adapter

For integrating mainframe applications with a large number of applications, we describe two approaches based on ESB. We consider two approaches in this category. The first approach relies on application server–based ESB, such as IBM WebSphere Enterprise Service Bus (WESB). This approach is suitable when the mainframe application is being integrated with Java/J2EE, XML, and SOAP-based applications. For integrating mainframe applications with a wider variety of applications, we use the ESB based on messaging software. An example of such an ESB is IBM WebSphere Message Broker (WMB), which is based on IBM messaging software called WebSphere MQ. This latter approach also provides higher scalability capability in terms of higher transaction volumes as well as provides for ensuring the delivery of messages between the service consumer and the service provider.

We start this chapter with brief descriptions of the two main types of mainframe applications and why the integration of these two types of applications is so important for large organizations. Next, we discuss some general features and considerations of the integration schemes described in this chapter, as well as various point-to-point options and two ESB-based options.

Mainframe Application Types

Two main types of applications run on mainframe computers: applications that run under IMS (IBM's Information Management System) and applications that run on CICS (IBM's Customer Information Control System).

Some people refer to mainframe applications as *legacy applications*. However, this is a misplaced and unjustified titled. Mainframe applications have not remained stagnant but have come a long way in terms of modernization. The modernization started at the operating system level, which has evolved from MVS to the modern z/OS system. Furthermore, currently both IMS and CICS transaction systems allow applications to be written in modern languages other than COBOL. Some of the modern programming languages supported on IMS and CICS systems include C, C++, Java, and PL/1. In addition, both CICS and IMS have added software components that allow the functionalities embedded in their applications to be exposed directly and/or indirectly as Web Services.

IMS Applications

IBM's Information Management System consists of a transaction processor and a hierarchal database. A *transaction* in this context is a request and execution of a set of programs/applications performing administrative functions and accessing a database on behalf of a user. In this chapter, we are mostly concerned with the transaction processor part of IMS because we are mostly interested in integrating applications/programs that run under IMS.

IMS has a long and interesting history, starting in 1966. Originally IBM developed IMS with two other NASA contractors for the Apollo program. IMS is still going strong after more than four decades of service, with a very impressive record. Originally, IMS was designed to work with IBM System/360 technology, but it has evolved into using the z/OS operating system and associated technologies. Also, IMS currently supports a number of programming languages, including COBOL,

C/C++, and Java. However, COBOL remains the dominant language for programming applications in IMS. Here are some interesting and impressive facts about IMS:

- IMS is part of everyday life. For example, bank ATMs almost all use IMS as the back-end system. All different types of industries and organizations use IMS—banks and financial institutions, manufacturing, government, power companies, and telephone companies.

- It is estimated that over 95 percent of Fortune 1000 companies use IMS.

- It is estimated that IMS processes over 50 billion transactions per day.

- Because of the wide use of IMS, it is considered to be among the top-ten largest revenue-producing "software companies" in the world.

- IMS provides extremely high performance in terms of the following:

  - **System availability**   Only two to three hours of planned and unplanned outages per year.

  - **Response time**   Measured in subseconds.

  - **Number of transactions**   A single IMS installation can handle more than 50 million transactions per day.

This chapter does not discuss integrating with mainframe hierarchical databases (such as IMS database), because this type of integration requires different tools and techniques for integration. For example, for IMS database integration, IMS offers the IMS DB resource adapter, also known as the *IMS JDBC Connector,* which is a Java Connector Architecture (JCA) resource adapter that enables a direct connection to IMS database assets from a J2EE runtime. This is a complementary adapter to the IMS TM resource adapter, which is discussed later in this chapter.

CICS Applications

CICS (Customer Information Control System) is also a transaction-processing software that primarily runs on the z/OS and z/VSE operating systems for mainframes. CICS was first released in 1969, not long after the first IMS release. CICS was first developed at IBM's Palo Alto laboratory in the U.S., but in 1974 development of CICS moved to Hursley in the U.K. CICS applications can be written in a variety of languages, including COBOL, C, C++, PL/1, Assembly, and Java. However, COBOL is the predominant language for developing CICS applications.

Here are some of the interesting and impressive facts about CICS:

- Ninety percent of the top 500 companies use CICS for their core business.
- CICS is used in all categories of industries as well as in government.
- CICS is installed on 85 percent of all z/Series computers.
- There are 30 million CICS users worldwide.
- More than 30 billion CICS transactions are processed per day.
- A CICS system supports about one million concurrent users.
- CICS is available on distributed platforms such as AIX, Windows, Solaris, UNIX, and HP-UX. On distributed platforms, CICS is known as *TX Series*.

The two types of CICS applications are based on the COMMAREA and 3270 terminal. COMMAREA is a block of contagious memory used by a CICS program to communicate with other programs. We will deal with both types of CICS applications in this chapter.

Preliminaries

To begin our discussion of the various schemes for integrating mainframe applications, recall from Chapters 7 and 8 that integration always starts from a point-to-point approach, in which we integrate the given application with only a small set of applications by building connections and interfaces with each pair of applications in the set. In this regard, it is important to note that Web Services themselves only provide point-to-point integration of applications. Once you have enabled an application to take part in at least one point-to-point integration, it is straightforward to employ an Enterprise Service Bus, which enables the application to be integrated with a large and more diverse set of applications. Therefore, in this chapter we first describe the point-to-point integration of a mainframe application with a more modern application such as Java/J2EE application. The changes we make to the mainframe application in order to enable it to communicate with the modern application in the point-to-point schema will also be needed when we employ an ESB for a wider integration of the mainframe applications. In describing the point-to-point integration schemes, we will use a Java/J2EE application as an example of a modern application, because currently these are the most common modern applications.

Two broad categories of integration schemes are used in the point-to-point approaches when it comes to mainframe integration. The first broad category employs a messaging system for integrations. Recall that we discussed the messaging systems in Chapter 6. The second broad category of integration schemes exposes the mainframe applications as Web Services.

The first category consists of two methods:

- In the first method, the mainframe application is enabled to communicate directly with the messaging software system. The messaging software system then talks to the Java/J2EE application.

- In the second method, the messaging system does not talk directly to the mainframe application; instead, the connection is made through a bridge.

The second category also consists of two methods:

- In the first method, the mainframe application is directly exposed as a Web Service without the use of any middle service components. Only some versions of CICS can be exposed by using this method.

- In the second method, the mainframe application's functionality is first wrapped in a middle service component, which is then exposed as a Web Service.

In describing these various approaches of integration, instead of using generic systems (such as a messaging system or an application), we will use specific IBM products that correspond to these systems. This is done for two reasons. First, products from different companies vary somewhat in their capabilities, and we are more certain that IBM products have the needed functionalities. Second, we strongly feel that IBM products, in many respects, are superior to other comparable products available on the market. In our discussion we will employ these IBM products for the following categories:

- Messaging system: WebSphere MQ (MQ)
- Application server: WebSphere Application Server (WAS)
- ESB (light): WebSphere Enterprise Service Bus (WESB)
- ESB: WebSphere Message Broker (WMB)

In addition to these products, we also refer to some IBM tools that can be used to implement the various integration schemes described in this chapter. Here are some of the tools mentioned in this chapter:

- WebSphere Developer for z-Series
- Rational Application Developer
- WebSphere Integration Developer

In some of the integration options discussed in this chapter, you'll see references to two IMS components: IMS Connect and Open Transaction Management Access (OTMA). IBM IMS Connect improves IMS TCP/IP access and enables easier access to IMS applications and data from the Internet. OTMA is a transaction-based, connectionless client/server protocol that provides an access path and an interface specification for sending and receiving transactions and data from IMS.

There is no one best solution for every situation; therefore, the description of each option covers the same set of aspects so that you can compare them and then decide on a particular option for your specific environment. Here's a list of the aspects discussed:

- Work required (on the mainframe)
- Technology constraints
- Guaranteed delivery
- Security
- Cost
- Time to production
- Real-time access and synchronous/asynchronous messaging
- Operating system requirements
- Additional hardware requirements
- Reuse
- Scalability
- Extendibility
- Performance
- Preferred data type and protocol
- Data enrichment
- Agility

Next we start describing various options that are available for mainframe integrations, starting with MQ-based approaches.

MQ Enablement

To use MQ with enablement, you need to significantly modify the CICS or IMS application using the MQ application programming interface called MQI, so that the application can receive and send MQ messages. You also need to do a substantial amount of work on the COBOL/mainframe side; however, this enablement results in a very scalable integration solution.

There are two ways to perform this type of integration:

- You can install MQ Servers on both sides of the connection; then, you can absolutely guarantee delivery because messages are persisted on both sides.

- You can replace one of the two MQ Servers (either on the mainframe side or the client application side) with an MQ Client. In this case, messages are not persisted on the MQ Client; therefore, to guarantee delivery, you must design the application on the side where MQ Client is installed with much more care. However, this second option reduces costs substantially.

Use the first method when message delivery must be 100-percent guaranteed, with no exception; you can use the second method when lower cost is a major consideration. As an example, consider the business case where a credit-card transaction must be reported to accounting by an asynchronous message so as not to block the sending application. For legal or contractual reasons, this message to accounting must be absolutely guaranteed, with no exceptions. In this case, you would use the first option. However, if the contractual or legal requirements are not so strict and lower cost is an important consideration, then the second option with MQ Client on one side of the connection should be employed.

This option requires the use of MQ CICS or MQ IMS adapters. These adapters are sets of CICS/IMS programs and resource definitions that enable a CICS/IMS system to run programs that call MQI. The remaining work involves employing a pattern in the implementation to avoid flooding the CICS/IMS transaction application. MQ CICS and MQ IMS adapters are well tested and therefore add reliability to your integration solution. Figure 9.1 shows a schematic view of this option.

Here is a brief discussion of the various aspects involved in this approach to integrating mainframe applications to help you decide whether this option is suitable for your situation.

Work Required   MQ enablement, in principle, requires a substantial amount of work using the MQI API to add code to a COBOL application to send and receive MQ messages. This applies to both CICS and IMS transaction applications. The API work is in addition to the work required to configure queues and queue managers. You can use the CICS adapter or IMS adapter supplied with MQ to significantly reduce the amount of work.

Technology Constraints   There are no technology constraints related to the operating system on the mainframe; you can use any operating system on which CICS or IMS applications run, including z/OS, MVS, and OS/390 (but, of course, not Windows or UNIX).

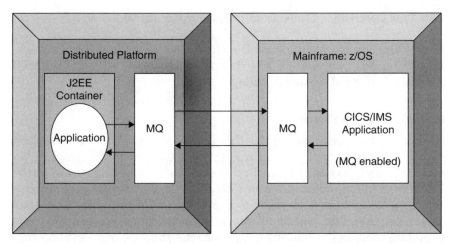

Figure 9.1   Point-to-point integration of mainframe applications via MQ enablement

Real-Time Access and Synchronous/Asynchronous Messaging   This solution allows for real-time access. The messaging can be synchronous or asynchronous.

Guaranteed Delivery   One of the major advantages of using MQ is a guaranteed delivery if the MQ Server is also installed on the other end. However, if only the MQ Client is deployed on one of the two ends, this guarantee may be compromised.

Operating System Requirements   This option is suitable for all operating systems on the mainframe side.

Additional Hardware Requirements   No additional hardware is required.

Security   MQ provides no security of its own. You must employ External Security Manager (ESM), which uses z/OS Security Authentication Facility (SAF) for security. Security can be implemented at the queue manager level or at the queue-sharing group level. Alternatively, you can deploy WebSphere MQ Extended Security Edition, which supports SSL through authentication, encryption, and message integrity.

Cost   Among the point-to-point options we discussed, this is one of the most expensive options in terms of software costs because of the cost of MQ Servers. (You can reduce the cost of this option by half if you only use the MQ Server on one side of the connection.) It is also the most expensive option in terms of software development resources and development time.

Data Type Centricity   This option is data type neutral.

Tools   You can use WebSphere Developer for zSeries, which is a work-station-based environment for writing and testing code, to add the MQI commands to existing applications.

MQ with CICS/IMS Bridge

Similar to the previous option, this point-to-point integration option involves a modern application connecting to a CICS or IMS COBOL application through MQ messaging. In this case, you use a bridge between the MQ server/client and the CICS or IMS application. The bridge eliminates the need for extensive changes to the CICS or IMS applications using MQI calls; therefore, you might consider this option if you want to avoid changing code on the mainframe. Figure 9.2 shows a high-level conceptual diagram of this option for a CICS application.

For an IMS application, you must install an additional Open Transaction Manager Access (OTMA) component on the mainframe in front of the IMS application. The OTMA talks to the MQ server/client through the bridge, as shown in Figure 9.3.

The CICS Bridge, which comes with CICS TS version 1.2, provides access to a large number of existing CICS applications which were written for 3270 terminals input and outputs. The heart of this bridge is a bridge exit program, which handles commands from existing 3270-based applications.

The primary advantages of using the bridge are as follows:

- It provides a simple interface and minimizes the need for programming on the mainframe side.

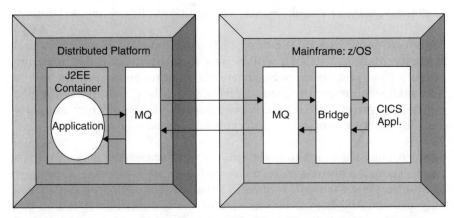

Figure 9.2   Point-to-point integration using MQ and a bridge for a CICS application

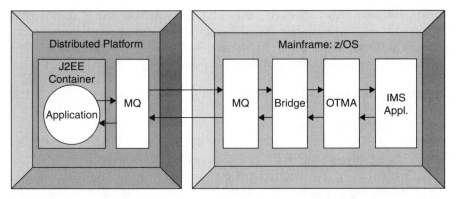

Figure 9.3 Point-to-point integration using MQ and a bridge for an IMS application

- You do not have to deal with the complexities of the 3270 data stream. It provides a Business Mapping Service (BMS) to decode the complex 3270 data stream into a symbolic map structure that the program uses. BMS loads a map set load module to obtain the mapping instructions. You only need to create a map set. You can maintain a pseudo-conversational state by chaining together a number of CICS transactions.

An alternative approach is the conversational model, in which the original message may not contain all the data to run the transaction. If the transaction issues a request that cannot be answered by any of the vectors in the original message, a message is put into a reply-to queue requesting more data. The client application gets this message and puts a new message back in the queue to satisfy the request.

Here is a brief discussion of the various aspects of this approach of integrating a mainframe application to help you decide whether this option is suitable for your situation.

Work Required This option requires only a minimal amount of coding, compiling, and linking on the mainframe side. For the CICS Bridge, you need to create a map set for each CICS application. You must also configure the queues and managers.

Technology Constraints z/OS is required on the mainframe. For the CICS Bridge, you need CICS version 1.2 or higher. For the IMS Bridge, you need Open Transaction Manager Access (OTMA).

Real-Time Access and Synchronous/Asynchronous Messaging The access is real time, and messages can be synchronous or asynchronous.

Cost   Because this option requires MQ Servers, it is one of most costly options. If you only use the MQ Client on the client application, you can cut the software cost in half. In terms of software development cost, this is one of least expensive options available.

Data Type Centricity   No particular type of data is preferred.

Tools   No specific tools are required.

Guaranteed Delivery   As in the previous case of MQ with enablement, the message delivery is guaranteed if you use MQ Servers on both sides of the connection. If you only use the MQ Client on the client application side, the message delivery is not guaranteed.

Operating System Requirements   The z/OS operating system is required on the mainframe side.

Additional Hardware Requirements   None.

Security   If you use the IMS Bridge, the security issues are the same as in the case of MQ enablement. If you are using the CICS Bridge, you must include an additional user ID/password pair in the message to the CICS transactions.

IMS SOAP Gateway

The IMS SOAP Gateway makes IMS applications accessible as Web Services through easy deployment and configuration steps. You don't have to change your IMS applications, but you do need to generate Web Services Definition Language (WSDL) files and XML converters using IBM WebSphere Developer for System z. The gateway usually runs on a separate machine (Windows, Linux, AIX), which can limit the scalability of this solution. The gateway communicates with the mainframe system using XML over TCP/IP. On the mainframe, the IMS Connect component with an XML adapter interacts with the IMS application through the use of Open Transaction Manager Access (OTMA), as shown in Figure 9.4.

Here is a brief discussion of the various aspects of this approach of integrating mainframe applications to help you decide whether this option is suitable for your situation.

Work Required   You can use WebSphere Developer for zSeries to easily generate the Web Services artifacts. For example, with WebSphere Developer for zSeries, you can generate a WSDL file from the COBOL copybook of an IMS application, which will also generate an XML

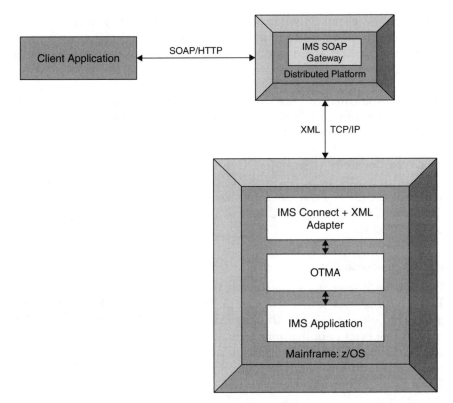

Figure 9.4   Point-to-point integration of an IMS application using a SOAP Gateway

converter to transform XML data in IMS Connect. Then, the overall application can send and receive XML data, without you needing to modify your existing IMS applications. To use this functionality, you need APAR PK24912 applied to IMS V9.1.

Technology Constraints   Requires IMS version 9 or higher, integrated with IMS Connect version 9. You need to be running z/OS on the mainframe.

Real-Time Access and Synchronous/Asynchronous Messaging   Only synchronous messages are allowed, but access is real time.

Guaranteed Delivery   The delivery of messages is not guaranteed.

Operating System Requirements   Gateway runs on multiple platforms, including Microsoft Windows XP, Windows 2000, AIX, and zLinux. It usually runs on a machine separate from the one on which the application is running.

Additional Hardware Requirements IMS Soap Gateway typically runs on a machine separate from the application. This machine can be running Windows XP, Windows 2000, or AIX, or it could be a mainframe running zLinux.

Security You can configure this solution for SSL to support secure communication using HTTPS between the end client and IMS SOAP Gateway, as well as between the IMS SOAP Gateway and IMS Connect.

Data Type Centricity This is an XML-centric solution.

Tools WebSphere Developer for zSeries can be used to generate WSDL files from COBOL copybooks and to generate an XML converter to use in IMS Connect.

IMS TM Resource Adapter

Previously known as IMS Connector for Java (IC4J), the IMS TM Resource Adapter is a J2EE Connector Architecture–based resource adapter you can deploy on the application server. It enables Java/J2EE and Web Services applications to access IMS applications on the mainframe through TCP/IP. The Java or J2EE application talks to the IMS applications through IMS Connect and OTMA, as shown in Figure 9.5. Therefore, IMS Connect and OTMA must be configured on the mainframe side.

With this option, you can quickly develop Java/J2EE or Web Services applications that run IMS transactions. For development, Rational Application Developer can be employed. Application Developer parses copybook information to describe the input/output messages of a target

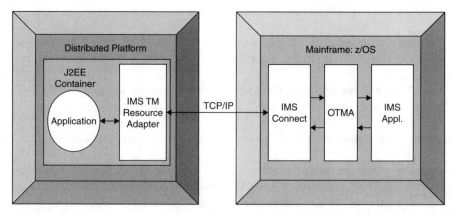

Figure 9.5 Point-to-point integration of an IMS application using an IMS TM Resource Adapter

IMS application, and it generates a J2EE application. Application Developer can also generate WSDL so that the target IMS application can be exposed as a callable Web Services. Minimal work is required on the mainframe side.

Here is a brief discussion of the various aspects of this approach of integrating mainframe applications to help you decide whether this option is suitable for your situation.

Work Required   You don't need to change the IMS application. You can use IBM tooling to develop the J2EE or Web Services application. Then you can deploy the application on a J2EE application server such as WebSphere Application Server.

Technology Constraints   z/OS is required on the mainframe. The IMS TM Resource Adapter runs in a WebSphere application on a number of platforms, including Windows, AIX, Linux, zLinux, and HP-UX.

Real-Time Access and Synchronous/Asynchronous Messaging   Messaging is typically synchronous and in real time.

Guaranteed Delivery   The delivery of messages is not guaranteed.

Operating System Requirements   This option requires the z/OS system on the mainframe.

Additional Hardware Requirements   The IMS TM Resource Adapter runs in a WebSphere application on a number of distributed platforms, including Windows, AIX, Linux, zLinux, and HP-UX.

Security   This option supports component-managed and container-managed security, including container-managed thread identity. This option supports SSL communication between the IMS TM Resource Adapter and IMS Connect.

Data Type Centricity   Data is transported in copybook format.

Tools   You can use Rational Application Developer, Web-Sphere Integration Developer, or WebSphere Developer for z-Series to parse the input and output of a target J2EE application and also to generate a WSDL file from the copybook.

Web Services Support in CICS V3.1

CICS Web Services Support in CICS TS V3.1 enables applications running in CICS TS V3.1 to participate in a heterogeneous Web Services environment as a service requester, a service provider, or both, using either HTTP or WebSphere MQ as the transport mechanism. Figure 9.6 provides a high-level view of this option.

Web Services Support contains three components:

- A pipeline process, which controls the processing of SOAP messages. CICS TS V3.1 also supplies some message handlers that process SOAP messages. The pipeline process uses a configuration file to determine which SOAP handler to invoke, as shown in Figure 9.7.

- Web Services Assistant, which is a tool you can use to generate WSDL and WSBIND files. The CICS application uses WSBIND files to transform application data to SOAP messages, and vice versa. Alternatively, you can use WebSphere Developer for z-Series to generate the WSDL and WSBIND files.

- CICS resources for management.

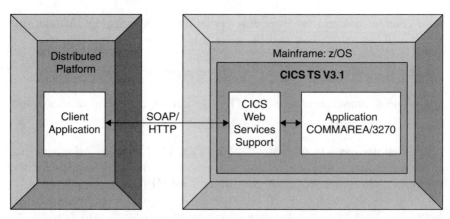

Figure 9.6   The CICS TS version 3 Web Services Support option for integrating CICS applications

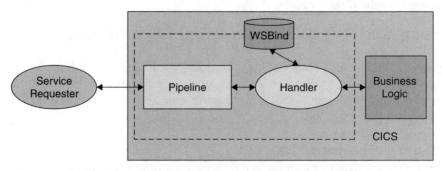

Figure 9.7   Detail working of Web Services Support in CICS version 3

An attractive additional feature of the CICS Web Services Support is the CICS Service Flow feature. You can use this feature to enable accessing terminal-oriented CICS applications, to aggregate multiple terminal-oriented interactions into a business flow process, or to aggregate terminal-oriented applications with COMMAREA applications.

The CICS Service Flow feature is a composition of WebSphere Developer Service Flow Modeler (SFM) and CICS Service Flow Runtime (SFR). SFR uses a component called Link3270 Bridge to access terminal-oriented applications.

Here is a brief discussion of the various aspects of this approach of integrating mainframe applications to help you decide whether this option is suitable for your situation.

Work Required   Developers need to generate WSDL and WSBIND files using either the Web Services Assistant tool or WebSphere Developer for z-Series. System programmers need to do the following:

- Create a PIPELINE resource definition and a PIPELINE configuration file.
- Install PIPELINE definitions and TCPIPSERVICE.
- Publish WSDL.

Technology Constraints   Requires z/OS and CICS TS V3.1 or higher.

Real-Time Access and Synchronous/Asynchronous Messaging   Access is in real time using synchronous messaging.

Guaranteed Delivery   Delivery can be ensured if you use WebSphere MQ as the transport mechanism.

Operating System Requirements   z/OS is required on the mainframe.

Additional Hardware Requirements   This option requires no additional hardware.

Security   SSL is supported; it provides the necessary security during data transport.

Cost   There is no additional cost; you must use V3.1 of CICS TS.

In summary, this option (also called *direct expose of the CICS applications*) should be used when expediency is the primary motivator. By eliminating the need to write new code, you can save development and testing time. However, the service requirement must match closely with the functionality and data that is already in the existing CICS application. Therefore, there should be no requirement for customizing the information flowing between the CICS application and the service consumer.

CICS Transaction Gateway

Older versions of CICS, such as V2.3, do not have native support for Web Services; hence, the functionalities of the CICS applications for such older systems cannot be exposed directly. Therefore, to expose the functionalities embedded in older CICS applications that run on V2.3 and earlier versions, an indirect approach must be employed. With this approach, the CICS applications are wrapped in a Java/J2EE class (for example, as a session EJB) that is then exposed as a Web Service. The approach uses an adapter (or a connector) to access the CICS application. This indirect expose pattern provides maximum control over the transportation of data, the aggregation of CICS functions, and the mapping of a required service contract (WSDL document) to the underlying implementation, represented by a COBOL copybook.

The main software component in this approach is a CICS Transaction Gateway (CICS TG), which includes a Java Connector Architecture (JCA) Resource Adapter. CICS TG for Multiplatforms V6.0 runs on a multitude of operating systems and platforms to support connectivity to all in-service (that is, all versions of) CICS servers. Here are some of the operating systems and platforms on which CICS TG V6.0 is supported:

- Linux on System z
- Linux on Intel
- Linux on POWER
- AIX
- HP-UX
- Sun Solaris (on SPARC)
- Various versions of Windows

CICS TG for Multiplatforms consists of the following runtime components:

- The Gateway daemon, which listens for incoming requests and manages the threads and connections necessary to ensure good performance.
- The Client daemon, which provides the communications to the CICS servers and non-Java APIs.
- A Java class library or JCA Resource Adapter, which is deployed into the client runtime environment. This resource adapter for J2EE Client is deployed into a J2EE application server.

A Java client can connect to a remote Gateway daemon using the TCP or SSL protocol. The Client daemon has the transport driver to connect to the CICS server as shown in the Figure 9.8.

The most common Java client resides in a J2EE application server. The application server and CICS TG can be deployed in three different topologies. We describe only the most common topology, where the J2EE application server is deployed on a distributed platform while the CICS TG is deployed on z/OS, which also hosts the CICS application.

A schematic but more detailed drawing in which the CICS application is exposed indirectly is shown in Figure 9.9. We will use this figure to explain how indirectly exposing CICS applications works.

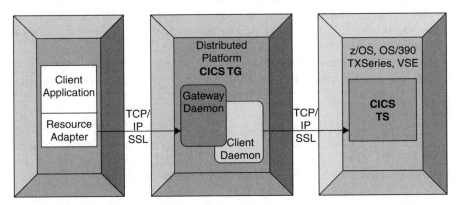

Figure 9.8   Option for integrating a CICS application using a CICS Transaction Gateway

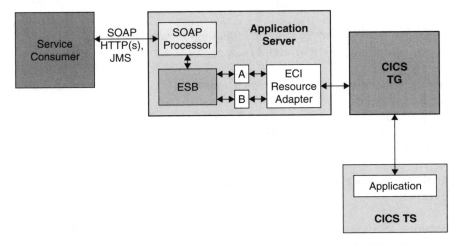

Figure 9.9   Detailed view of integrating a CICS application using CICS TG

In this approach, you start by using a tool to read the COBOL copybook and create application-specific classes (which are displayed as A and B in Figure 9.9). An example of this type of tool is the CICS/IMS Data Binding Wizard in IBM Rational Developer for System z. The classes, such as A and B, understand the CICS functions and data, and they handle talking to CICS using JCA. The particular resource adapter that is used is CICS ECI, which is deployed in the J2EE application server runtime.

Next, you write a WSDL service contract, which is then used in tooling to generate a class skeleton, along with a SOAP processing class that handles incoming SOAP requests. The processing is done in Java code, which is easy to write. The handling code maps the incoming method calls to the access classes, aggregate functions, and transform data as required.

One advantage of this approach is that you do not need to know much about the resource adapter or even anything about COBOL, except to use the copybook with the wizard in the tool. You simply invoke Java classes to perform your work.

Here is a brief discussion of the various aspects of this approach of integrating mainframe applications to help you decide whether this option is suitable for your situation.

Work Required   This option requires the use of the IMS/CICS Binding Wizard in the IBM Rational Developer for System z to generate application-specific classes from the copybook. A WSDL service contract must also be created, which is then used to generate skeleton classes along with a SOAP processing class. Code must be written to handle the incoming method calls, aggregate functions, and transform data as required.

Technology Constraints   Requires z/OS. This approach can be used with any in-service version of CICS.

Real-Time Access and Synchronous/Asynchronous Messaging   Access is in real time using synchronous messaging.

Guaranteed Delivery   Delivery can be ensured if you use WebSphere MQ as the transport mechanism.

Operating System Requirements   This option requires z/OS on the mainframe.

Additional Hardware Requirements   This approach requires no additional hardware.

Security   SSL is supported; it provides the necessary security during the data transport.

Summary of Point-to-Point Integration

In this section we summarize some of the results of the point-to-point integration approaches for the two types of mainframe applications.

We start with the integration schemes for IMS applications. As pointed out previously, there is no one best solution for all situations. Whereas the integration schemes based on MQ are best when high transaction volumes are expected, the approach that relies on IMS TM Resource Adapter might be the best if loose coupling between the mainframe and the Web Services being exposed is desired. Table 9.1 provides a summary comparison of the various approaches for integrating IMS applications.

Similar considerations apply to the CICS applications integration approaches. No single approach is best for all situations. Once again, the MQ-based approaches provide the best solution if very high transaction volumes are desired. However, if the work needed is minimal and CICS TS V3.1 is available, then directly exposing the CICS applications might be a good choice. Table 9.2 provides a comparison of the various aspects of the different integration approaches available.

ESB-Based Integration Options

The point-to-point integration schemes described in the previous sections are suitable when the mainframe applications need to be integrated with one or two other applications. However, if you need to integrate

TABLE 9.1   Comparison of Various Point-to-Point Integration Approaches for IMS Applications

Option/Aspect	MQ Enabled	MQ Bridge	IMS SOAP Gateway	IMS TM Resource Adapter
Work required on mainframe	Substantial	Minimal	Some	Some
Guaranteed delivery	Yes	Yes	No	No
Real-time access	Yes	Yes	Yes	Yes
Synchronous/ asynchronous	Both	Both	Synchronous	Both
Additional hardware	No	No	Yes	No
Operating system required	z/OS	z/OS	z/OS	z/OS
Data type centricity	None	None	XML	None
Cost	High	High	Medium	—
Technology constraints	z/OS	z/OS, OTMA	IMS V9 and higher	z/OS
Security	Yes	Yes	Yes	Yes

TABLE 9.2   Comparison of Various Point-to-Point Integration Approaches for CICS Applications

Option/Aspect	MQ Enabled	MQ Bridge	CICS Web Services Support	CICS Transaction Gateway
Work required on mainframe	Substantial	Minimal	Some	Some
Guaranteed delivery	Yes	Yes	Possible	No
Real-time access	Yes	Yes	Yes	Yes
Synchronous/ asynchronous	Both	Both	Synchronous	Synchronous
Additional hardware	No	No	No	Yes
Operating system required	z/OS	z/OS	z/OS	z/OS
Data type centricity	None	None	XML	XML
Cost	High	High	Low	Medium
Technology constraints	z/OS	z/OS, OTMA	CICS V3.1	All CICS versions
Security	Yes	Yes	Yes	Yes

mainframe applications with a substantial number of other applications, point-to-point integration is not suitable because the number of connections required between the applications explodes quickly as the number of applications being integrated increases. For such situations, an ESB offers a flexible, comprehensive, and scalable solution to the problem of mainframe integration.

Recall from Chapter 8 that an ESB offers the following three basic capabilities:

- Content- and context-based routing of messages
- Communications protocol transformation or switch
- Message transformation

Message format transformation involves transforming data from one format to another format; for example, a flat file format can be transformed into an XML format. Similarly, one transport protocol such as HTTP can be transformed into another form, such as an MQ message. This allows an application that can only communicate through HTTP to talk to an application that can only communicate through MQ. Participants need not know the location or identity of other participants. For example, requesters don't need to be aware that a request can be serviced by any of several providers. Service providers can be added and removed without disruption. The ESB forms the backbone of a Service-Oriented Architecture (SOA).

An ESB supports many interaction types, including one-way, request/response, asynchronous, synchronous, and publish/subscribe. It also supports complex event processing, in which a series of events may be observed to produce one event as a consequence of the relationships in the series.

Figure 9.10 shows a conceptual diagram of a basic ESB. It provides a number of hooks or hubs for connecting applications of various kinds to the ESB and therefore to each other. The hooks are simply adapters for synchronous services (MQ, HTTP, Web Services, and so on) and asynchronous services (MQ input and output nodes). Each type of hub caters to one type of protocol and one type of data. For example, a SOAP/HTTP-type hub will be suitable to connect an application to the bus that communicates over HTTP using SOAP messages. To perform its functions, the ESB contains various component types that might include dispatchers, request handlers, routing and rules engines, transformation engines, persistence nodes, delegates, exception handlers, and a logging facility.

To connect the mainframe to the ESB and to the other applications, you must perform the steps outlined in one of the options discussed for point-to-point integration. Then the mainframe can be connected to an

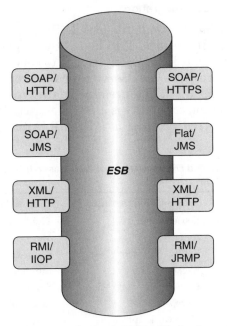

Figure 9.10 Conceptual diagram of a basic ESB with hooks or hubs for connecting applications

appropriate hub/hook in the ESB. For example, if you have enabled the mainframe for MQ, you can connect it to an MQ hook. Alternatively, if you have installed a SOAP Gateway, you can connect the mainframe through the SOAP/HTTP hook.

Table 9.3 summarizes the advantages and disadvantages of ESB-based integration compared to point-to-point integration.

Based on these benefits, if you decide that the use of an ESB for integrating mainframe applications is the best choice for a given situation, the next question to ask is which kind of ESB to deploy. In Chapter 8, we discussed three different kinds of ESBs:

- Application server based, such as WebSphere Enterprise Service Bus (WESB)

- Messaging system based, such as WebSphere Message Broker (WMB)

- Hardware-based integration devices, such as the WebSphere DataPower devices from IBM

Each kind of ESB has its pros and cons. For mainframe integration, usually only the first two kinds of ESBs are used. We discuss mainframe integration based on these two types of ESBs next.

WebSphere ESB–Based Integration

IBM WebSphere ESB is a standards-based ESB based on the WebSphere application server. It uses the JMS bus of the application server as a messaging backbone. It is primarily meant to serve as a Web Services environment. It provides Web Services–based connectivity and services-oriented integration. The preferred data type is XML, and data format transformation capability is mostly restricted to different forms of XML. The preferred protocol is HTTP(S). Although this ESB can

TABLE 9.3   Advantages and Disadvantages of ESB-Based Integration Compared to Point-to-Point Integration

Feature	ESB-Based Integration	Point-to-Point Integration
Coupling	Loose coupling	Tight coupling
Agility	Agile	More rigid
Extendibility	Easily extended	Less extendable
Reuse	Excellent reuse	Limited reuse
Integration scale	Large-scale integration	Small-scale integration
Scalability	More scalable	Less scalable
Initial work required	More work upfront	Less work upfront
Cost	More costly	Generally less costly

connect applications other than J2EE/Java and Web Services, it is primarily meant to work with these applications only.

A very attractive feature of WebSphere ESB is the low cost (comparatively speaking). It is also easy to set up. What's more, you can install WebSphere ESB on a variety of operating systems, including z/OS, various Windows operating systems, Linux, zLinux, HP-UX, AIX, and Solaris. It supports HTTPS and SSL and, therefore, provides data security during transit.

Figure 9.11 shows one possible scenario for using WebSphere ESB for integrating a CICS mainframe application with other XML/SOAP and Java-based applications. In this example, a CICS application running in CICS TS V3.1 is first exposed as a Web Service using a method described in our point-to-point integration discussion and then it is connected to the WebSphere Enterprise Service Bus (WESB), which allows it to

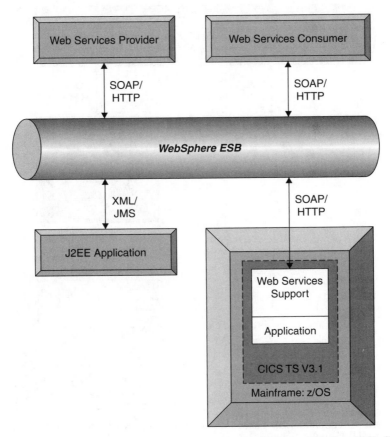

Figure 9.11   WebSphere ESB–based CICS application integration with other XML, SOAP, and Java/J2EE applications

interact with other applications based on Web Services (SOAP/HTTP), XML, and Java. The other option for CICS applications to use for integration using WESB is to first employ the CICS Transaction Gateway for exposing the CICS applications as Web Services.

Similarly, Figure 9.12 shows one possible way to integrate an IMS mainframe application with other XML/SOAP and Java-based applications using IMS SOAP Gateway, which first exposes IMS applications as Web Services. This second choice would have to use IMS TM Resource

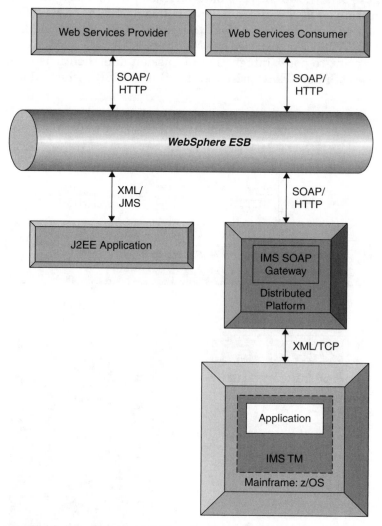

Figure 9.12   WebSphere ESB–based IMS application integration with other XML, SOAP, and Java/J2EE applications

Adapter inside a J2EE container, such as WebSphere Application Server, to enable IMS applications to take part in a WESB-based integrated IT environment.

WebSphere Message Broker–Based Integration

The WESB-based integration just described is a good approach if the following conditions are satisfied:

- Applications that are to be integrated with the mainframe applications are Java, XML, and Web Services–based only.
- There is no requirement for guaranteeing the delivery of the messages.
- The transaction volumes are expected to be low.

However, if any of these three conditions are not satisfied, a more powerful ESB is needed that can provide for integration of a more diverse set of applications, guarantee the delivery of messages, and be able to handle large transaction volumes.

WebSphere Message Broker (WMB) is an advanced ESB. It is based on the WebSphere MQ MOM (message-oriented middleware). Quite often this is the only standard way to guarantee delivery of messages. Message Broker provides a very scalable, reliable, proven method for mainframe integration. It is also flexible in terms of data type neutrality and is capable of data transformation from any-to-any formats.

As an advanced ESB, WebSphere Message Broker also supports a much wider variety of protocol transformation. You can use it to integrate applications with a wide variety of application types, including Java/J2EE, Web Services, C++, and mainframe legacy applications. WebSphere Message Broker also provides data enrichment and mediation. It is more expensive than WebSphere ESB.

You can install WMB on numerous operating systems, including AIX, HP-UX, Linux, zLinux, Solaris, various versions of Windows, and z/OS. Data security is supported through the use of secure protocols (such as SSL and HTTPS).

A sample scenario for integrating a mainframe application using WebSphere Message Broker is shown in Figure 9.13. The example shows that a CICS application is being integrated with a diverse set of applications using WMB as an ESB. The CICS application was first MQ enabled. Then a WebSphere MQ server is used to communicate with the ESB and, through it, to the rest of the applications in the integrated structure. The other option would have been to use an MQ bridge first, which would have reduced the necessary programming changes on the

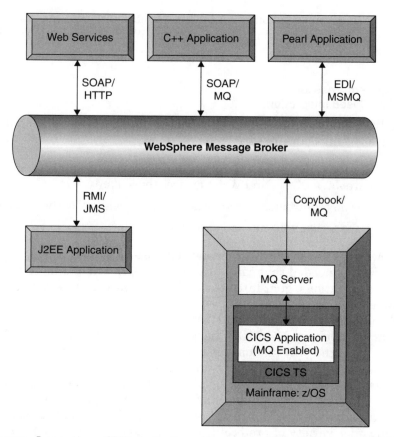

Figure 9.13 Integrating a CICS application with a variety of applications using WMB

mainframe side but would have retained the scalability of the solution in terms of transaction volume.

Figure 9.14 shows another example of mainframe integration with a diverse set of applications. This time the mainframe applications being integrated are IMS applications, and an MQ bridge and an MQ server are employed. In addition, OTMA is also used. The other choice—which would have maintained the high transaction volume and guarantee of message delivery capabilities—would have been to use only an MQ server. However, this second choice would have required substantial changes on the mainframe side.

Comparison of WMB and WESB

Table 9.4 provides a summary comparison of two ESB-based approaches for integrating mainframe applications. Generally speaking, WMB provides a more powerful approach, but it is more expensive and takes more

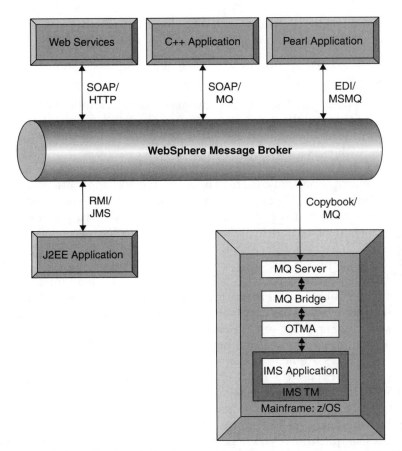

Figure 9.14 IMS applications being integrated with a variety of other applications using WMB

TABLE 9.4   Comparison of WESB-Based Integration and WMB-Based Integration

Feature	Message Broker ESB	WebSphere ESB
Scalability	High volume	Lower volume
Reliability	Proven, reliable	Newer product
Guaranteed delivery	Yes	No
Data type centricity	No preferred data type	XML centric
Protocols	Any protocol can be used	HTTP is preferred
Preferred language	None	Java/J2EE
Cost	Comparatively expensive	Much lower cost
Time to production	More time needed	Fast setup

time to set up. On the other hand, WESB is much cheaper and is easy to set up, but it has limited capabilities compared to WMB ESB.

Conclusion

In this chapter, we reviewed the various options available for integrating mainframe applications in a Service-Oriented Architecture. This was made possible by first exposing the mainframe applications as services, either as Web Services or MQ-based services.

We started the chapter by reviewing basic facts about the two major types of mainframe applications. These two types of applications are IMS applications and CICS applications. You learned that these two types of applications constitute the backbone of the IT structure of almost all major corporations and large organizations (including governments). Therefore, it is imperative that methods be found to integrate these mainframe applications in a Service-Oriented Architecture.

We first considered point-to-point integration of the mainframe with other applications in an enterprise. In a point-to-point integration, each distinct pair of applications involves a separate connection and integration scheme. For point-to-point integration of mainframe applications, we focused on exposing the functionalities embedded in IMS applications and CICS applications as services of some kind. Sometimes it is convenient to expose the functionalities embedded in these applications as Web Services, while at other times it is more prudent to expose the functionalities as messaging-based services.

For these two types of mainframe applications (IMS applications and CICS application), you learned there are four different methods of integrating in the point-to-point approach. Two of these four methods expose the mainframe applications' functionalities as services, which are based on messaging software such as WebSphere MQ, whereas the other two methods expose the mainframe applications' functionalities as Web Services. Although the Web Services provide the advantage of being based on open standards, the services based on the messaging system (MQ) generally provide a more scalable solution as well as guarantee delivery of messages between the service provider and service consumer.

Of the two MQ-based methods of integrating IMS and CICS applications, one method, called MQ enablement, requires substantial changes on the mainframe side. However, this method provides the most scalable solution in terms of the volume of transactions. The second method, using an MQ server, additionally employs an MQ bridge, which reduces the need to change the mainframe applications substantially.

The remaining two methods for integrating IMS applications involve IMS SOAP Gateway and IMS TM Resource Adapter. Both of these expose the IMS applications' functionalities as Web Services. The Web Services exposed through the IMS SOAP Gateway have tight coupling with the existing functionality in the IMS application, and they require a distributed platform to host SOAP Gateway, which can limit the scalability of the solution in regard to the transaction volume. In case of the IMS TM Resource Adapter, a distributed platform is also required as well as a J2EE container such as WebSphere Application Server. However, this latter approach offers loose coupling between the exposed Web Services and the IMS applications, because the IMS applications are exposed indirectly through the use of J2EE components (also called service components) such as Enterprise Java Beans (EJBs). The scalability is not a serious issue in this latter approach because J2EE components are designed for high transaction volumes.

In the case of CICS applications, the remaining approaches are directly exposing CICS applications as Web Services and indirectly exposing them as Web Services using CICS Transaction Gateway and Resource Adapter. The first approach can be applied only if a new version (version 3.1 and higher) of CICS Transaction Server is in use on the mainframe. In this first approach, there is tight coupling between the CICS applications' functionalities and the exposed services. If you are using an older version of CICS Transaction Server on the mainframe, the second approach of indirectly exposing the CICS applications as Web Services must be employed. This approach has the advantage that there is loose coupling between the exposed services and the functionalities embedded in the CICS applications. This loose coupling is the result of using J2EE components (such as EJBs) as the front end for exposing the CICS applications as Web Services.

These point-to-point approaches for integrating mainframe applications are suitable if the mainframe application is being integrated with one or two other, more modern applications, such as a Java/J2EE application. If the number of applications is larger, an Enterprise Service Bus–based integration approach of indirectly connecting the applications to the mainframe application should be employed. The use of an ESB for integration purposes greatly reduces the number of connections required and provides loose coupling between the applications. Individual applications can be added or removed easily from the integrated structure without affecting other applications in the structure.

In this chapter, we described various approaches that employ ESB for integrating mainframe applications with other, more modern applications. These approaches are based on two major types of ESBs. The first type is based on the application server. IBM's WebSphere Enterprise Service Bus (ESB), which is based on WebSphere Application Server (WAS), is an example of such an ESB. These ESBs primarily cater to Web Services, XML, and J2EE-centric applications. In order to use such an ESB for integrating mainframe applications, the mainframe applications typically have to be exposed as Web Services first using one of the point-to-point techniques described earlier.

The second type of ESB is based on the messaging software. The prime example of such an ESB is the IBM WebSphere Message Broker (WMB), which is based on the WebSphere MQ messaging software from IBM. This type of ESB is much more scalable in terms of transaction volume. Also, a more diverse set of applications can be integrated with the mainframe applications via these ESBs. These ESBs can also be used to guarantee delivery of messages between the service consumer and service provider. In order to use this kind of ESB, it is necessary to expose the mainframe application first, either as a Web Service or a messaging-based service using one of the methods described earlier for point-to-point integration.

Chapter 10

Integrating Package Applications

In addition to mainframe applications, which form the backbone of IT systems of large enterprises, the IT system of a large organization typically has a number of package applications. Examples of such package applications include Customer Relationship Management (CRM) applications and Enterprise Resource Planning (ERP) applications. SAP, PeopleSoft, Oracle, and JD Edwards are some of the software suppliers for these types of applications. Some of the advantages of these package applications for large organizations include risk reduction, introduction of best practices and processes, speed of implementation, and more accurate estimation of the cost of the software. Frequently these package applications are also referred to as *Enterprise Information Systems (EISs)*. For such large organizations it is also important to integrate these package applications with the other applications in the IT systems in order to provide a consistent and unified view of data and functionality to both the internal and external customers.

Most, if not all, of the schemes for integrating these package applications rely on the use of adapters. Adapters are simply software components or subsystems that allow package applications to talk to other applications using the interfaces provided by the package applications. Modern ways of integrating these applications use adapters in conjunction with a J2EE application server to connect the EIS with the modern applications. Alternatively, the adapters can be used with an Enterprise Service Bus (ESB) to integrate the EIS with a wider variety of applications. (Many times in this chapter we will refer to application servers and Enterprise Service Buses as *brokers* because these application servers and ESBs can mediate between different applications.) In addition, sometimes the EIS supplier provides an infrastructure to expose some of the functionality and data embedded in the EIS application as Web Services. For example, such is the case for SAP by integrating an application server with their EIS. The first two options are shown schematically in Figures 10.1 and 10.2. In general, the adapter can be deployed either at the EIS side or the application server/ESB side, or somewhere in between. However, most commonly the adapter is deployed at the application server or ESB side. We will discuss adapters in some detail in the following sections.

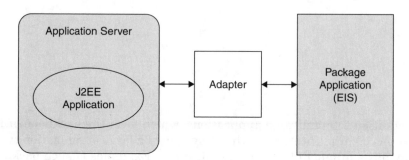

Figure 10.1 Integration of a package application with a modern application using an adapter

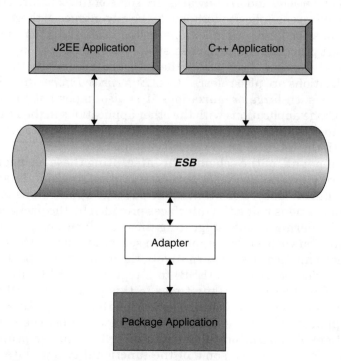

Figure 10.2 Integration of a package application to a wider range of applications through the use of an adapter and ESB

The remaining sections of the chapter are organized as follows: First, we describe the adapter and integration of package applications in general. J2EE Connector Architecture (JCA) is discussed next. Compliance with JCA reduces the number of adapters needed for a given package application by a large factor. Following this we illustrate the use of adapters by considering a specific package, namely SAP applications. We describe the SAP system and the various interfaces exposed by the SAP system, and then we describe the WebSphere adapter for the SAP system. Finally, integrating package applications by exposing their functionality as Web Services is briefly discussed.

Adapters

In general, an EIS adapter is specific to an EIS and an integration point (broker), such as a specific application server or a specific ESB. Examples of application servers include WebSphere Application Server (WAS) and JBoss Application Server. Examples of an ESB include WebSphere Enterprise Service Bus (WESB) and WebSphere Message Broker. Examples of an EIS include SAP's ERP and CRM applications. Therefore, in general, each combination of an EIS and the integration point (broker) requires a separate adapter.

An EIS-specific adapter contains two outlets (that is, interfaces), as shown in Figure 10.3: one interfacing with the respective EIS and one interfacing with the integration broker. The outlet to the EIS understands its given application interface. The outlet to the integration broker supports the interface of the integration broker. In this way, the adapter is an abstraction layer and shields the integration broker from the peculiarities of an EIS. The integration broker must understand only one protocol and one data format when communicating with the adapters.

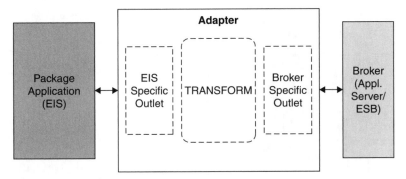

Figure 10.3 Two faces of an adapter

It is common that a fairly complex package application can be accessed by various interfaces. An adapter is not limited to supporting only one interface per package application; rather, it can bundle different interfaces of the same package application. This can be achieved by configuring the adapter with the description of the exchanged data and the interface type to be used with the EIS/package application (see Figure 10.4). This information is stored in configuration files and enables the adapter to cope with EIS-specific application data of various data types and access mechanisms during runtime.

In addition to performing data transformations, another characteristic of an adapter is that it may run in its own process. Therefore, the integration broker does not have to access the EIS/package application directly, thus resulting in the decoupling of the availability of the broker for other applications. This decoupling also means that the EIS/package application can be accessed without making any modifications.

Because the adapter runs in its own process, it can support bidirectional communication between the integration broker and the package application, as shown in Figures 10.5 and 10.6. In the case where the data

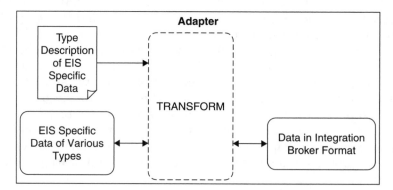

Figure 10.4   Data transformation driven by the type description within an adapter

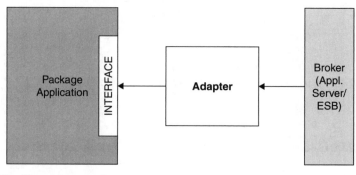

Figure 10.5   Request processing

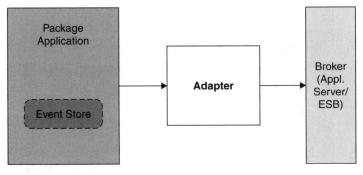

Figure 10.6   Event processing

gets forwarded to the package application from the integration broker, the scenario is called *request processing* or *outbound processing*. Request processing is usually based on the existing interfaces of the package application. These existing interfaces are called directly by the adapter. In the second case, the events are generated independently in the package application, which are forwarded to the integration broker by the adapter for processing. This second scenario is called *event processing*.

If the EIS/package application cannot be configured to submit events to an external component directly, special functionality must be introduced that enables an adapter to retrieve or pull the event by itself. Normally, this is done using an Event Store in the EIS, which buffers the events and extends the adapter via a mechanism for detecting (and pulling) the events stored there.

J2EE Connector Architecture (JCA)

Before the introduction of J2EE Connector Architecture (JCA), for each combination of application server (broker) and EIS (package application), a different adapter was needed. For example, three separate adapters were needed to integrate an SAP application with WebSphere Application Server, JBoss Application Server, and WebLogic Application Server, as shown in Figure 10.7. This led to a proliferation of adapters and made the integration of package applications with modern applications very complex and cumbersome.

JCA simplified the integration of package applications by defining a standard interface to an application server/broker. This standard interface means that the EIS vendor has to provide only a single adapter to integrate their package application with a number of different application servers, each of which is JCA compliant. Thus, for example, SAP has to provide a single adapter that will integrate an SAP application with modern applications running on any application server that supports JCA.

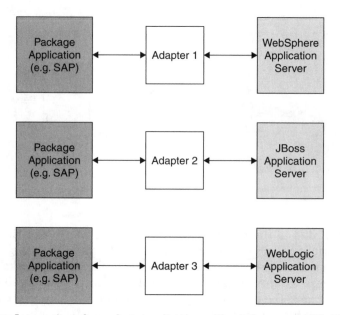

Figure 10.7 Integration of a package application without the use of JCA. Note three different adapters are needed, one for each brand of application server.

This is illustrated in Figure 10.8, which shows that the same adapter can be used with any of the three brands of application server (namely, WebSphere Application Server, JBoss Application Server, and WebLogic Application Server), in contrast to the situation shown in Figure 10.7, where three different adapters are needed.

Multiple resource adapters (that is, one resource adapter per type of EIS) can be plugged into an application server. This capability enables application components deployed on the application server to access a number of the underlying EISs.

To achieve a standard system-level pluggability between application servers and EISs, the JCA defines a standard set of system-level contracts between an application server and the EIS. The adapter implements the EIS side of these system-level contracts. The adapter usually runs in the address space of the application server.

An adapter is a system-level software driver used by an application server or an application client to connect to an EIS. By plugging into an application server, the adapter collaborates with the server to provide the underlying mechanisms, the transactions, security, and connection-pooling mechanisms.

JCA defines three system-level contracts between the application server and the EIS: one for outbound connectivity, one for inbound connectivity, and one for life cycle and thread management. We first discuss the JCA-defined system-level contract for outbound connectivity.

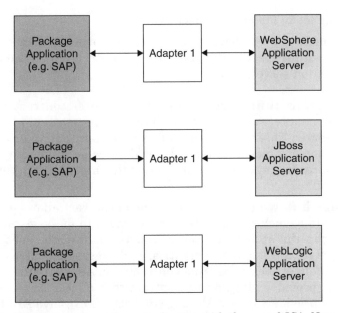

Figure 10.8 Integration of a package application with the use of JCA. Note that only one adapter is needed, which can be used with any number of brands of application servers.

JCA's Contract for Outbound Connectivity

The J2EE Connector Architecture defines the following system-level contracts between the EIS and the application server:

- **Connection management contract** This type of contract lets an application server pool connections to an underlying EIS, and lets application components connect to an EIS. This leads to a scalable application environment that can support a large number of clients requiring access to EISs.

- **Transaction management contract** This is a contract between the transaction manager and an EIS that supports transactional access to EIS resource managers. This contract lets an application server use a transaction manager to manage transactions across multiple resource managers. This contract also supports transactions that are managed internally to an EIS resource manager without the need to involve an external transaction manager.

- **Security contract** This type of contract enables secure access to an EIS. This contract provides support for a secure application environment, which reduces security threats to the EIS and protects valuable information resources managed by the EIS.

JCA's Contract for Inbound Connectivity

JCA also defines the following system-level contracts for inbound connectivity (with respect to the application server) between the EIS and the application server:

- **Transaction inflow contract** This type of contract allows a resource adapter to propagate an imported transaction to an application server. This contract also allows a resource adapter to flow in transaction-completion and crash-recovery calls initiated by an EIS, and ensures that the ACID properties of the imported transaction are preserved.

- **Message inflow contract** This type of contract allows a resource adapter to asynchronously deliver messages to message end points residing in the application server independent of the specific messaging style, messaging semantics, and messaging infrastructure used to deliver messages. This contract also serves as the standard message provider pluggability contract that allows a wide range of message providers—Java Message Service (JMS), Java API for XML Messaging (JAXM), and so on—to be plugged into any J2EE technology–compatible application server via a resource adapter.

JCA's Life Cycle and Thread Management Contract

The following system-level contracts defined by JCA relate to the adapter's life cycle management and thread management:

- **Life cycle management contract** This type of contract allows an application server to manage the life cycle of an adapter. This contract provides a mechanism for the application server to bootstrap an adapter instance during its deployment or application server startup, and to notify the adapter instance during its "undeployment" or during an orderly shutdown of the application server.

- **Work management contract** This type of contract allows an adapter to do work (monitor network end points, call application components, and so on) by submitting work instances to an application server for execution. The application server dispatches threads to execute submitted work instances. This allows an adapter to avoid creating or managing threads directly, provides a mechanism for an adapter to do its work, and allows an application server to efficiently pool threads and have more control over its runtime environment. The adapter can control the security context and transaction context with which work instances are executed.

In the next two sections, we consider the WebSphere brand adapter for integrating a specific package application. WebSphere adapters are available for a wide range of package applications. Because these adapters are JCA compliant, they can be used to integrate with any brand of application server or enterprise bus. We start with a brief introduction to SAP and the various interfaces that can be used for integration. Then we cover the WebSphere adapter for SAP integration.

Introduction to SAP and Its Interfaces

SAP implements a three-tier architecture that includes a back-end database, which can be a database from any of the major database software suppliers. The middle tier consists of application server instances. These instances distribute the workload. The front end uses a specific fat client SAP graphical user interface (SAPGUI) to access the back-end system. The more recent SAP releases also support web browsers as a front end.

Earlier releases of SAP business applications were packaged in modules, which were written in Advanced Business Application Programming (ABAP) and ran on the SAP application server. More recent releases, such mySAP.com, have extended support for additional Internet technologies. The new SAP Web Application Server includes the full functionality of a J2EE application server. The new SAP NetWeaver is the current technology platform that supports business applications on both technology stacks: ABAP and Java.

SAP applications integration must support the various releases of SAP enterprise engine as well as various interfaces, including the following:

- Application Link Enabling (ALE) and Intermediate Documents (IDocs)
- Remote Function Call (RFC)
- Business Application Programming Interface (BAPI)
- Batch Data Communications (BDC)
- Electronic Data Interface (EDI)
- Web Services (SAP Web Application Server 6.20 and later)

Note that the BDC and EDI interfaces are beyond the scope of this chapter, and the last option exposes only some of the functionality as Web Services. We will not elaborate on this interface because its use is straightforward.

ALE and IDocs

ALE is used to integrate business processes between different SAP and non-SAP back-end systems. It allows controlled data exchange between and SAP and non-SAP applications. IDocs are used by ALE to pass data in and out of the SAP applications. IDocs contain information in a predefined format (structured ASCII) and may be understood as the serialized form of business data objects. Asynchronous communication is used by ALE.

RFCs

RFCs are SAP-specific remote procedure calls that are used to communicate among distributed SAP modules. ABAP function modules can be declared as remote enabled and made accessible to an RFC client remotely. The SAP system can act as an RFC server or as an RFC client. RFCs represent a synchronous communication style.

WebSphere Adapter for SAP Software

WebSphere Adapter for SAP Software provides a comprehensive way to interact with SAP software by allowing multiple ways to work with applications and data on the SAP server. This adapter supports both outbound processing (from application to adapter to SAP server) and inbound processing (from SAP server to adapter to the application). In the case of outbound processing, all CRUD (create, retrieve, update, delete) operations on the data on the SAP server are supported. In the case of inbound processing, an event that occurs on the SAP server is sent to the adapter. The ALE Inbound and Synchronous Callback interfaces start event listeners that detect the events. Conversely, the Advanced Event Processing interface polls the SAP server for events. The adapter then delivers the event to an end point, which is an application or other consumer of the event from the SAP server.

Figure 10.9 shows an overview of the outbound processing interfaces. Here is a summary description of these interfaces:

- **BAPI interfaces** Through its BAPI interfaces, the adapter issues remote function calls (RFCs) to RFC-enabled functions, such as a Business Application Programming Interface (BAPI) function. These remote function calls create, update, or retrieve data on an SAP server and return the results to the calling application. BAPI calls are useful when you need to perform data retrieval or manipulation and a BAPI or RFC function that performs the task already exists.

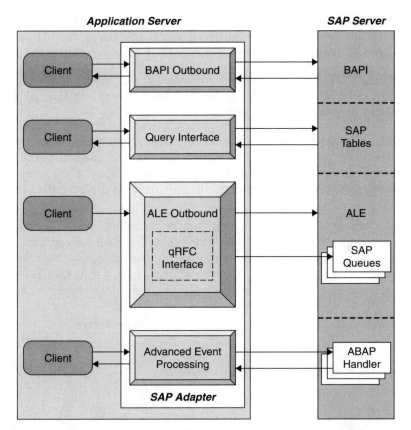

Figure 10.9 Outbound SAP interactions via the use of the WebSphere SAP adapter

- **Query interface** The Query interface for SAP Software retrieves data from specific SAP application tables. It can return the data or check for the existence of the data. You can use this type of interaction with SAP if you need to retrieve data from an SAP table without using an RFC function or a BAPI.

- **ALE** In the case of Application Link Enabling (ALE), SAP's Intermediate Data Structures (IDocs) are used for the exchange of data. For outbound processing, you send an IDoc or a packet of IDocs to the SAP server. The ALE interface, which is particularly useful for batch processing of IDocs, provides asynchronous exchange. You can use the queued transactional (qRFC) protocol to send the IDocs to a queue on the SAP server. The qRFC protocol ensures the order in which the IDocs are received. It is often used for system replications or system-to-system transfers.

- **Advanced Event Processing interface**   Lastly, in the case of Advanced event processing interface, you send data to the SAP server. The ABAP handler on the SAP server then processes the data.

Similarly, Figure 10.10 shows an overview of inbound processing interfaces. WebSphere Adapter for SAP provides the following three interfaces for inbound processing:

- **Synchronous Callback interface**   The adapter listens for events and receives notifications of RFC-enabled function calls from the SAP server through the use of this interface. The adapter then sends the request to a predefined application and returns the response to the SAP server.

- **ALE Inbound Processing interface**   In this case, the adapter listens for events and receives IDocs from the SAP server. The communication is asynchronous. In addition, the IDocs can be received through a queue on the SAP server, which ensures that the IDocs are received in the proper order. The adapter uses a data source to persist

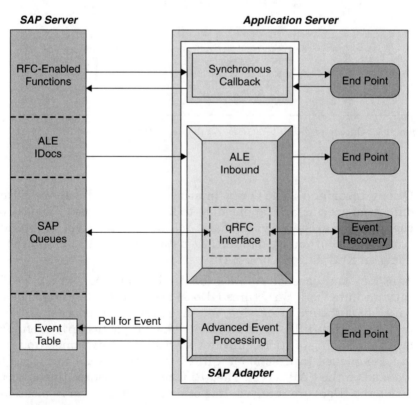

Figure 10.10   Inbound processing interfaces

the event data, and event recovery is provided to track and recover events in case of abrupt termination.

■ **Advanced Event Processing interface**   In this case, the adapter polls the SAP server for events. When it discovers events to be processed, it sends the events to the end point (application/component).

Exposure as Web Services

As mentioned previously, some of the package applications (EISs) directly expose some of their functionality and data as Web Services. For example, SAP directly exposes some of its functionality as Web Services. Any external application that has a network connection can use such functionality, thus providing another integration method for these package applications.

However, many times this direct exposure is not enough because the functionality needed by a consumer application may not be wholly contained in a single package application. In addition, because only some of the functionality of a given package application is exposed directly as Web Services, there is sometimes still a need to expose the remaining functionality as Web Services. The method described previously in this chapter that employs adapters to integrate the package application with modern applications (particularly Java/J2EE applications) comes in handy. This is because once the functionality and data contained in the package applications have been integrated with J2EE components, it is easy to expose these components as Web Services. The methods to expose J2EE components as Web Services is discussed in some detail in Chapter 15; therefore, refer to Chapter 15 for further information on this subject. Exposing a package application as Web Services using this indirect method is shown schematically in Figure 10.11.

Conclusion

In this chapter, we described the integration of package applications, which are sometimes referred to as *Enterprise Information Systems (EISs)*, with other application types in the enterprise. We focused on the use of adapters, which can be used along with brokers (application servers or ESBs) to integrate these types of applications. We started out with a general description of the adapters and then we described the J2EE Connector Architecture (JCA), which reduces the number of different adapters needed for a given package application. Compliance of both the broker and the adapter with JCA specifications greatly simplifies the integration of package application.

Next, we demonstrated the use of adapters for integration by considering a specific package application system, namely SAP. For this we

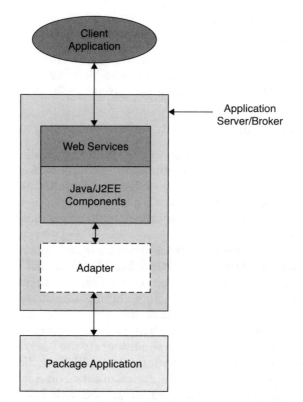

Figure 10.11   Indirectly exposing a package application using an adapter and Java/J2EE components

first discussed the SAP application and the various interfaces you can use to connect to such an application. Next, we described the WebSphere Adapter for SAP Software, which provides a compressive way to access the functionality and data embedded in an SAP application.

Lastly, we discussed how you can indirectly expose the functionality and data pertaining to a package application as Web Services. This indirect method involves first integrating the package application with J2EE/Java components in an application server via the use of an adapter. Then the Java/J2EE component is exposed as Web Services using the bottom-up method described in Chapter 15 of this book. In this bottom-up approach, you first use the Java2WSDL automated tool with a Java class to generate a WSDL document for the service. Then you use the automated tool WSDL2Java to generate the binding and the artifacts needed on the server side and the client side. After the EIS has been exposed as a service, any other application can use the service either by integrating in a point-to-point manner or by connecting the EIS to an ESB through a SOAP/HTTP port.

Understanding and Developing Web Services

11

XML

XML is probably the most important pillar of Web Services. XML documents are often used as a means for passing information between the service provider and service consumer. XML also forms the basis for WSDL (Web Services Description Language), which is used to declare the interface that a Web Service exposes to the consumer of the service. Additionally, XML underlies the SOAP protocol for accessing a Web Service. Lastly, UDDI (Universal Description, Discovery, and Integration), which is used to publish and discover a Web Service, is also based on XML.

Web Services often pass information using XML documents. Therefore, the applications that implement Web Services or the applications that act as the consumer of Web Services must be able to interpret the information contained in an XML document. In addition, these applications must be able to extract and process the information contained in an XML document. Furthermore, they must be able to assemble XML documents from the results of this business processing.

In this chapter, we describe the concepts and techniques for the use of XML that are important in implementing Web Services and their clients. We start with an overview of the XML language. This overview includes the basic concepts as well as a description of the basic structure of an XML document. Next, we discuss the concept of namespaces, which is used to avoid the collision of names in different spaces and to extend the use of the vocabulary defined in one specific domain to other domains. Schemas, which define the structure and grammar for a particular type of XML document, are discussed following namespaces. Finally, we discuss the various models you can use for parsing, processing, creating, and editing an XML document.

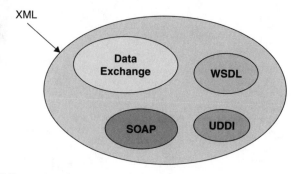

Figure 11.1   XML space and use

Overview

XML has been adopted as a popular middleware-independent standard format for the exchange of data and documents. In addition, XML forms the basis for the other three standards relating to Web Services mentioned previously. This is shown schematically in Figure 11.1.

XML syntax is similar to HTML, but it serves a different purpose than that of HTML. HTML is a language used to describe how the data should be displaced. On the other hand, XML is designed to describe what the data is. Just as in HTML, there are tags in XML. However, in XML, tags describe what the data *is* instead of how data should be displayed, as is the case for HTML. A sample portion of an XML document is shown in Listing 11-1.

Listing 11-1

```
Listing 11.1: Sample XML code snippet
1       <product>
2           <name>Blue Device</name>
3           <price currency="US">99.99</price>
4       </product>
```

Another important difference between XML and HTML is that XML does not force the use of specific tag names, thus allowing programmers to invent their own tags. The following phrases are used in conjunction with "tags":

- **Open tags**   Example: <name>
- **Close tags**   Example: </name>
- **Elements**   Example: <name>Blue Device</name>
- **Attributes**   Example: <price currency="US">

The general structure of an XML document is shown in Figure 11.2.

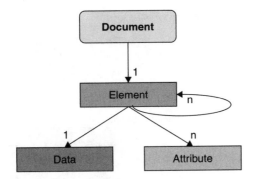

Figure 11.2 The general structure of an XML document

This figure shows that a basic XML document consists of a top element. Note that there can only be one top element in a valid XML document. This top element may consist of data (the payload), an attribute, and any number of other elements in a recursive manner. A sample portion of a simple XML document is shown in Listing 11-2. This document contains a top element named "address," which has a single attribute used to specify the country. This top element has also five child elements, which provide information on the name of the person, the street address, the city, and the postal code. Each of these child elements has data (that is, a payload) contained in them. For example, the data for the name element is "John Smith."

Listing 11-2

```
Listing 11.2: Basic XML document structure
1    <address country="USA">
2            <name>John Smith</name>
3            <street>43 Walcut St</street>
4            <city>Dublin</city>
5            <state>Ohio</state>
6            <postal-code>45561</postal-code>
7    </address>
```

XML Namespaces

The namespace is an important concept in XML, and we will employ this feature as a technique to increase reuse across multiple WSDL documents and across the enterprise and beyond. Therefore, we'll describe this concept and discuss how this concept is implemented.

An XML namespace comprises a collection of element type names and attribute names. A namespace is identified by a URI reference. As an example, consider the three different namespaces shown in Figure 11.3.

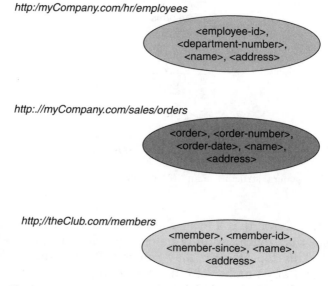

http:/myCompany.com/hr/employees

http:.//myCompany.com/sales/orders

http;//theClub.com/members

Figure 11.3 Namespaces

The element's name and the address of the namespace (http:/myCompany .com/hr/employees) refer to the names and addresses of the employees of the company (myCompany). The identical element type name of the namespace http:.//mCompany.com/sales/orders holds the name for the supplier for myCompany. Finally, myCompany's tennis club management also decides to store their member data in XML format with the element types of name and address.

A namespace is declared through the reserved namespace attribute xmlns or through an attribute that is prefixed with "xmlns:" and followed by a name without a colon. The namespace attribute can be provided in any element of an XML document. The value of the namespace attribute is the namespace name (that is, the URI reference). An example of a namespace prefix declaration is shown here:

```
<address  xmlns:myC="http://myCompany.com/hr/employees">
```

Now we can use the prefix to qualify any name of the element. A more complete example of the use of the prefix is shown in Listing 11-3.

Listing 11-3

```
Listing 11.3: Example of the use of a namespace prefix
1     <myC:address xmlns:myC="http://myCompany.com/hr/employees">
2         <myC:name>John Smith</myC:name>
3         <myC:street>43 Walcut St</myC:street>
4         <myC:city>Dublin</myC:city>
```

```
5            <myC:state>Ohio</myC:state>
6            <myC:postal-code>45565</myC:postal-code>
7         </myC:address>
```

This namespace declaration binds the namespace prefix myC to the namespace URI http://myCompany.com/hr/employees. Because all elements are prefixed with myC, they all belong to the namespace URI.

There is another way to declare and use a namespace that does not employ a prefix. It is called a *default namespace*. The following is an example of a default namespace declaration:

```
<address xmlns="http://myCompany.com/hr/employees">
```

In this case, the attribute xmlns provides a default name for the namespace in its attribute value. The use of the default declaration of the namespace is demonstrated in Listing 11-4. Figure 11.4 shows a schematic view of the listing. All subordinate elements are assumed to belong to the default namespace, provided they are not prefixed with a reference to another namespace URI or do not declare a default namespace of their own.

Listing 11-4

```
Listing 11.4: Use of default namespace declaration
1        <address xmlns= "http://myCompany.com/hr/employees"
2            <name>John Smith</name>
3            <street>45 Walcut St</street>
4            <city>Dublin</city>
5            <state>Ohio</state>
6            <postal-code>45565</postal-code>
7        </address>
```

XML Schemas

An XML schema defines the grammar and structure of XML instance documents of a particular type. An XML schema is itself an XML instance. The top element of a schema is named "schema." The namespace for

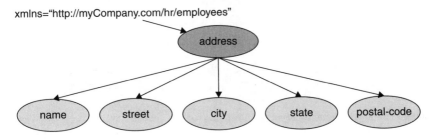

Figure 11.4 Schematic view of Listing 11-4

a schema definition is http://www.w3.org/2001/XMLSchema, which is linked to the prefix xsd. Note that this namespace prefix is conventionally used to denote XML schema definitions. In principle, any other prefix could be used as well. The following shows the top element named schema:

```
<xsd:schema xmlns:xsd="http://www.w3.org/2001/XMLSchema">
        .
        .
        .
        </xsd:schema>
```

The schema element can contain several subordinate element types, such as the following:

- element
- attribute
- simpleType
- complexType
- include
- import

The relationship to the top schema element is shown in Figure 11.5. Here's a brief description of these subelements of the top element schema:

- **element**   This subelement declares an element used in an XML instance. A declaration includes the name and type.
- **attribute**   This subelement declares an attribute used in an XML instance. A declaration includes the name and type.
- **simpleType**   This subelement defines a simple type. A simple type in an XML schema is a built-in type, a list of simple types, a union of simple types, or a restriction of a simple type.

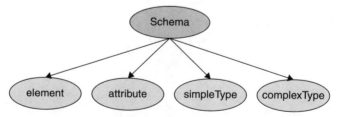

Figure 11.5   Basic elements of an XML schema

- **complexType**   This subelement defines a complex type. The complex type definition typically contains XML elements and carries attributes. The elements appearing in a complex type are declared or referenced within the type definition. Attributes appearing in a complex type similarly are declared within the type definition.

- **include**   This subelement is used to import an element definition defined in another schema. The other schema must belong to the same XML namespace.

- **import**   This subelement is used to import an element definition defined in another schema that belongs to a different namespace. Through the use of include and import, reuse is possible with XML schema definitions.

Out of these subelements, probably the most important type is the complexType. The structure of this subelement is shown in Figure 11.6. The complexType can have any number of attributes but can have only one of the following: sequence, all, choice, or group. Under *sequence,* we can have any number of elements, but these elements must appear in the specific order. In case of *all,* we can have any number of elements. All these elements must appear, but the order is not important. In case of *choice,* only one of the allowed elements can appear in an XML instance. An example of the complex element types is shown in Listing 11-5.

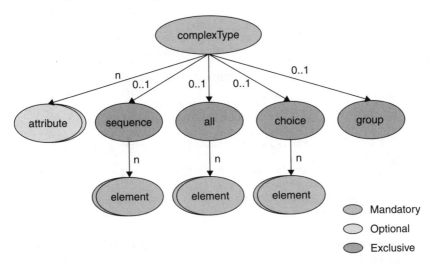

Figure 11.6   Structure of XML complex type

Listing 11-5

```
Listing 11.5: An example of a complexType
1    <xsd:complexType name="nameType">
2        <xsd:sequence>
3            <xsd:element name="title" type="xsd:string">
4            <xsd:element name="firstName" type="xsd:string">
5            <xsd:element name="middleName" type="xsd:string">
6            <xsd:element name="lastName" type="xsd:string">
7        </xsd:sequence>
8    </xsd:complexType>
```

A complete sample schema is shown in Listing 11-6.

Listing 11-6

```
Listing 11.6: An example of a complete schema
1    <?xml version="1.0" encoding="UTF-8">
2    <xsd:schema xmlns:xsd="http://www.w3.org/2001/XMLSchema"
3        targetNamespace="http://simple.example.com/CInfoXmlDoc"
4        xmlns="http://simple.example.com/CInfoXmlDoc"
5            elementFormDefault="qualified"
6        <xsd:complexType>
7            <xsd:sequence>
8                <xsd:element name="Name" type="xsd:string/>
9                <xsd:element name="Address">
10                   <xsd:complexType>
11                       <xsd:sequence>
12                           <xsd:element name="Street"
13                                    type="xsd:string"/>
14                           <xsd:element name="City"
15                               type="xsd:string" />
16                           <xsd:element name="State"
17                               type="xsd:string" />
18                           <xsd:element name="Country"
19                               type="xsd:string" />
20                       </xsd:sequence>
21                   </xsd:complexType>
22               </xsd:element>
23               <xsd:element name="HomePhone" type="xsd:
string" />
24               <xsd:element name="Email" type="xsd:string" />
25           </xsd:sequence>
26       </xsd:complexType>
27   </xsd:schema>
```

A sample XML instance that conforms to this schema is given in Listing 11-7.

Listing 11-7

```
Listing 11.7: An example XML instance document that conforms to
schema in Listing 10.6
1       <?xml version='1.0' encoding='UTF-8'?>
2       <ContactInformation
3           xmlns='http://simple.example.com/CInfoXmlDoc'
4           xmlns:xsi:'http://www.w3.org/2001/XMLSchema-instance'
5           xsi:schemaLocation='http://simple.example.com/
CinfoXmlDoc
6               file:./CInfoXmlDoc.xsd'>
7           <Name>John Smith</Name>
8           <Address>
9               <Street>45 Walcut St</Street>
10              <City>Dublin</City>
11              <State>Ohio</State>
12              <Country>USA</Country>
13          </Address>
14          <HomePhone>9891234567</HomePhone>
15          <Email>xyz@abc.com</Email>
16      </ContactInformation>
```

XML Processing/Parsing Models

A common way for Web Services interaction to the exchange of data between the service provider and service consumer application is through XML instance documents. A number of processing models are available for the applications to use when dealing with the information contained in an XML document instance. In the case of Java/J2EE applications, five choices are available for XML processing models:

- **SAX** The Simple API for XML is an event-driven parsing/programming model.
- **StAX** The Streaming API for XML provides a pull, event-based parsing/programming model.
- **DOM** The Document Object Model provides an in-memory tree-transversal programming model.
- **XML data-binding** Provides an in-memory Java content class-bound programming model.
- **XSLT** Extensible Stylesheet Language Transformation provides a template-based programming model.

The most common processing models have been SAX and DOM, but StAX is quickly catching up. These three methods, along with XSLT, are available through the JAXP APIs (Java APIs for XML Processing). The XML data binding is available through JAXB technology.

The processing of an XML instance document includes two distinct tasks. Processing not only includes parsing a source XML document so that the content is made available to the application for processing, but it also includes writing or producing an XML document from the content generated by an application. Parsing an XML document into an equivalent data structure so that it can be employed by an application is often called *deserialization* or *unmarshalling*. In a similar manner, writing a data structure into an equivalent XML document representation is often called *serialization* or *marshalling*. Some processing models include both types of processing. An example of such processing models is DOM. On the other hand, some processing models support only one category of processing. An example of such a processing model is SAX.

Next, we briefly describe each of these processing models.

SAX Processing Model

SAX is an event-driven model in which you have to implement event handlers to manage events generated by the parser when it encounters the various tokens of the XML language. Because a SAX parser generates a transient flow of events, it is advisable to process the source document in the following manner: First, intercept the relevant type of events generated by the parser. You can use the information passed as parameters of the events to help identify the relevant information that needs to be extracted from the source XML document. Once this is extracted from the XML document, the application logic can be applied to the information obtained.

In a typical scenario, an application may have to maintain some context so that it can logically aggregate information from the flow of events. Such aggregation is typically done before any business logic is applied. There are two ways of applying business logic when using SAX parsing:

- The business logic is invoked as soon as the information is extracted or after minimal aggregation. This approach is referred to as *stream processing*. In this approach, the document can be processed in one step.

- In the second approach, the application invokes the business logic after it completes parsing the document and has completed consolidating the extracted information. This approach involves two steps to complete the processing of an XML document.

In many cases, the consolidated information may in fact be domain-specific objects, which can be passed directly to the business logic. There are pros and cons to both of these approaches, as we discuss next.

The greatest advantage of the first approach (stream processing) is that it lets an application immediately start processing the content of the source document. In some configurations, the application does not even have to wait for the entire document to be retrieved. This includes retrieving the document from an earlier processing stage when implementing pipelines, or even retrieving the document from the network when exchanging documents between applications.

However, some disadvantages and issues are associated with stream processing. For example, a document may appear to be well formed and even valid for most processing. However, there may be unexpected errors by the end of the document that cause the document to be broken or invalid. An application using the stream processing notices these problems only when it comes across erroneous tokens or when it cannot resolve an entity reference. In other cases, the application might realize the document is broken if the input stream from which it is reading the document unexpectedly closes, as with the end-of-file exception. Therefore, an application that wants to implement a stream processing model may have to perform the document parsing and the application's business logic within the context of a transaction.

With the second approach, parsing the document and applying business logic are performed in two steps. Before invoking its business logic, the application first ensures that the document and the information extracted from the document are valid. Once the document data is validated, the application invokes the business logic, which may be executed within a transaction if needed.

One of the disadvantages of the SAX processing model is that it provides no facility to produce XML documents. However, it is still possible to generate an XML document by initiating a properly balanced sequence of events (method calls) on a custom serialization handler. The handler intercepts the events and, using an XSLT identity transformation operation, writes the events in the corresponding XML syntax. The difficulty lies in generating a proper sequence of events. Furthermore, that generated sequence of events is prone to error and should be considered only for performance reasons.

To summarize, consider using SAX processing model when

- the XML document may potentially be very large and memory usage is an issue.

- your applications only consume documents without making any structural modifications and there is no need to generate XML documents.

- the document needs only be processed once.

- you want to implement stream processing, which is well suited for very large documents.

- you have to effectively extract and process only parts of a document.
- the XML document structure and the order of information map well to the domain-specific objects.
- you are familiar with event-based programming.
- there is no need to generate/write XML documents.

One last important thing to note about the SAX processing model is that it is a push model, in which the parser pushes the event onto the application, which may not be prepared to handle the event. In such a case, the information associated with that event will be lost and cannot be recovered. This push model is shown schematically in Figure 11.7.

StAX Processing Model

StAX (Streaming API for XML) is a new API that is fast becoming the most common processing model for Java applications. Like SAX, this processing model is based on streaming. *Streaming* refers to a programming model in which XML infosets are transmitted and parsed serially at application runtime, often in real time, and often from dynamic sources whose contents are not precisely known beforehand. Moreover, stream-based parsers can start generating output immediately, and infoset elements can be discarded and garbage collected immediately after they are used. (Note that *infoset* is short for *information set,* which refers to the collection of information items of a particular XML document.) Although stream processing provides a smaller memory footprint, reduced processor requirements, and higher performance in

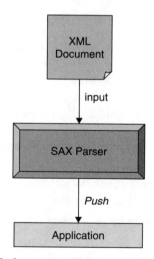

Figure 11.7   SAX push model of streaming XML processing

certain situations, the primary trade-off is that you can only see the infoset state at one location at a time in the document. You are essentially limited to the "cardboard tube" view of a document, the implication being that you need to know what processing you want to do before reading the XML document.

Unlike SAX, StAX is a *pull streaming processing model,* which is a programming model in which a client application calls methods on an XML parsing library when it needs to interact with an XML infoset— that is, the client only gets (pulls) XML data when it explicitly asks for it. This pull streaming model is shown schematically in Figure 11.8.

Pull parsing provides several advantages over push parsing when working with XML streams:

- With pull parsing, the client controls the application thread and can call methods on the parser when needed. By contrast, with push processing, the parser controls the application thread, and the client can only accept invocations from the parser.

- Pull parsing libraries can be much smaller, and the client code to interact with those libraries can be much simpler than with push libraries, even for more complex documents.

- Pull clients can read multiple documents at one time with a single thread.

- A StAX pull parser can filter XML documents such that elements unnecessary to the client can be ignored, and it can support XML views of nonXML data.

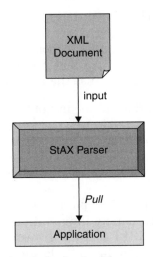

Figure 11.8   StAX pull streaming processing model

In addition to these advantages for parsing by StAX, StAX offers full support for marshalling the infoset into an XML document. Recall that SAX does not offer such a facility, at least one that can be used easily.

Another advantage that StAX has is that StAX-enabled clients are generally easier to code than SAX clients. Although it can be argued that SAX parsers are marginally easier to write, StAX parser code can be smaller and the code necessary for the client to interact with the parser simpler.

In summary, you should use the StAX processing model when any of the following apply:

- You are dealing with very large documents and memory usage is an issue.

- You are familiar with event-based programming.

- The document must be processed only once.

- There is need for marshalling and unmarshalling XML documents.

- You want high performance.

DOM Processing Model

In the DOM processing model, the parser casts the XML document into a tree-like data structure (see Figure 11.9). You write code to traverse the tree. Most commonly, processing the XML input data involves two steps:

1. The DOM parser generates a tree-like data structure that models the XML source document. This structure is called a *DOM tree.*

2. The application searches for the relevant information in the tree and extracts, consolidates, and processes it further. Then the application can create domain-specific objects from the consolidated data. The cycle for searching, extracting, and processing can be repeated as many times as is needed because the DOM tree persists in memory.

There are some limitations to the use of the DOM processing model. The DOM model was designed to be a platform- and language-independent interface. Because of this, the Java binding of the DOM API is not particularly Java friendly. For example, the binding does not use the java.util.Collection API. However, in general, it is slightly easier to use than the SAX model.

A great advantage of the DOM parser is that most implementations of this parser allow both marshalling and unmarshalling of the XML document. In addition, XSLT identity transformation can be used to achieve serialization back to the XML document.

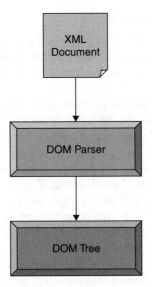

Figure 11.9   DOM processing model

Another convenience for developers is the use of XPath in conjunction with the DOM processing model. XPath can be used to locate and extract information from a source document DOM tree. By allowing you to specify path patterns to locate element content, attribute values, and subtrees, XPath not only greatly simplifies but may even eliminate tree-transversal code. Because XPath expressions are strings, they can be easily parameterized and externalized in a configuration file. Consequently, more generic and reusable programs can be created.

In summary, the DOM processing model should be used when any of the followings conditions exist:

- You want to process or generate XML documents.

- You want to process the XML document more than once.

- The document is not very large and memory usage is not an issue.

- You want to manipulate an XML document and need fine-grained control over the document structure that you want to create or edit.

- You want random access to parts of the document. For example, you want to go back and forth within the document.

- You want to benefit from the flexibility of XPath and apply XPath expressions on the DOM tree.

- You want to implement data binding but you cannot use JAXB technology because the document either has no schema or it conforms to a DTD schema definition rather than to an XSD schema definition.

XML Data-Binding Processing Model

In contrast to the SAX, StAX, and DOM processing models, the XML data-binding processing model allows the processing of the content of an XML document without being concerned with XML document representation (infosets or meta-data).

In this processing model (as implemented by JAXB technology), first a binding compiler is used, which binds a source XSD schema to schema-derived Java content classes, as shown in Figure 11.10. JAXB binds an XML namespace to a Java package. In the next step of processing, the XSD schema instance documents can be unmarshaled into a tree of Java objects, as shown in the following Figure 11.11. The Java objects created are the instances of the Java classes generated by the binding compiler using the XSD schema. Applications can access the content of the source document using Java Bean–style getter and setter accessor methods. Furthermore, you can create or edit in-memory content tree and then marshal the tree into an XML document instance of the source schema. During the process of marshalling or unmarshalling, validation can be performed to ensure that the document about to be processed or created satisfies the constraints expressed in the XSD schema.

The following steps are involved in using JAXB schema–derived classes to process an incoming XML document:

1. Set up the JAXB context (JAXBContext) with the list of schema-derived packages that are used to unmarshal the document.
2. Unmarshal an XML document into a content tree. Also, perform the validation of the document if enabled by the application.
3. Directly apply the business logic to the content tree or extract and consolidate information from the content tree and then apply the business logic on the consolidated information. This consolidated information may very well be domain-specific objects that expose a more adequate, schema-independent interface.

This processing model also supports serialization to XML (see Figure 11.12). In other words, it supports marshalling a content tree to

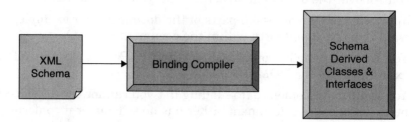

Figure 11.10 Schema-derived classes and interfaces in JAXB technology

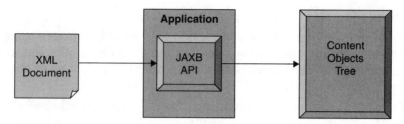

Figure 11.11 Objects generated from an XML instance document

an XML document. The following steps are required for marshalling a content tree:

1. Modify an existing content tree, or generate a new tree, from the application's business logic output.

2. Validate the in-memory content tree against the source schema. This step is optional.

3. Marshal the content tree into an XML document, as shown schematically in Figure 11.12.

It is important to note that when no well-defined schema is available, JAXB technology may be cumbersome to use due to tight coupling between the schema and the schema-derived classes. Also note that the more abstract the schema is, the less effective the binding is.

In summary, use an XML data-binding model such as JAXB when one of the following conditions exists:

- You are either creating or consuming XML documents.

- You want to deal directly with Java objects and are not concerned with XML document representation.

- You do not need to maintain certain aspects of an XML document, such as comments and entity references.

- You want to process the content tree multiple times.

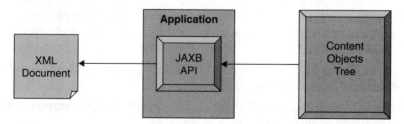

Figure 11.12 Marshalling of a content tree into an XML instance document

- You need random access to parts of the document.

- Memory usage may be less of an issue. It should be noted, though, that a JAXB implementation, such as the standard implementation, creates a Java representation of the content of a document that is much more compact than the equivalent DOM tree.

- You previously were implementing XML data binding manually with DOM, and an XSD schema is available.

XSLT Processing Model

XSLT is a higher level processing model than the SAX, StAX, DOM, and XML data-binding models. XSLT should be considered complementary to these models, and should be used along with these other models. XSLT requires writing of rules and templates that are applied when specified patterns are encountered in the source document. The application of the rules adds new fragments or copies fragments from the source tree to a result tree. The patterns are expressed in the XPath language, which is used to locate and extract information from the source document.

When using XSLT, one typically writes style sheets, which are themselves XML documents. Compared to the other processing models, XSLT processing provides the flexibility that comes with scripting. In an XML-based application, XSLT processing is usually used along with one of the other three processing models. The XSLT API available with JAXP provides an abstract for the source and result of a transformation, allowing the developer not only the ability to chain transformations but also to interface with other processing models, such as SAX and DOM. Figure 11.13 summarizes the steps necessary to use XSLT in conjunction with DOM to create a new XML document from an existing one using XSLT transformations.

In summary, XSLT should be used under the following conditions:

- You want to change the structure or insert, remove, or filter the content of an XML document.

- You need to perform complex transformations. Because XSLT is a functional declarative model, it is easier to design complex transformations by coding individual rules or templates than by hard-coding procedures.

- You want the ability to be flexible and allow future changes in the schemas of documents you are processing.

- You need to minimize performance overhead for large documents that contain a significant amount of data.

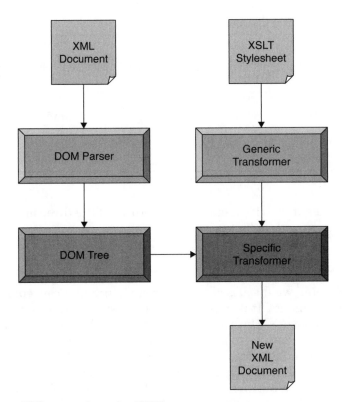

Figure 11.13   XML processing using XSLT

■ You potentially have more than one transformation for the same document. Although one transformation can be hand-coded using another
API, multiple transformations—because of the scripting nature of the
style sheets—are better performed using XSLT transformations.

Summary Recommendations

You should use the processing model that best suits your requirements.
If you are required to deal with the content and structure of a document,
consider using DOM, StAX, or SAX—they provide more information
about the document itself than the data-binding model does. However,
if you are more concerned with the actual domain-oriented objects, consider using JAXB. In addition, use JAXB if the document content has
representation in Java that is directly usable by the application implementing the service provider or service consumer. DOM, when used with
XPath, can be very powerful if the focus is on the content and structure
of the data. DOM can be more flexible if the schema for the document
does not exist or is not well defined.

TABLE 11.1   Summary of Recommendations

	StAX	SAX	DOM
API type	Pull streaming	Push streaming	In-memory tree
Ease of use	High	Medium	High
Memory usage	Good	Good	Varies
XPath capability	No	No	Yes
Forward only	Yes	Yes	No
Write XML	Yes	No	Yes
Create, update, delete	No	No	Yes

Table 11.1 summarizes some of the features of the three most popular XML processing models.

Conclusion

In this chapter, we discussed the basic structure and concepts of XML instance documents. It is important to understand these structure and concepts because XML forms the basis of WSDL, SOAP, and UDDI. Some of the concepts we touched upon are XSD schemas (which describe the structure and grammar of a particular type of XML instance document) and namespaces. Namespaces are used to avoid the collision of names in different business domains and to extend a tag's name vocabulary across different domains. Within the context of namespaces, we discussed the use of include and import elements, which allow us to include the definition of a set of tags defined in another schema.

A very important practical side of XML use in Web Services is the exchange of data between service provider and service consumer through the use of XML instance documents. In this context, both the service provider application and the service consumer application must be able to parse, process, edit, and create XML instance documents. A large part of this chapter was devoted to describing the various processing/parsing models available to the developer of Web Services. The various parsing/processing models we discussed include SAX, StAX, DOM, XML data-binding model (JAXB), and XSLT transformations. We also discussed the conditions under which each of these models should be employed.

In the next chapter you will begin to see direct application of XML. You learn about SOAP, which is one of the four standards that constitute Web Services. SOAP is based on XML and it defines a common message format for exchanging messages between the service provider and service consumer.

Simple Object Access Protocol (SOAP) is an XML-based messaging specification. It describes a message format and a set of serialization rules for data types, including structured types and arrays. This XML-based information can be used for exchanging structured and typed information between peers in a decentralized, distributed environment. In addition, SOAP describes the ways in which SOAP messages may be transported to realize various usage scenarios. In particular, it describes how to use Hypertext Transfer Protocol (HTTP) as a transport for such messages. SOAP messages are essentially service requests sent to some end point on a network. The end point may be implemented in a number of different ways, including an RPC server, a Java servlet, a Component Object Model (COM) object, and a Perl script, which may be running on any platform.

A SOAP message is fundamentally a one-way transmission between SOAP nodes, from a SOAP sender to a SOAP receiver. In other words, a SOAP message may pass through a number of intermediaries as it travels from the initial sender to the ultimate recipient.

SOAP Messages

The basic structure of a SOAP message is depicted in Figure 12.1. The top element of a SOAP message is the Envelope element, with an optional Header element and a mandatory Body element as the children elements. If a Header element exists, it must be the first child of the Envelope element. The Envelope element identifies the XML document as being a SOAP message and therefore must be the root element of the message. The Body element contains the actual data (payload) to be transmitted. The Header element is an extension hook that can be used to extend SOAP in arbitrary ways. Envelope and its two children

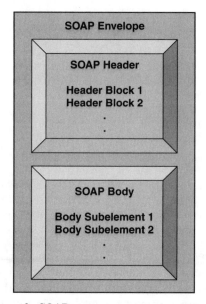

Figure 12.1   The structure of a SOAP message

(Header and Body) are defined in the namespace http://schemas
.xmlsoap.org/soap/envelop/.

A preliminary example of a SOAP message is shown in Listing 12-1.

Listing 12-1

```
Listing 12.1 : An example of a SOAP message
1     <?xml version='1.0' ?>
2     <env:Envelope xmlns:env="http://www.w3.org/2003/05/soap-envelope">
3      <env:Header>
4         <m:reservation xmlns:m="http://mycompany.example.org/reservation"
5             env:role="http://www.w3.org/2003/05/soap-envelope/role/next"
6             env:mustUnderstand="true">
7             <m:date>2008-11-29</m:date>
8         </m:reservation>
9       <n:passenger xmlns:n="http://mycompany.example.com/employees"
10             env:role="http://www.w3.org/2003/05/soap-envelope/role/next"
11             env:mustUnderstand="true">
12             <n:name>John Smith</n:name>
13         </n:passenger>
14     </env:Header>
15     <env:Body>
16         <p:itinerary
17             xmlns:p="http://mycompany.example.org/reservation/travel">
```

```
18          <p:departure>
19              <p:departing>Boston</p:departing>
20              <p:arriving>Dallas</p:arriving>
21              <p:departureDate>2001-12-14</p:departureDate>
22              <p:departureTime>Early Morning</p:departureTime>
23              <p:seatPreference>Window</p:seatPreference>
24          </p:departure>
25          <p:return>
26              <p:departing>Dallas</p:departing>
27              <p:arriving>Boston</p:arriving>
28              <p:departureDate>2001-12-20</p:departureDate>
29              <p:departureTime>mid-morning</p:departureTime>
30              <p:seatPreference/>
31          </p:return>
32      </p:itinerary>
33    </env:Body>
34  </env:Envelope>
```

This listing provides a SOAP message requesting a return ticket reservation from an airline for a passenger traveling from Boston to Dallas. The SOAP message starts (line 1) with a declaration that it is an XML document. This SOAP message contains both a Header element and a Body element. As mentioned before, Header is optional but Body is mandatory. In this example, Header (lines 3–14) has two blocks, each of which uses its own namespace, corresponding to the reservation and passenger tags, respectively. These two blocks carry two pieces of information. One is the date of the transaction, and the other is the name of the passenger. How these pieces of information are used will become clear later in this section. The SOAP Body element (lines 15–33) in this example has only one subelement. This subelement has the tag itinerary. The structure in this subelement carries the request information both for the out-bound flight and the in-bound flight. The Header element and the Body element are contained within the top element (Envelope), which is defined in the namespace http://www.w3.org/2003/05/soap-envelope.

We discuss the four important elements encountered in a SOAP message in the next section. Then we discuss some of the attributes and the related processing model. This is followed by a discussion of the various SOAP message-exchange types and then a discussion of the SOAP HTTP bindings.

SOAP Elements

SOAP defines four important elements in the namespace http://schemas.xmlsoap.org/soap/envelope/. The three elements—Envelope, Header, and Body–have been mentioned before. The fourth element is Fault.

This section describes these elements, starting with the top element, Envelope.

Envelope

Envelope is the root element of all SOAP messages and identifies the XML document as a SOAP message. It is defined in the following manner:

```
<env:Envelope  xmlns:env='http://schemas.xmlsoap.org/soap/
envelope/'>
          <!—the header and body elements go here   -->
</env:Envelope>
```

The Envelope element has two child elements: An optional Header element and a mandatory Body element. Both of the child elements are defined in the namespace http://schemas.xmlsoap.org/soap/envelope/. The Header element, if present, must precede the Body element.

Header

The Header element, if present, must be the first child of the root element Envelope. It is defined in the following manner:

```
<env:header xmlns:env='http://schemas.xmlsoap.org/soap/
envelope/'>
            <!—extensions go here -->
</env:header>
```

A SOAP header is an extension mechanism that provides a way to pass information in SOAP messages that is not part of the application payload. Such "control" information includes, for example, passing directives or contextual information related to the processing of the message. This allows a SOAP message to be extended in an application-specific manner. The immediate child elements of the Header element are called *header blocks,* and they represent a logical grouping of data that can be targeted individually at SOAP nodes encountered along the message's path from the sender to the ultimate receiver.

It is important to note that the SOAP specification defines no extensions of its own, but user-defined extension services such as transaction support, authentication, digital signatures, locale information, and so on, could be implemented by placing this information inside the Header element. Header blocks can have the attributes mustUnderstand and actor. These attributes are described later in this chapter.

A Header element can have any number of child elements that are not in the namespace 'http://schemas.xmlsoap.org/soap/envelope/'. In Listing 12-1, there are two child elements: passenger and reservation.

Body

The Body element is the mandatory child of the SOAP Envelope element. If the Header element is present, the Body element must follow it; otherwise, it is the first child of the Envelope element. It is defined in the following manner:

```
<env:Body xmlns:env='http://schemas.xmlsoap.org/soap/envelope/'>
         <!-- message payload goes here -->
</env:Body>
```

This element carries the payload of the message. The payload is for the exchange of information between the initial SOAP sender and the SOAP node that assumes the role of the ultimate SOAP receiver in the message path. The message payload is typically a request to perform some form of service and, optionally, to return some result. In the case of a response message, the payload is typically the result of some previous request or a fault (that is, error).

The Body element can have any number of child elements, but each must be qualified with a namespace, and the namespace must not be 'http://schemas.xmlsoap.org/soap/envelope/'. However, if a fault does occur, it could be a Fault element in the namespace 'http://schemas .xmlsoap.org/soap/envelope/'. This Fault element is described next.

Fault

The Fault element is the direct child of the Body element, and it indicates an error condition has occurred while processing the message. This typically occurs in a response message. The Fault element is defined in the following manner:

```
<env:Fault xmlns:env='http://schemas.xmlsoap.org/soap/envelope/' >
         < !-- fault details go here  -->
</env :Fault>
```

The Fault element has five child elements: Code, Reason, Detail (optional), Node (optional), and Role (optional). All these elements belong to the namespace 'http://schemas.xmlsoap.org/soap/envelope/'. The element Detail carries application-specific information. The Node element specifies, through a URI, the SOAP node that generated this fault. The Role element identifies the role played by the node that created the fault. The Reason element is used to convey the reason for the fault in a human-readable form, typically as a string. The Code element has two subelements: Value (mandatory) and Subcode (optional). The use of these elements and subelements is illustrated in Listing 12-2, which provides an example of a SOAP fault message.

Listing 12-2

```
1    Listing 12.2: SOAP Fault example
2    <?xml version='1.0' ?>
3     <env:Envelope xmlns:env="http://www.w3.org/2003/05/soap-envelope"
4           xmlns:rpc='http://www.w3.org/2003/05/soap-rpc'>
5      <env:Body>
6        <env:Fault>
7          <env:Code>
8            <env:Value>env:Sender</env:Value>
9            <env:Subcode>
10               <env:Value>rpc:BadArguments</env:Value>
11           </env:Subcode>
12         </env:Code>
13          <env:Reason>
14            <env:Text operation not allowed</env:Text>
15          </env:Reason>
16          <env:Detail>
17            <myC:myFaultDetails
18                xmlns:myC="http://mycompany.example.org/faults">
19                <myC:message>Division by zero not allowed</myC:
message>
20            </myC:myFaultDetails>
21          </env:Detail>
22        </env:Fault>
23      </env:Body>
24    </env:Envelope>
```

In the example, the top-level Value uses a standardized XML qualified name (of type xs:QName) to identify that this is an env:Sender fault, which indicates that it is related to some syntactical error or inappropriate information in the message. The env:Subcode element is optional. If it is present, as it is in this example, it qualifies the parent value further. In this example, env:Subcode denotes that an RPC-specific fault, rpc:BadArguments, is the cause of the failure to process the request.

A simplified structure of a fault message is shown schematically in Figure 12.2.

SOAP Attributes and Processing Model

SOAP defines three attributes that are closely related to how a SOAP node processes information in a SOAP message. These attributes are role, mustUnderstand, and relay. The meaning and use of these three attributes are covered in this section.

The role Attribute

SOAP defines the (optional) env:role attribute (syntactically, xs:anyURI) that may be present in a header block. It identifies the role played by the intended target of that header block. A SOAP node is required to

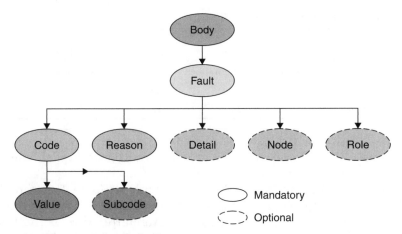

Figure 12.2   The structure of a fault message

process a header block if it assumes the role identified by the value of the URI. How a SOAP node assumes a particular role is not part of the SOAP specifications. SOAP defines three standard values of this attribute:

- none
- next
- ultimateReceiver

We explain these roles with the help of an example, shown in Listing 12-3. In this example, in Header Block1 the role attribute is set to the URI myCompany.com/Log. Any node that assumes this application-defined role must log the message.

Every SOAP node receiving a message with a header block that has an env:role attribute of "next" must be capable of processing the contents of the element, because this is a standardized role that every SOAP node must be willing to assume. A header block thus attributed is one that is expected to be examined and (possibly) processed by the next SOAP node along the path of a message, assuming that such a header has not been removed as a result of processing at some node earlier in the message path. Note that Header Block1, where the role attribute is set to the specific URI of myCompany/Log, must also be willing to play the role of "next" node. This is also true when the role attribute is set to the value ultimateReceiver, because the last node is obviously also the next node in the chain of nodes.

If the attribute role is missing, as is the case of Block3 in the example, it is targeted at the node that assumes the ultimate receiver node. Therefore,

TABLE 12.1   Applicable Standardized Roles

Role Node	Absent	None	Next	Ultimate Receiver
Initial sender	Not applicable	Not applicable	Not applicable	Not applicable
Intermediary	Yes	No	Yes	No
Ultimate receiver	Yes	No	Yes	Yes

the value ultimateReceiver of the attribute can be set explicitly or set implicitly by not having the attribute.

Note that the Body element does not have a role attribute. Therefore, the body is always targeted to be processed by the ultimate receiver node.

Table 12.1 summarizes the applicable standardized roles that may be assumed at various SOAP nodes. ("Yes" and "No" mean that the corresponding node does or does not, respectively, play the named role.)

Listing 12-3

```
Listing 12.3
1    <?xml version="1.0" ?>
2    <env:Envelope xmlns:env="http://www.w3.org/2003/05/soap-envelope">
3       <env:Header>
4          <m:Block1 xmlns:m=http://myCompany.com
5             env:role="http://myCompany.com/Log">
6             ...
7             ...
8          </m:Block1>
9          <n:Block2 xmlns:n="http://myCompany.com"
10            env:role="http://www.w3.org/2003/05/soap-
11               envelope/role/next">
12            ...
13            ...
14         </n:Block2>
15         <o:Block3 xmlns:o="http://myCompany.com">
16            ...
17            ...
18         </o:Block3>
19      </env:Header>
20      <env:Body >
21         ...
22         ...
23      </env:Body>
24   </env:Envelope>
```

The mustUnderstand Attribute

The mustUnderstand attribute is complementary to the role attribute. The purpose of this attribute is to ensure that SOAP nodes do not ignore header blocks that are important to the overall purpose of the application. When this attribute is set to a value of "true", the targeted SOAP node *must* process the block according to the specification of that block. Such a block is colloquially referred to as a *mandatory header block*. In fact, the processing of the SOAP message must not even start until the node has identified all the mandatory header blocks targeted at itself and has "understood" them. Understanding a header means that the node must be prepared to do whatever is described in the specification of that block.

A mustUnderstand value of "true" means that the SOAP node must process the header with the semantics described in that header's specification, or else generate a SOAP fault. Processing the header appropriately may include removing the header from any generated SOAP message, reinserting the header with the same or an altered value, or inserting a new header. The inability to process a mandatory header requires that all further processing of the SOAP message cease and that a SOAP fault be generated. The message is not forwarded any further.

Table 12.2 summarizes how the processing actions for a header block are qualified by the mustUnderstand attribute with respect to a node that has been appropriately targeted through the role attribute.

The relay Attribute

SOAP defines another attribute, called relay. It is of type Boolean and can assume a value of "true" or "false". This attribute indicates whether the header block targeted at a SOAP node must be relayed if it is not processed. If the message is processed by the targeted SOAP node, the header block must be removed from the outbound message. The default behavior for an *un*processed header block targeted at a role played by a SOAP intermediary is that it must be removed before the message is relayed.

If the attribute rely is set to "true" for the header block targeted at the node with the role "next", it ensures that each intermediary has a chance to examine the header, because one of the anticipated uses of the "next" role is with header blocks that carry information expected to persist along a SOAP message path. Note that setting the relay attribute

TABLE 12.2   Processing Actions for Various Values of the mustUnderstand Attribute

mustUnderstand Node	True	False	Absent
Intermediary	Must process	May process	May process
Ultimate receiver	Must process	May process	May process

is meaningless for header blocks that are targeted at ultimateReceiver and none.

Listing 12-4 shows the use of the relay attribute in one of the header blocks.

Listing 12-4

```
Listing 12.4: An example of the use of attribute relay
1   <?xml version="1.0" ?>
2   <env:Envelope xmlns:env="http://www.w3.org/2003/05/soap-envelope">
3     <env:Header>
4       <m:Blockm xmlns:p=http://myCompany.com
5         env:role=http://myCompany.com/Log
6           env:mustUnderstand="true">
7       ...
8       ...
9       </m:Blockm>
10      <n:Blockn xmlns:q="http://myComapny.com"
11        env:role="http://www.w3.org/2003/05/soap-envelope/role/next"
12        env:relay="true">
13      ...
14      ...
15      </n:Blockn>
16      <r:Blockr xmlns:r="http://myCompany.com">
17      ...
18      ...
19      </r:Blockr>
20    </env:Header>
21    <env:Body >
22      ...
23      ...
24    </env:Body>
25  </env:Envelope>
```

SOAP Message Exchange Types

A SOAP message is fundamentally a one-way transmission between SOAP nodes, from a SOAP sender to a SOAP receiver. However, SOAP messages can be combined to obtain more complex interaction patterns, such as RPC-type request/response and "back-and-forth" conversational messages. We discuss the RPC-type request/response interaction next.

Remote Procedure Call (RPC)

One of goals of the SOAP specification is to define a uniform representation for RPC invocations and responses carried in SOAP messages. This is done using the flexibility and extensibility of XML.

To make an RPC request for invocation, the following items are needed:

- The address of the targeted node that will ultimately process the request

- The name of the method/procedure you want to invoke

- The required parameters' names and values to invoke the method/procedure, including any output parameter and return value

- Optionally, data that may be carried as a part of SOAP header blocks

It is important to note that the preceding information differs in subtle ways from the information needed to invoke other nonSOAP types of RPC. For example, the first item requires the address information of the SOAP node that "contains" or "supports" the target of the RPC. It is obviously the node that adopts the role of ultimate Receiver. The ultimate recipient can identify the target of the named procedure or method by looking for its URI. The way in which the target URI is made available depends on the underlying protocol binding. For example, the URI identification information can be carried in a SOAP header block. The other possibility is to carry the URI information outside the SOAP message. Such is the case for HTTP SOAP binding.

Listing 12-5 shows an example of an RPC request for credit card payment. The travel reservation application provides credit card information, and the successful completion of the different activities results in the card being charged and a reservation code returned. This reserve-and-charge interaction between the travel reservation application and the travel service application is modeled as a SOAP RPC. As seen in this example, the RPC information itself is carried in the "body" of the SOAP message. It is contained in a structure, which houses the reservation information and credit card information. The credit card information itself is contained in a substructure. This latter struct has three elements: name, card number and expiration date. The method invoked has the name chargeReservation.

Listing 12-5

```
Listing 12.5: An example of RPC SOAP request
1    <?xml version='1.0' ?>
2    <env:Envelope xmlns:env="http://www.w3.org/2003/05/soap-envelope" >
3      <env:Header>
4        <t:transaction
5            xmlns:t=http://thirdparty.example.com/transaction
```

```
6                env:encodingStyle=http://example.com/encoding
7                env:mustUnderstand="true" >45</t:transaction>
8      </env:Header>
10     <env:Body>
11       <c:chargeReservation
12         env:encodingStyle="http://www.w3.org/2003/05/soap-encoding"
13         xmlns:c="http://myCompany.example.com/">
14         <r:reservation
15           xmlns:r="http://myCompany.example.com/reservation">
16           <r:code>AB324QZ</r:code>
17         </r:reservation>
18         <o:creditCard
19             xmlns:o="http://mycompany.example.com/financial">
20             <n:name xmlns:n="http://mycompany.example.com/employees">
21               John Smith
22             </n:name>
23             <o:number>9876543212345678</o:number>
24             <o:expiration>2010-07</o:expiration>
25         </o:creditCard>
26       </c:chargeReservation>
27     </env:Body>
28    </env:Envelope>
```

Next we turn our attention to a RPC response. The response is also returned as a SOAP message. Let's assume that the response has two output parameters. The first output parameter provides a reference to the reservation code, and the second output parameter provides a URL where the details of the reservation can be viewed. As in the case of RPC, the response is returned in the body of the SOAP message, within a struct. The struct has the name of the RPC request (chargeReservation) with the word "Response" appended to it. The two output parameters are included as two elements in this struct. Listing 12-6 shows the response SOAP message.

Listing 12-6

```
Listing 12.6: A sample SOAP message for a RPC response
1    <?xml version='1.0' ?>
2    <env:Envelope xmlns:env="http://www.w3.org/2003/05/soap-envelope" >
3      <env:Header>
4        <t:transaction
5          xmlns:t="http://thirdparty.example.com/transaction"
6          env:encodingStyle="http://example.com/encoding"
7          env:mustUnderstand="true">45</t:transaction>
8      </env:Header>
9      <env:Body>
10       <r:chargeReservationResponse
11         env:encodingStyle="http://www.w3.org/2003/05/soap-encoding"
12         xmlns:r="http://myCompany.example.org/">
```

```
13          <r:reservationCode> AB324QZ</m:reservationCode>
14          <r:viewReservationAt>
15              http://myCompany.example.com/reservations?code= AB324QZ
16          </r:viewReservationAt>
17        </r:chargeReservationResponse>
18      </env:Body>
19        </env:Envelope>
```

SOAP HTTP Binding

SOAP messages may be exchanged using a variety of "underlying" protocols. An example of such an underlying protocol is HTTP. The specification for how SOAP messages may be passed from one SOAP node to another using an underlying protocol is called a *SOAP binding*.

SOAP defines a standard binding to only one protocol, namely HTTP. HTTP defines a well-known message-exchange pattern and a well-known connection model. In HTTP, the client specifies a server by a URL and connects to it by using the TCP/IP network. Then it issues an HTTP request message and receives an HTTP response message over the same TCP connection. Therefore, in the HTTP protocol, there is an implicit correlation between the request and the response, and an application using HTTP binding can deduce the correlation between a SOAP message sent in the body of an HTTP request message and a SOAP message returned in the HTTP response. In a similar manner, HTTP identifies the request server end point via a URI, the Request-URI, which can also serve as the identification of a SOAP node at the request server.

The HTTP binding to SOAP restricts the use of HTTP to two methods: POST and GET. The binding allows two ways to exchange SOAP messages. In the first method, the HTTP POST method is used to convey SOAP messages in the bodies of HTTP request and response messages. In the second method, the HTTP GET method in an HTTP request is used to return a SOAP message in the body of an HTTP response. The first usage pattern is the HTTP-specific instantiation of a binding feature called the *SOAP request/response message-exchange pattern,* whereas the second uses a feature called the *SOAP response message-exchange pattern.* SOAP offers guidance on circumstances when applications may use one of the two specified message-exchange patterns. The HTTP GET response exchange pattern is used when you are reasonably sure this exchange is for retrieval of information only and does not require a change in the state of the server from which the information is being requested. Such interactions are considered safe and idempotent in the HTTP specification. We'll now discuss examples of both types of HTTP bindings, starting with HTTP GET.

HTTP GET Usage

SOAP response message exchange patterns are limited to the HTTP GET method. In this pattern, the response to an HTTP GET request is in the form of a SOAP message sent in an HTTP response. Listing 12-7 shows the HTTP GET request. This is used to request travel information from a travel website with the following URI:

```
http://myCompany.example.com/reservations?code= AB324QZ
```

At this site the travel itinerary can be viewed.

Listing 12-7

```
Listing 12.7: Example of HTTP GET request
GET /myCompany.example.com/reservations?code= AB324QZ   HTTP/1.1
Host: myCompany.example.com
Accept: text/html;q=0.5, application/soap+xml
```

The preferred representation of the information from the source is indicated in the HTTP header. In this example, the preferred representation is

```
application/soap+xml
```

which is meant for consummation by an application rather than by a browser.

The response to the preceding GET request is shown in Listing 12-8. In this case, the response is returned as a SOAP message in the body of an HTTP response.

Listing 12-8

```
Listing 12.8: Response to HTTP GET request of listing 12-7
1    HTTP/1.1 200 OK
2    Content-Type: application/soap+xml; charset="utf-8"
3    Content-Length: 367
4
5    <?xml version='1.0' ?>
6    <env:Envelope xmlns:env="http://www.w3.org/2003/05/soap-envelope">
7      <env:Header>
8        <m:reservation
9           xmlns:m="http://myCompany.example.com/reservation"
10          env:role="http://www.w3.org/2003/05/soap-
11              envelope/role/next"
12          env:mustUnderstand="true">
13          <m:date>2008-07-13</m:date>
14       </m:reservation>
15      </env:Header>
16      <env:Body>
```

```
17      <rdf:RDF xmlns:rdf="http://www.w3.org/1999/02/22-rdf-syntax-
18                        ns#"
19            xmlns:x="http://myCompany.example.com/vocab#"
20          env:encodingStyle="http://www.w3.org/1999/02/22-rdf-syntax-
21                        ns#">
22        <x:ReservationRequest
23          rdf:about="http://myCompany.example.com/reservations?code=
24                        AB324QZ ">
25          <x:passenger>John Smith</x:passenger>
26          <x:outbound>
27            <x:TravelRequest>
28              <x:to>Chicago</x:to>
29              <x:from>Dallas</x:from>
30              <x:date>2008-07-12</x:date>
31            </x:TravelRequest>
32          </x:outbound>
33          <x:return>
34            <x:TravelRequest>
35              <x:to>Dallas</x:to>
36              <x:from>Chicago</x:from>
37              <x:date>2008-07-13</x:date>
38            </x:TravelRequest>
39          </x:return>
40        </x:ReservationRequest>
41      </rdf:RDF>
42    </env:Body>
43  </env:Envelope>
```

HTTP POST Usage

The SOAP request/response message-exchange pattern is restricted to the HTTP POST method if HTTP binding is used. This pattern is available to all applications. It can be used for general exchange of XML data or RPCs.

An example of an RPC exchange with the request is shown in Listing 12-9 and the response is shown in Listing 12-10.

In Listing 12-9, the request is directed to the server myCompany .example.com, and the SOAP request is sent in the body of an HTTP POST request. In this case, the request is directed at the method chargeReservation. The HTTP POST response is shown in Listing 12-10. For brevity, the details have been omitted. The appearance of the code "200" in the first line of the HTTP response header indicates that the POST request is successful.

Listing 12-9

```
Listing 12.9: An example of RPC request using HTTP POST method
1    POST /Reservations HTTP/1.1
2    Host: myCompany.example.com
3    Content-Type: application/soap+xml; charset="utf-8"
```

```
4    Content-Length: 367
5
6    <?xml version='1.0' ?>
7    <env:Envelope xmlns:env="http://www.w3.org/2003/05/soap-envelope" >
8        <env:Header>
9            <t:transaction
10                xmlns:t="http://thirdparty.example.com/transaction"
11                env:encodingStyle="http://example.com/encoding"
12                env:mustUnderstand="true" >45</t:transaction>
13        </env:Header>
14        <env:Body>
15            <m:chargeReservation
16                env:encodingStyle=http://www.w3.org/2003/05/soap-
encoding
17                xmlns:m="http://myCompany.example.com/">
18                <m:reservation xmlns:m="http://myCompany.example.com/
reservation">
19                    <m:code> AB324QZ </m:code>
20                </m:reservation>
21                <c:creditCard xmlns:c="http://myCompany.example.com/
financial">
22                    <n:name xmlns:n="http://myCompany.example.com/
employees">
23                        John Smith
24                    </n:name>
25                    <c:number>6789234512345678</c:number>
26                    <c:expiration>2010-10</c:expiration>
27                </c:creditCard>
28            </m:chargeReservation>
29        </env:Body>
30    </env:Envelope>
```

Listing 12-10

```
Listing 12.10: The HTTP POST response to the request shown in Listing 12.9
1    HTTP/1.1 200 OK
2    Content-Type: application/soap+xml; charset="utf-8"
3    Content-Length: 167
4
5    <?xml version='1.0' ?>
6    <env:Envelope xmlns:env="http://www.w3.org/2003/05/soap-envelope" >
7        <env:Header>
8            ...
9            ...
10        </env:Header>
11        <env:Body>
12            ...
13            ...
14        </env:Body>
15    </env:Envelope>
```

Conclusion

In summary, SOAP is an XML-based message format that can be used to exchange typed and structured information between peers (applications) in a distributed environment. SOAP also describes a set of rules for serialization and deserialization. Although a SOAP message can be transported by any transport protocol, the SOAP specification describes a specific binding to HTTP. Furthermore, SOAP supports a number of message-exchange patterns, including remote procedure calls.

In the next chapter, we describe the third of the four standards that make up Web Services. This third standard is called Web Services Description Language (WSDL) and is used to describe the Web Services in a language and platform independent manner. Once again, this standard is based on XML.

13

WSDL

In order for a service consumer (application) to use the service provided by a service provider application, a formal description of the service is required that contains the description of the interface exposed by the service and information on where that service can be found on the network. Such a formal specification is provided by the Web Services Description Language (WSDL). A WSDL document is an XML-based document that describes a formal contract between the service provider and the service consumer. Detailed information on the WSDL 1.1 standard can be found at http://www.w3.org/TR/wsdl. A WSDL document is an XML instance. The schema from which such a document instance is derived is located in the target namespace http://schemas.xmlsoap.org/wsdl/. In addition to the WSDL specification, WS-I Basic Profile provides guidance on how to write the WSDL documents so that service interoperability across different platforms can be made more certain. In general, WS-I Basic Profile puts further restrictions on the WSDL standard.

A WSDL document describes two aspects of a service: the abstract interface exposed by the service and the description of the concrete implementation. The abstract interface describes the general interface structure, which includes the operations (that is, methods) in the service, the operation parameters, and abstract data types. This description of the interface does not depend in any way on the concrete implementation, such as the concrete network address, the concrete data structures, and the communication protocol. An abstract interface can have many corresponding implementations, giving the service consumer a choice of implementation and allowing it to pick the implementation that best suits its technical capabilities. The concrete implementation description binds the abstract interface description to a concrete network address, communication protocol, and concrete data structures. The concrete implementation description is used to bind to the service and invoke its various operations (methods).

In the next section, we start first with an overview of a WSDL document using an example of a weather service. For simplicity, we assume that this service has only one operation: getWeather. This operation takes information needed to identify the city of the world and return weather information for the current day. Next, we describe the general structure of a WSDL document. Following this we discuss in detail the abstract interface part of a WSDL document as well as the implementation part of the WSDL document. We then discuss the logical relationship between the different elements of a WSDL document as well as describe the SOAP extensibility elements related to SOAP binding.

Overview

In this section, we provide an overview of WSDL by considering a simple example of a weather service. The service has only one operation: getWeather. This operation takes input information related to identifying a city in the world and returns the weather of that city for the current day. The information required for city identification includes the city name, the state/province, and the country. The returned weather information includes temperature, weather conditions (sunny, cloudy, and so on), wind direction, and wind speed.

We start the discussion by first focusing on the interface description in the WSDL document. The part of the WSDL document that describes the interface portion for the weather service is shown in Listing 13-1.

Listing 13-1

```
Listing 13.1: Example of interface description
1    <definitions name="globalWeatherService"
2       targetNamespace=http://globService.com/ns/globalWeather/wsdl
3       xmlns:tns=http://globalService.com/globalWeather/wsdl
4       xmlns:SOAP-EXT=http://schemas.xmlsoap.org/wsdl/soap/
5       xmlns=http://schemas.xmlsoap.org/wsdl/>
6       <types>
7          <schema
8          targetNamespace=http://globalService.com/ns/globalWeather/wsdl
9             xmlns=http://www.w3.org/2001/XMLSchema>
10            <complexType name="inputType">
11               <sequence>
12                  <element name="City" type="xsd:string"/>
13                  <element name="State"  type="xsd:string"/>
14                  <element name="Country" type="xsd:string"/>
15               </sequence>
16            </complexType>
17            <complexType name="outputType">
18               <sequence>
19                  <element name="temperature" type="xsd:int">
```

```
20                    <element name="condition" type="xsd:string">
21                    <element name="windSpeed"  type="xsd:decimal">
22                    <element name="windDirection" type="xsd:string">
23              </sequence>
24          </complexType>
25        </schema>
26     </types>
27     <message name="inputParameters">
28          <part name ="input" type="inputType"/>
29     </message>
30     <message name="outputParameters">
31          <part name="output" type="outputType"/>
32     </message>
33     <portType name="weatherServicePortType">
34          <operation name="getWeather">
35                <input message="tns:inputParameters"/>
36                <output message="tns:outputParameters"/>
37          </operation>
38     </portType>
```

The main element of this interface is the portType (lines 33–35). This element contains all the operations a service of this kind will support. In this example, the port is named weatherServicePortType, and it supports only one operation: getWeather. As shown in the listing, the operations themselves are represented as XML elements. In our example, this operation is a request/response operation because it contains an input message and an output message. In general, you can have several types of operations, including a one-way operation.

An operation contains all the messages exchanged between the service provider and service consumer. In addition, you can define additional fault elements that can appear as direct child elements of the element operation.

We have defined two messages (lines 27–29 and lines 30–32). The message inputParameters defined in lines 27–29 is linked by name to the input element of the operation getWeather. Hence, this message represents the data that is sent from the service consumer to the service provider when the operation getWeather is invoked. Similarly, the message outputParameters defined in lines 30–32 represents the data that is sent from the service provider to the service consumer as a response message.

In our example, each of the two messages consists of one part. However, in general, a message can have multiple parts, thus giving a structure to the message. A part is linked to types. For example, in Listing 13-1, the message inputParameters consists of only one part that refers to one complex type named inputType. This complex type has three elements: City, State and Country. Each of these child elements are of the string type.

TABLE 13.1   Summary of Abstract Interface Definition Elements

Element	Short Description
types	A container of all abstract data types definitions. WSDL 1.1 prefers the use of XML schema types definitions.
part	Each part is associated with a data type.
message	A message represents a logical unit of data that consists of one or more part elements.
operation	An operation abstractly defines a service method. It may consist of an input message, an output message, and, optionally, several fault messages.
portType	A collection of operations is called a portType and must be named.

The types element is the container of all the abstract data types. Parts may pick up individual type definitions out of this container. It is important to note that the parts do not have to use the abstract data types defined in the types container element. Instead, types definitions can be directly attached to the parts definition.

Note that the abstract data type inputType and outputType definitions employ XML-type schema definitions. However, the WSDL specification allows other types systems to be used.

Table 13.1 summarizes what we have covered about the abstract interface definition part of WSDL.

Next, we discuss the WSDL service implementation description, which is required in order for the service consumer to find out about the concrete network address and communication protocol for the service.

For the weather service, Listing 13-2 shows the implementation description part of the WSDL document.

Listing 13-2

```
Listing 13.2: Example of a service implementation description
1     <binding name="weatherServiceSoapBinding"
2          type="tns:WeatherServicePortType">
3          <SOAP-EXT:binding style="rpc"
4               transport=http://schema.xmlsoap.org/soap/http/>
5          <operation name="getWeather">
6               <SOAP-EXT:operation saopAction=""/>
7               <input>
8                  <SOAP-EXT:body use="encoded"/>
9               </input>
10              <output>
11                 <SOAP-EXT:body  use="encoded"/>
12              </output>
13          </operation>
14     </binding>
15     <service name= "WeatherService">
```

```
16          <port name="WeahterServicePort"
17                 binding="tns:WeatherServiceSoapBinding">
18              <SOAP-EXT:address
19                  location=http://myComapny.com/servlet/rpcrouter/>
20          </port>
21      </service>
22  </definitions>
```

In this implementation description, the main element is the binding element. It associates the abstract interface description to a specific implementation. It contains information about the transport protocol and the concrete data format employed by the service. In this listing, the binding associates the abstract port type WeatherServicePortType to a specific port named WeatherServicePort. For this purpose, the binding name WeatherServiceSoapBinding (compare codes on lines 1–2 and lines 15–16) is used.

In this example, we are using SOAP over HTTP, as indicated by code line 4. In addition, we are employing an RPC interaction style. This is indicated by setting the attribute style to rpc on line 3. The abstract operation from the service interface description getWeather (see Listing 13-1) is mapped to concrete SOAP messages (lines 7–12). Furthermore, the input and output messages are SOAP encoded for transfer.

It should be noted that the SOAP binding–associated elements, which are identified by the prefix SOAP-EXT, extend the WSDL-defined elements. For each protocol, such as SOAP, a different binding is defined to describe the mapping from the abstract WSDL interface description to the concrete protocol description. These are called *extensibility elements*.

An important element of the implementation description is the port element, which is used to provide a network address for the service. A service client may bind to a port and invoke methods on the service according to the concrete data format specified in the WSDL document. The same service may be offered at different ports that use different data formats. A client may choose between the different ports. It is important to note that the port and binding have been separated. This is because the binding is reusable, and multiple ports can use the same binding.

Finally, a service element encapsulates all the ports. This service element may be a starting point for a service client to discover the service.

Table 13.2 summarizes the part of the WSDL document that describes service implementation:

Figure 13.1 shows schematically the relationships among the different elements of the service implementation description as well their relationships to the abstract port type.

In the next section, we take a brief look at the overall structure of a WSDL document.

TABLE 13.2   Summary of Service Implementation Elements in WSDL

Element	Description
binding	A binding element binds a port type to a specific transport protocol and data format.
port	A port describes the network address of a particular implementation of the service.
service	A service element encapsulates all the available ports. These ports may share the same service types but employ different network addresses. There may also be concrete service implementations of several port types.

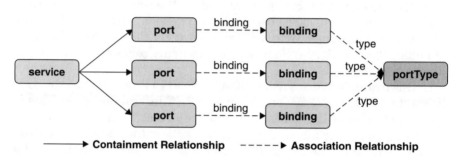

Figure 13.1   Relationships among the service implementation elements as well their relationship to the port type element

Containment Structure

Figure 13.2 summarizes the overall containment structure of a WSDL document. The structure has a top element called "definitions," which is shown in dark gray in the figure. All the elements that correspond to the abstract interface description are shown in medium gray, whereas the elements that correspond to the implementation part of the WSDL description are shown in light gray. The structure has tree-like hierarchy. The figure also shows how the abstract port type containment structure has an equivalent binding containment structure. In other words, the structure under the portType element looks identical to the containment tree underneath the binding element. Each binding related to a distinct port type maps a concrete protocol implementation to this port type.

In addition to this structure, there are associations between different elements that are established through the use attributes and their values. You have already seen some of these associations earlier in this chapter. For example, you have seen that a message consists of different parts, and the parts types can be defined through the types elements. An individual data type defined in the types element may appear multiple times in several messages. Also, a specific message is reusable and may appear in the description of several operations. Similarly, bindings may also be reusable.

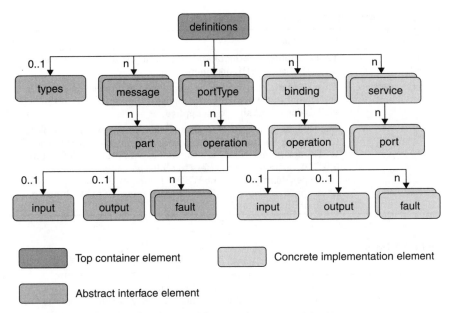

Figure 13.2 A WSDL document's tree-like containment structure

The tree-like structure of the WSDL shown in Figure 13.2 is helpful in visualizing some of the relationships between different elements of a WSDL document. However, it does not provide a complete picture of these relationships. For example, the structure cannot by itself provide information about which abstract data types belong to which messages. Therefore, starting with the next section, we look into the details of each element to discover these types of relationships. For this purpose, we first look at the elements and their attributes belonging to the abstract interface description.

Elements of Abstract Interface Description

We'll start our discussion of these elements with the top element, definitions, which is the container of all elements. Within this element we define various namespaces as well.

The definitions Element

This element constitutes the top container of all the other elements of a WSDL document. It has three attributes: name, targetNamespace, and xmlns. Table 13.3 provides a summary of these attributes.

Listing 13-3 shows an example of the use of the definitions element in a WSDL document.

TABLE 13.3   Attributes of the definitions Element

Attribute	Description
name	This attribute is optional and is used to provide a hint about the content of the WSDL document.
targetNamespace	This attribute can be used to introduce the namespace to which the element declaration and type definition contained in the WSDL document should be applied.
xmlns	The schema processor uses xmlns to determine where to look for the element declarations and type definitions used within the WSDL document. Usually, a tns namespace prefix is defined in a WSDL document that refers to all local element declarations and types definitions of the WSDL document. Another common namespace prefix is SOAP-EXT, which refers to SOAP binding extensibility elements.

Listing 13-3

```
Listing 13.3: An example of the use of the definitions element
1    <definitions name="weatherForecastService"
2         targetNamespace=http://myCompany.com/ns/weatherService/wsdl
3         xmlns:tns=http://myCompany.com/ns/weatherService/wsdl
4         xmlns:SOAP-EXT=http://schemas.xmlsoap.org/wsdl/>
5         <documentation>
6              WSDL document describing a Weather forecast service
7         </documentation>
8         <!---- The remaining WSDL document goes here    -->
9              ......
10   </definitions>
```

Note in this example that the namespace assigned to the target-Namespace attribute and the namespace prefix tns are the same. These two assignments help the WSDL processor to locate the local definitions when they are used.

The types Element

The types element is the direct child of the definitions element; it encapsulates all the abstract data type definitions. These abstract data types are then used in definitions of message elements (see the next subsection). Although WSDL specifications allow other kinds of abstract data type definitions, the use of XML schemas are preferred for this purpose.

Listing 13-4 is an example of a types element that contains three elements.

Listing 13-4

```
Listing 13.4: An example of types element
1    <types>
2         <schema
```

```
3          targetNamespace=http://myCompany.com/ns/weatherService/wsdl
4          xmlns=http://www.w3.org/2001/XMLSchema>
5          <element name="City"    type="xsd:string"/>
6          <element name="State"   type="xsd:string"/>
7          <element name="Country" type="xsd:string"/>
8       </schema>
9    </types>
```

In this example, we have defined three elements that can be directly used in the definitions of the message, and there is no need to always directly link to data type definitions. Note that we have overwritten the default namespace (WSDL namespace) to refer to the XMLSchema namespace and that these three elements can be unqualified. (A qualified name means that the namespace is included explicitly in the name.)

An import point regarding the interoperability issue: The WS-I Basic Profile recommends that all XML schema elements of the types container have a valid target namespace.

The message and part Elements

A message element abstractly represents one input or output parameter for an operation. For example, for a SOAP RPC type request, a message element can represent the abstract type for the input parameter. Similarly, for an RPC response, a message element may represent the abstract data type for the output parameter. In addition, a message can combine the parameters of each possible error response. A message element has one mandatory attribute called "name." Its value must be unique within the scope of a WSDL document.

Messages consists of one or more part elements. Part elements describe the logical parts of a message. A part can have the three attributes described in Table 13.4.

Listing 13-5 provides an example of a message element that uses the element attribute of the part child element.

TABLE 13.4   Three Attributes of the part Element

Attribute	Description
name	This attribute is mandatory, and its value must be unique within the scope of the containing message.
element	This attribute refers by name to a schema element declaration.
type	A part element can directly refer to the type without referring to an element declaration. This requires the use of the type attribute. Attribute elements and types are mutually exclusive.

Listing 13-5

```
Listing 13.5: an example of a message which employs the
attribute element of the part child element
1      <message name="getWeatherIn">
2              <part name="CityIn" element="tns:City"/>
3              <part name="StateIn" element="tns:State"/>
4              <part name="CountryIn" element="tns:Country"/>
5      </message>
```

The element attribute here refers to the element's declaration in the types container (see Listing 13-4). Note that a second method of defining the same message can be used instead. This second method employs the type attribute to define the types of the part elements. Listing 13-6 shows such a definition of a message element.

Listing 13-6

```
Listing 13.6: Alternate way to define the message element
1      <message name="getWeatherIn">
2              <part name="CityIn" type="xsd:string"/>
3              <part name="StateIn" type="xsd:string"/>
4              <part name="CountryIn" type="xsd:string"/>
5      </message>
```

The WSDL message element and part element definitions have a significant effect on SOAP binding. This effect will be discussed later.

The WS-I Basic Profile further emphasizes that the element attribute and the type attribute of the port element must not be used at the same time. In other words, these two attributes are mutually exclusive.

The operation Element

The operation element is a direct child of the portType element. (The portType element will be described later in this section.) A portType can contain any number of operation elements. An operation is an abstract description of a service call and therefore describes the set of abstract messages exchanged between the service client and service provider for executing a call.

Four different types of operations can be defined in WSDL. These types of operation are differentiated by their ordering and the presence of input, output, and fault messages. The four types of operations are summarized in Table 13.5.

For Web Services, only two of these types are important: the request/response type operation and the one-way type operation. The WSDL specification defines SOAP bindings for these two types only. The containment structure of the request/response type and the one-way type of operations are depicted in Figure 13.3.

TABLE 13.5   Four Types of Operations Supported by WSDL

Operation Type	Description
Request/response	In this type of operation, the service end point receives a message and sends a correlated message back. It contains one input element, one output element, and, optionally, one or more fault elements. The ordering of these elements is significant.
One-way	In this case, the service end point just receives a message and there is only an input element specifying the operation.
Notification	The service end point sends a message and there is only an output element specifying the operation.
Solicit/response	In this case, the service end point sends a message and receives a correlated message. There is an output element, an input element, and, optionally, one or more fault elements. The order of these parameters is significant.

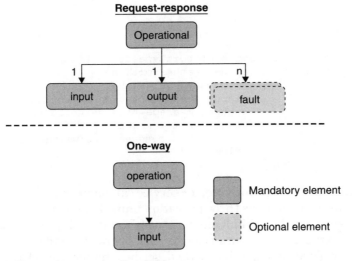

Figure 13.3   Two common types of operations

The input, output, and fault Elements

The input, output, and fault elements are direct children of the operation element and sometimes are referred to as *operation units*. The fault element can appear more than once. For request/response operations, the input represents the service request whereas the output represents the response. These three elements have two attributes each, as described in Table 13.6.

The portType Element

This element is the container of all the abstract operations and describes a specific service interface. This element has one attribute, "name,"

TABLE 13.6   Two Attributes of the input, output, and fault Elements

Attribute	Description
name	This attribute is optional for the input and output elements but is mandatory for the fault element. This name must be unique within the scope of a portType.
message	This attribute refers by name to the linked abstract message for the operation unit. Recall that messages are reusable units. Several operations can possibly result in identical faults and associated fault messages.

which is mandatory. The value of this attribute must be unique within the scope of a WSDL document. Listing 13-7 provides an example of a portType element declaration.

Listing 13-7

```
Listing 13.7:  An example of portType definition
1        <portType name="getWeatherPortType">
2               <operation name="getWeather">
3                       <input message="tns:getWeatherIn"/>
4                       <output message="tns:getWeatherOut"/>
5                       <fault  name="weatherForecastFailure"
6                                      message="tns:WeatherNotFound"/>
7               </operation>
8        </portType>
```

In this example, the operation or service call name is getWeatherPort-Type. This operation has three operation units. For each operation unit, the message attribute implements a "uses" relationship to the message (that is, to the abstract data type for each operation unit).

The portType element abstractly describes the service call characteristics, such as the operations and the data type expected and returned by the service. However, to be able to use this service, a service client still needs information about the specific protocol binding and the network address. These issues are covered in the next section, where we discuss the elements and attributes corresponding to the implementation part of the WSDL description of the service.

Elements of the Implementation Part

We first discuss the binding elements and then we discuss the service elements. There are two binding elements: binding and operation. These two elements contain elements that are not declared in WSDL namespace, and they contain extensibility elements.

The binding and binding operation Elements

As shown earlier in Figure 13.2, the structure of the binding element is similar to the structure of the portType element. This similarity is because a binding maps the abstract portType description to a concrete implementation. The binding element contains an operation element, but may contain other extensibility elements that provide binding-specific information. The operation element may also contain extensibility elements. The example provided in Listing 13-8 contains SOAP binding extensibility elements.

Listing 13-8

```
Listing 13.8: Example of binding containing SOAP extensibility elements
1    <binding name="WeatherServiceSoapBinding"
2                    type="tns:WeatherServicePortType">
3        <!--SOAP binding extensibility elements    -- >
4        <SOA-EXT:binding stype="rpc"
5                transport=http://schemas.xmlsoap.org/soap/http?>
6        <operation name="getWeather">
7            <!-- SOAP operation extensibility element   -- >
8            <SOAP-EXT:operation saopAction+""/>
9            <input>
10               <SOAP-EXT:body use="encoded"/>
11           </input>
12           <output>
13               <SOAP-EXT:body use="encoded"?>
14           </output>
15        </operation>
16    </binding>
```

The binding element has two attributes: name and type. The name attribute is required and specifies the name of the binding. It should be unique within the WSDL document. The type attribute is also required, and its value refers to the portType it binds. As various ports may correspond to the same port type, the type attribute along with the name attribute uniquely identify a binding. There is only one attribute called name, that belongs to the binding operation. Its value specifies the name of the binding operation, and its value must be identical to the value of the mapping portType name attribute.

The binding input, output, and fault Elements

The binding operation element has three child elements. It may have an input element, an output element, and optionally one or more fault elements. This structure is identical to the structure of the operation element belonging to the element portType. All three of these elements have one attribute each, each called "name." For the input and output elements, the name attribute is optional. However, this attribute is mandatory for a fault element.

The service and port Elements

A service element is a container of port elements; therefore, we discuss the port element first. A port element contains an extensibility element that specifies the network address of a given service implementation. This element has two attributes. The first attribute, name, is required and specifies the name of the port (that is, the name of a specific service implementation). The second attribute, binding, is also required and refers to the binding for which port provides a specific network address.

As indicated previously, the service element groups all related port elements. Each port is linked to the same port type and therefore provides semantically equivalent functionality at different network addresses. The service element has one required attribute: name. The name attribute specifies the name of the service and must be unique within the scope of the WSDL document. Listing 13-9 provides an example of a service element definition.

Listing 13-9

```
Listing 13.9: Example of a WSDL service element
1    <service  name="weatherForeCastService">
2        <port name="premierForecast"
binding="tns:weatherServiceSoapBinding">
3            <SOAP-EXT:address
4                    location=http://myCompany.com/servlet/forecaster/>
5        </port>
6    </service>
```

Logical Relationships

Now that we have gone over all the important elements and attributes of a WSDL document, we are in a position to summarize the logical relationships among these different elements. These relationships are shown schematically in Figure 13.4. Some of these relationships are established through the use of attributes and child elements.

SOAP Binding

WSDL specifications contain three bindings: SOAP, HTTP, and MIME. You have previously seen some examples of SOAP binding. The extensibility elements of each of these bindings are defined in separate namespaces. We will only cover the SOAP binding here. In general, the

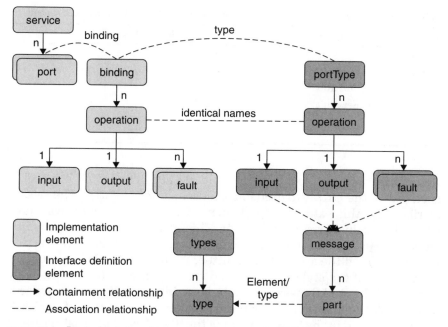

Figure 13.4   Logical relationships among elements of a WSDL document

concept of extensibility elements allows for the definition of arbitrary protocol bindings, although WSDL specifications only contain the afore-mentioned three bindings.

In discussing the implementation part of the WSDL Web Services description, we have already covered some example of SOAP exten-sibility elements. In this section, we will take a more detailed look at these types of elements, which are always contained in WSDL elements corresponding to the implementation part. As previously mentioned, these SOAP extensibility elements carry the prefix SOAP-EXT and their namespace corresponds to the URI http://schemas.xmlsoap.org/wsdl/soap/.

The SOAP extensibility elements we discuss here are shown in Table 13.7, along with the corresponding WSDL elements that contain them.

These extensibility elements are described in the following subsections.

SOAP binding Extensibility Element

This SOAP extensibility element is the direct child of the WSDL binding element. It is mandatory for SOAP binding and has two attributes. The first attribute is transport, which is used to specify the communication protocol used for the SOAP message. The WS-I Basic Profile limits the

TABLE 13.7   SOAP Extensibility Elements and the Corresponding WSDL Container Elements

SOAP Extensibility Elements	WSDL Container Elements
binding	binding
operation	operation
body, header, headerFault	input
body, header, headerFault	output
fault	fault
address	port

communication protocols to HTTP and HTTPS. The HTTP protocol is specified as the URI http://schemas.xmlsoap.org/soap/http/. The second attribute for this extensibility element is called style, and it can have one of two values: rpc or document. This attribute provides a default value for each operation at this higher level. An operation can override this selection. If the attribute is omitted, the default value is document. If the value of the style attribute is document, the content of the body element of the SOAP message can be an arbitrary XML instance document. SOAP does not place any restrictions on the structure of the XML instance carried in the body element of the SOAP message. Listing 13-10 shows a sample XML instance contained in the body element of a SOAP message. This message can be used by the service provider to update a customer's address.

Listing 13-10

```
Listing 13.10: Example of a SOAP document style message
1    <SOAP-ENV:Envelope
2        xmlns:SOAP-ENV=http://schemas.xmlsoap.org/soap/envelope/>
3        <SOAP-ENV:Body>
4            <add:address xmlns:add=http://myCompany.com/ns/employees>
5                <add:name>
6                    <add:firstName>John</add:firstName>
7                    <add:lastName>Smith</add:lastName>
8                </add:name>
9                <add:streetAddress>45 Alpine Street</add:streetAddress>
10               <add:city>New York</add:city>
11               <add:state>New York</add:state>
12               <add:postalCode>43321</add:postalCode>
13           </add:address>
14       </SOAP-ENV:Body>
15   </SOAP-ENV:Envelope>
```

SOAP operation Extensibility Element

This SOAP extensibility element is the direct child of the WSDL operation element. It provides operation scope information and has two attributes: style and soapAction. The value of style attribute is used to indicate the operation type (that is, rpc or document) and is used to override the style declared in the SOAP binding extensibility element. The second attribute, soapAction, is used to specify the value of the soapAction HTTP header for the operation. The SOAP specification requires the presence of a soapAction header when embedding SOAP into HTTP protocol. The WS-I Basic Profile requires that all style attributes for different operation extensibility elements have identical values.

SOAP body Extensibility Element

This extensibility element is used to define the mapping of abstract message parts into a SOAP message body element. It is important to note the difference between the SOAP body extensibility element and the SOAP message body element. The SOAP body extensibility element appears in the WSDL document, whereas the SOAP message body element appears in the SOAP message itself (see Chapter 12). A SOAP body extensibility element may have up to four attributes. These attributes are described in Table 13.8.

SOAP fault Extensibility Element

This element is the direct child of the WSDL fault element; it defines the mapping of the abstract message representing the fault data to the SOAP message Fault element. As described in Chapter 12, the SOAP message Fault element consists of several child elements, one of which is details.

TABLE 13.8   Attributes of the SOAP body Extensibility Element

Attribute	Description
parts	This attribute contains a set of abstract message parts that belong to the SOAP message body. Not all message abstract parts must appear in the SOAP message body.
use	This attribute is mandatory and has two possible values: literal and encoded. If the value is literal, the abstract message part is directly written in the body of the SOAP message. However, if the value is encoded, the abstract message part is first encoded and then put in the message body.
encodingStyle	If the value of the use attribute is set to encoded, the value of the encodingStyle attribute determines how the abstract message parts would be encoded before being put in the SOAP message body.
namespace	This attribute is used to specify the namespace of the operation name (that is, of the elements comprising all operation parameters). The value of this attribute is the same as the WSDL operation name. Hence, the namespace attribute helps a consumer to select which Web Services implementation to invoke.

This details element carries the application-specific error information. The SOAP fault extensibility element maps directly into this SOAP message details element content. The SOAP fault extensibility element has four attributes, three of which are identical to the first three attributes described in Table 13.8. They have exactly the same meaning. The fourth attribute is the name attribute, which is a required attribute. The value of the name attribute should exactly match the value of the name attribute of the WSDL fault element.

SOAP header and headerFault Extensibility Elements

The SOAP header extensibility element describes how abstract message parts are mapped as content of the SOAP message header element. The SOAP header extensibility element has five attributes. The first three attributes are identical to the ones described in Table 13.8 and have exactly the same meaning. The two remaining attributes—message and part—refer to the abstract specification of the header. The message attribute describes the abstract message representing a SOAP message header entry. It is important to point out that this identification is required because a SOAP message may contain more than one header entry. The part attribute describes the part of the header. The part attribute along with the message attribute is used to define the SOAP message header entry.

SOAP address Extensibility Element

This extensibility element is the direct child of the WSDL port element. This element is used to specify the network address of a given implementation of a service. The specification is provided through the attribute location. Listing 13-11 provides an example of the use of this extensibility element.

Listing 13-11

```
Listing 13.11: Example of the use of SOAP Address extensibility
element
1    <service name="WeatherForecastService" >
2        <port name="weatherServicePort"  binding=
"WeatherServiceSoapBinding"
3            <SOAP-EXT:address
4                    location=http://myCompany.com/servlet/
weatherService/>
5        </port>
6    </service>
```

Conclusion

This chapter covered the contents of a WSDL document. A WSDL document is a formal description of a service and is considered a formal contract between a service provider and a service consumer. The document has two parts. The first part of the document describes abstractly the interface offered by the service provider to the service consumer. This first part describes the abstract data types, the operations, and the input and output abstract messages corresponding to a given service. The second part of the document deals with the concrete implementation of the service. This part has information on the network address, communication protocol, and concrete data types for the service. For this second part, WSDL relies on the extensibility elements that allow protocol-specific bindings. In particular, we covered the SOAP bindings and the related SOAP extensibility elements and attributes. In addition, WSDL specifies HTTP and MIME bindings. Other bindings may also be defined. We also discussed some of the restrictions placed on the WSDL document by the WS-I Basic Profile. The purpose of the WS-I Basic Profile is to ensure that services deployed on different platforms can interoperate.

If there are only a few services and a few service consumers, the WSDL documents might be sufficient for service deployment and use because a WSDL document can be exchanged manually between the service provider and service consumer, for example, via email. However, in a dynamic situation where new services and new versions of old services are continually being added, there should be a central repository where the service provider can publish its services (and the associated requirements for use) and the service consumers can discover the services. The published information should not only include the WSDL document but also other information that allows a service consumer to discover and choose between alternatives.

In the next chapter, we discuss the concept of a central repository and the associated interface called Universal Description, Discovery, and Integration (UDDI). This type of central repository allows for the discovery of service end point implementation, interface information, and business-related information.

UDDI Registry

In addition to the WSDL description of a service and the SOAP message format, a central place is needed where the service provider can advertise the services it offers and the service consumers can find the service they require. Such a central place is called a *service registry*. A common analogy for a service registry is the library card catalog. This catalog is used to enter information about new books as they arrive in the library and to look up the location of a book when it is needed. Another analogy is the telephone directory, where service providers advertise their services in Yellow and White Pages and the consumers use the directory to find the services they need.

The Universal Description, Discovery, and Integration (UDDI) specification defines a standard way for registering, unregistering, and looking up Web Services. Figure 14.1 summarizes the basic working of a UDDI-based registry. First, a service provider registers a service with the UDDI registry. Then, the service consumer looks up the service in the UDDI registry. Lastly, the service consumer binds to the service provider and uses the service. Note that once the service consumer finds a service, the registry has no role to play between service provider and service consumer. The service consumer directly binds with the provider to use the service.

Three categories of information are stored in the UDDI registry. These categories are

- **General business and organization information** This includes name, description, address, and so forth. This could be compared to the White Pages of the telephone directory.

- **Descriptions of businesses according to standard taxonomies** This could be according to the types of services they offer or geographical location. This category could be compared to the Yellow Pages of the telephone book.

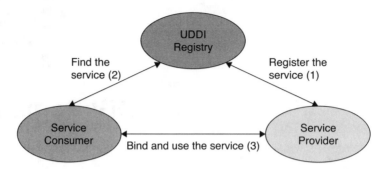

Figure 14.1   Basic working of a UDDI registry

- **Lists of services, binding, and service-specific technical information**   This category could be compared to the Green Pages of the telephone book.

In addition to providing a model for storing information about services and businesses, the UDDI specification defines an XML schema for SOAP messages and two APIs for applications needing to use the registry. The two APIs are

- **Inquiry API**   Used to look up and browse the service registry
- **Publishers API**   Used to register services with the registry

The following section provides an overview of UDDI and the associated storage model, which includes tModel and associated taxonomies. We then discuss the tModel in detail, including the dual role played by a tModel, both as a technical fingerprint and as an abstract namespace. We then discuss the various categorization and identification schemes vital to the workings of UDDI registries. Binding templates, used to store technical information about a service and its end point, are discussed next. Then we cover the authoring of a WSDL document so that it can be properly referenced in a tModel and a binding template. The UDDI inquiry and publishing APIs are covered, and then we discuss currently available and future commercial products that incorporate some of the registry ideas discussed in this chapter.

Overview and Basic Data Model

The role of the UDDI registry in Web Services is similar to the role played by a search engine on the Internet. The power of the search engine comes from the keywords used to classify contents. In a similar manner, a fine-grained search for a Web Service is possible only if the service is classified properly. The classification and identification taxonomies present in the UDDI registry provide a starting point for describing Web Services. Equally important is to classify the businesses or organizations that offer Web Services.

The structure that describes the taxonomies present in a UDDI registry is called a *tModel,* which is a very important abstraction in UDDI that takes a considerable amount of time to understand fully. The complexity of the tModel comes from the dual role it plays in a UDDI registry. tModel is used to define both a service's technical interface and a taxonomy (or namespace) that specifies the categorization or identification scheme. The complexity also comes from the fact that tModels are referenced, unlike other structures that hold containment relationships among themselves.

UDDI Data Model

The basic data model used in UDDI consists of a hierarchy of five basic data types, which are defined through XML schemas. These five data types are businessEntity, businessService, bindingTemplate, tModel, and publisherAssertion. The following subsections provide brief descriptions of these data types.

businessEntity   This data type contains information on a business or organization, such as the name of the business/organization, the address of the business/organization, and a contact phone number of the business/organization. This data type is at the top of the data model hierarchy.

businessService   This data type represents the aggregation of services belonging to a specific category offered by a service provider. A service provider identified through a businessEntity may offer several types or collections of Web Services. The businessService data type provides overall Web Service–level information, such as the name of a service aggregate, a description, or a service categorization.

bindingTemplate   This data type exposes the service end point address required for accessing a distinct Web Service from a technical point of view. It may also be used to describe technical characteristics of a service implementation or to refer to remotely hosted services. The businessService data type may contain more than one bindingTemplate.

tModel   tModel is short for *technical model.* This data type is used to expose Web Services interface information. A reference to a tModel may indicate that a Web Service complies with a certain distinct specification or standard or some specific convention. A tModel helps a client of a service to interact properly with the service. In other words, a tModel provides a technical specification for a fingerprint that helps the client determine whether the technical capabilities of the service meets its requirement. The second role of a tModel is that it represents a value system to identify and categorize information entities. This role is discussed later in more detail.

publisherAssertion   This data type complements the information contained in the businessEntity data type. It is especially useful for very large organizations that have many subsidiaries and may not be adequately represented by the businessEntity data type. The publisherAssertion data type is used to describe relationships between business entities.

Figure 14.2 schematically describes the relationships among the five data types of the UDDI data model. businessEntity serves as the

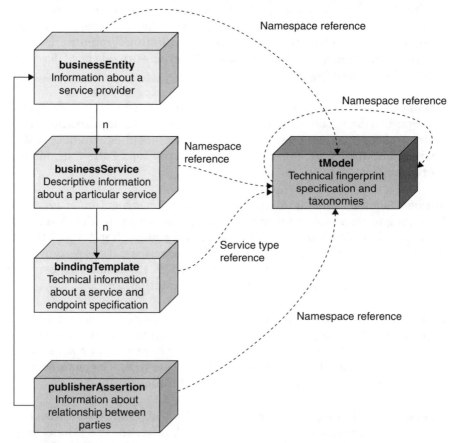

Figure 14.2   Relationships among the five entities of the UDDI data model

container of businessServices, which means there can be several businessServices belonging to a given businessEntity, but a businessService
can belong to only one businessEntity. In a similar manner, there is containment relationship between businessService and bindingTemplate.
Therefore, a bindingTemplate can belong only to a single businessService, but a businessService can have more than one bindingTemplate.

It is clear from Figure 14.2 that tModel has fundamentally different
relationships. It does not have a containment relationship with the
other elements; rather, it is always referenced from other elements.
Also, tModel is referenced in different roles by different elements. businessEntity, businessService, tModel, and publisherAssertion refer to
a tModel as a *namespace,* whereas bindingTemplate refers to it as a
service type. An interesting thing to notice is the use of tModel to refer
to itself like a namespace for classification or taxonomy. Because of the
special and different roles a tModel plays, we discuss the tModel data
structure in more detail next.

tModel

The tModel fulfills two important goals of the UDDI registry. The first
goal is to provide a facility to describe Web Services well enough that
a consumer of a service can interact with the service in a well-defined
manner. The second goal is to provide a means to describe Web Services
well enough that the description is useful during searches. The first goal
is met by tModel via the technical fingerprint of a service, whereas the
second goal is met by tModel by acting in the role of a namespace or
taxonomy. We discuss these two roles next.

Technical Fingerprint Role

The specification of how a consumer interacts with a service is stored
in the tModel. In this role, the tModel acts as service type. An example
might be a specification that refers to the wire protocol and interchange
formats, such as SOAP over HTTP. After standard protocol definitions
such as these are registered as a tModel, services can express their
compliance with them by referring to them in the bindingTemplate.

A common use of the technical fingerprint involves referring to a
Web Service WSDL in the bindingTemplate (which is described later in
this chapter). Listing 14-1 provides an example of a tModel registered
in a UDDI registry. This model pertains to a credit-check protocol. The
model refers to a WSDL document in the overviewURL element. This
illustrates an important point about tModel when used as a technical
fingerprint. The tModel only stores metadata and not the actual data.
In Listing 14-1, the tModel points to a WSDL document rather than
storing the information itself. Also note that the UDDI registry assigns

a universally unique identifier (UUID) to the tModel it stores. This identifier appears as the value of the attribute tModelKey. In our example, this attribute value is AAAAAAAA-1234-5678-AAAA.

Listing 14-1

```
Listing 14.1: An example of tModel used as a service fingerprint
1    <tModel xmlns="urn:uddi-org:api"
2          tModelKey="UUID:AAAAAAAA-1234-5678-AAAA">
3        <name>myCompany:creditcheck</name>
4        <description xml:lang="en">Check credit</description>
5        <overviewDoc>
6              <overviewURL>http://myComapny.schema.com/creditcheck.wsdl
7              </overviewURL>
8        </overviewDoc>
9        <categoryBag>
10             <keyedReference
11                 tModelKey="UUID:CD153257-086A-4237-B336-
6BDCBDCC6635"
12                 keyName="Consumer credit reporting services"
13                 keyValue="95.21.22.176.234"/>
14           <keyedReference
15                 tModelKey="UUID:C1ACF26D-9672-4404-9D70-
39B756E62AB4"
16                 keyName="types"
17                 keyValue="wsdlSpec"/>
18        </categoryBag>
19    </tModel>
```

Once a tModel has been registered in a UDDI registry and a service wants to adhere to the WSDL referenced in the tModel, the service can indicate this by referencing the tModel in the bindingTemplate using the identifier, as shown in Listing 14-2 (bindingTemplate is explained later in the chapter).

Listing 14-2

```
Listing 14.2: Example of a bindingTemplate referencing a tModel
1    <bindingTemplates>
2        <bindingTemplate
3            serviceKey="CCCCCCCC-CCCC-CCCC-CCCC "
4            bindingKey="DDDDDDDD-DDDD-DDDD-DDDD ">
5            <accessPoint  URLType="https">
6                  https://myCompany.com/creditcheck
7            </accessPoint>
8            <tModelInstanceDetails>
9                <tModelInstanceInfo
10                     tModelKey="UUID: AAAAAAAA-1234-5678-AAAA "/>
11            </tModelInstanceDetails>
```

```
12          </bindingTemplate>
13      </bindingTemplates>
```

Note that the bindingTemplate also includes a service end point, which also will be discussed in more detail later in this chapter. Now we turn our attention to the second type of role played by a tModel in a UDDI registry.

Abstract Namespace Reference Role

Note in lines 9–18 of Listing 14-1 that tModelKeys are being referenced in the categoryBag element of the credit-check tModel. (The category-Bag element is discussed later in this chapter.) This shows the second use of tModel—as an abstract namespace or taxonomy. The keyedReference element contains the element tModelKey, which itself consists of two elements called keyName and keyValue. The keyedReference element refers to a name in a given namespace defined by the tModel, which is represented by its key.

In lines 9–18, a reference is made to two tModels for classification purposes. In one case, the service is classified as type "wsdlSpec" in the uddi-org:types (UUID:C1ACF26D…) taxonomy, which means that the service description exists as a WSDL document. The uddi-org:types taxonomy is defined as a preregistered (canonical) tModel in the UDDI programmers specification. Therefore, it is always present in any UDDI registry and uses the same key. Also, the specification defines the valid values in the uddi-org:types taxonomy.

Various kinds of taxonomies can be used for classification and identification. The classification information exists in the categoryBag, whereas the identification information is coded into identifierBag. These two entities—categoryBag and identifierBag—are discussed in detail in their own separate section because, in addition to tModel, they can be used inside a businessEntity.

Next, we discuss the structure of a tModel.

Structure of a tModel

Figure 14.3 summarizes the structure of a tModel. The top structure includes one mandatory element, called "name," and four optional elements. The four optional elements are description, overviewDoc, identifierBag, and categoryBag. The overviewDoc has two child elements called overviewURL and description. These elements and subelements are briefly described in Table 14.1.

Next, we discuss the containment structures of categoryBag and identifierBag.

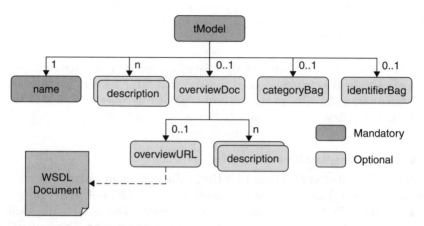

Figure 14.3 Structure of a tModel

TABLE 14.1   Elements of a tModel Structure

Element	Description
name	This is a mandatory element and should be a meaningful string name for a tModel.
description	This is an optional element that is used to describe the purpose of the tModel.
overviewDoc	This element is also optional and is a container for the overviewURL and description elements.
identifierBag	This is again an optional element and is used to maintain identification information for the tModel. The following section will detail this element.
categoryBag	This is also an optional element that is used to maintain classification information for the tModel. This element will also be discussed in detail in the following section.
overviewURL	This is again an optional element. It points to an overview document such as a WSDL document describing the Web Services interface and implementation.

Categorization and Identification Schemes

A common use of a UDDI registry is to help client applications find business and service information. Therefore, a formal way to identify businesses is needed. A formal identification system helps clients find out who is offering a service as well as provides them important criteria for deciding whether or not to use the service.

The identifierBag is a containment structure that UDDI provides for the introduction of identification systems and related identifications. In general, any identification system may be employed. However, the UDDI specification explicitly mentions few of these identification systems. Those mentioned in the specification include Thomas Register, Data Universal Numbering System (DUNS), and Global Location Numbers (GLNs). Thomas Register supplies unique provider identification digits. DUNS numbers are nine-digit identification sequences providing unique identifiers for single business entities. DUNS numbers are managed by Dun & Bradstreet. GLNs are unique 13-digit identification sequences identifying physical, legal, or functional locations within a business. These numbers are maintained by the EAN International Association.

The identifierBag can be optional in a businessEntity as well as in a tModel. The basic structure of an identifierBag is shown in Figure 14.4. It has three parameters: tModelKey, keyName, and keyValue. Such a triplet is called a *keyed reference*. Table 14.2 provides a brief description of each of these three elements.

In addition to the identified business, one should also be able to search a UDDI directory according to a distinct category. This would be the case if one is searching for a previously unknown service. In that case, the search could be based on distinct categories, such as the category of the product, the industry it belongs to, the region in which a service provider operates, or the technical requirements for invoking a service.

Similar to identifierBag, categoryBag is a container of information on categories. The technical structure of categoryBag is similar to that of identifierBag, as shown in Figure 14.4. The categoryBag contains keyed

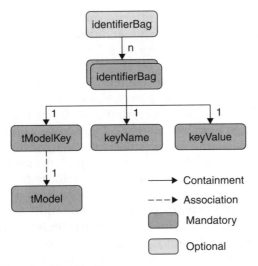

Figure 14.4 Structure of an identifierBag

TABLE 14.2   Parameters of an identifierBag

Parameter	Description
tModelKey	This parameter is mandatory and points to a tModel. For example, the distinct tModel represents the DUNS or GLN identifier system.
keyName	The keyName is a human-readable form of the identifier system plus the business entity.
keyValue	This parameter is also mandatory and contains the identifier according to the selected identifier system.

references to tModels identifying the actual classification system, along with keyNames and keyValues. The information in the categoryBag helps a consumer decide whether the service or the service provider belongs to the right category. A category can occur inside a businessEntity, businessService, or tModel. Once again, in general, any category can be employed. UDDI specifications mention some categories explicitly. These explicitly mentioned categories include the North American Industry Classification System (NAICS) and the Universal Standard Product and Services Classification (UNSPSC) system. UDDI also has a number of built-in taxonomies, including a taxonomy named uddi-org:types (in other words, the keyName attribute has this value). This is represented by a distinct tModel. This built-in taxonomy supports the categorization of tModels. Possible category values are wsdlSpec, soapSpec, and xmlSpec.

Binding Template

A binding template contains information on the service end point. It also represents or refers to the technical information about a Web Service. The complete structure of a binding template is shown in Figure 14.5.

We first discuss the service end point information in a binding template. Two elements can have information on the service end point: accessPoint and hostingRedirector. They are mutually exclusive and both are a direct child of the bindingTemplate element. The accessPoint element is used to code the service end point information directly into the bindingTemplate itself. The value of this must be interpreted according to the URL type attribute value. For example, if the attribute has the value http, the content of the accessPoint element represents a URL. The presence of hostingRedirector (in place of accessPoint) indicates that the binding template points to another bindingTemplate, which ultimately provides the service end point information. This element is used if more than one service description can benefit from one bindingTemplate.

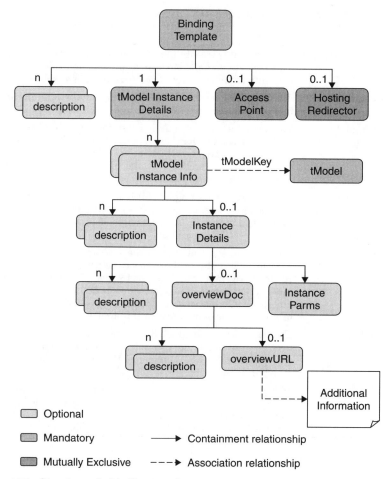

Figure 14.5 Structure of a binding template

The attribute bindingKey maintains the UUID value of the target bindingTemplate.

The remaining elements (elements other than accessPoint and hostingRedirector) shown in Figure 14.5 are used to provide technical information about a Web Service. The top element in this hierarchy is tModelInstanceDetails, which is a container element. This element and all its subordinates are described briefly in Table 14.3. The most important information carried by this substructure is information about the wire protocol and data exchange formats and links to the tModels associated with the binding template.

TABLE 14.3   tModelInstanceDetails and Its Subelements

Element	Description
tModelInstanceDetails	This element is a container of tModelInstanceInfo elements. This collection of all tModelInstanceInfo and tModel elements is called the *technical fingerprint* of a Web Service.
tModelInstanceInfo	This element refers to a tModel and optionally contains an instanceDetails element.
instanceDetails	This optional element contains associated bindingTemplate-specific information for the referenced tModel. This information may include wire protocol and data-exchange format info not expressed in the tModel. This information is carried by the subelements instanceParms and overviewDoc.
instanceParms	This element is a string type. It holds bindingTemplate-specific tModel usage parameters or setting information. For example, it may carry the port name of an associated WSDL implementation description.
overviewDoc	This element is a container for the overviewURL element. It contains information or links to a remote information source related to the proper usage of the tModel referenced within the bindingTemplate. It is an optional element and, if present, may add to the information contained in the instanceParms element, or it may be the only source for this kind of information.
overviewURL	This element may hold a URL reference to an additional overview document. For example, this reference may point to a file holding the WSDL implementation description of the Web Services.
description	This is an optional string type element that may appear at different places in the binding template. It is intended to carry information about the accessPoint, the use of tModel, and the use or purpose of the instanceDetails element.

Use of WSDL in the UDDI Registry

Recall from Chapter 13 that the WSDL document consists of a service interface part and a service implementation part. You learned earlier in this chapter that the bindingTemplate and tModels also provide the same information. Therefore, it may be possible that the bindingTemplate and tModels can delegate this information to a WSDL document. It turns out that this is possible if the WSDL document is authored or partitioned in a particular way. This particular way of partitioning a WSDL document is slightly different from the partitions we talked about in Chapter 13. In this way of grouping, you group the portType and binding elements in one file, which we will refer to as the WSDL interface and binding file. The service element containing the port elements is grouped in another file, which we will refer to as the WSDL implementation file. This implementation file imports the WSDL interface and binding file.

As an example, let's again consider the weather forecast service. We name the WSDL interface and binding file weatherServiceInterface .wsdl, and we call the WSDL implementation file weatherServiceImpl .wsdl. Listing 14-3 provides the implementation file that imports the interface and binding file.

Listing 14-3

```
Listing 14.3: An Example of a WSDL implementation file which imports the
interface and binding file
1      <definitions name="weatherService"
2              targetNamespace=http://myCompany.com/weather.wsdl
3              xmlns:tns=http://myCompany.com/weather.wsdl
4              xmlns:SOAP-EXT=http://schemas.xmlsoap.org/wsdl/soap/
5              xmlns:imported=http://myCompany.com/ns/weatherInterface/wsdl
6              xmlns=http://schemas.xmlsoap.org/wsdl/
7              <import location=
8                      http://www.myCompany.com/wsdlFiles/
weatherServiceInterface.wsdl
10                     namespace=http://myCompany.com/ns/
weatherServiceInterface.wsdl/>
11             <!-- The service element containing ports elements go here
- - >
12             …..
13     </definitions>
```

In this WSDL implementation file, the location attribute of the import element carries the physical location of the imported interface and binding file. The namespace prefix "imported" refers to the target namespace of the elements contained in the interface and the binding file named weatherServiceInterface.wsdl.

Now that we have discussed this particular partition of the WSDL file, we are in a position to discuss how to refer to the WSDL files in a tModel and in a bindingTemplate for registering a Web Service in a UDDI registry. For tModel, we refer to the WSDL interface and binding file, whereas with the bindingTemplate we refer to the WSDL implementation file.

In case of the tModel, a uddi-org:types taxonomy value of wsdlSpec classifies the tModel to refer to the WSDL interface and binding document. This value is specified in the categoryBag element of the tModel. The URL of the WSDL interface and binding document is contained in the value of the overviewURL element, which is a subelement of the overviewDoc element.

Let's continue with the weather service example. Listing 14-4 shows how the reference to the WSDL interface and binding document is made (see lines 7–9). Note that the value of the tModelKey attribute in the keyedReference element is a UUID and points to a tModel representing the UDDI built-in uddi-org:types category system. The keyName and keyValue attributes determine that this weather service tModel is a link to a WSDL document.

Listing 14-4

```
Listing 14.4: a tModel containing a reference to the WSDL interface and
binding document
1   <tModel tModelKey="…." >
2       <name> Weather service tModel </name>
3       <description>This example illustrates the reference to a WSDL
4               interface and binding file in a tModel
5       </description>
6       <overviewDoc>
7         <overviewURL>
8             http://www.myCompany.com/wsdlFiles/weatherServiceInterface.wsdl
9         </overviewURL>
10      </overviewDoc>
11      <categoryBag>
12        <keyedReference
13            tModelKey="uuid:CDDCF34D-1234-4404-9D40-41C842G32sd7"
14            keyName="uddi-org:types"
15            keyValue="wsdlSpec"/>
16      </categoryBag>
17   </tModel>
```

Next, let's look at how the WSDL implementation document is referred to in a bindingTemplate. Note that the accessPoint element of the bindingTemplate directly holds the exact network address of the Web Services, as shown in Listing 14-5.

Listing 14-5

```
Listing 14.5:  Network address of a Web Service encoded directly in the
bindingTemplate
1     <bindingTemplate bindingKey="…" servicekey="…">
2         <description> Weather service bindingTemplate</description>
3         <accessPoint URLType="http">
4             http://www.myCompany.com/servlets/weatherServlet
5         </accessPoint>
6         <!- -    tModelInstanceDetails goes in here - - >
7     </bindingTemplate>
```

Because the accessPoint completely holds the information on the Web Services network address, there is no need to replicate this information elsewhere. Therefore, the attachment of the WSDL implementation document, which also carries the network address of the Web Services, is not required. However, to illustrate how a WSDL implementation document can be linked if further tModel usage information must be attached, let's assume that we also want to attach a WSDL implementation document to the binding template. The tModelInstanceDetails element shown in Listing 14-6 completes the code for the example shown in Listing 14-5.

Listing 14-6

Listing 14.6: Attaching a WSDL implementation document to a bindingTemplate

```
1    <tModelInstanceDetails>
2        <tModelInstanceInfo tModelKey="…">
3            <instanceDetails>
4                <overviewDoc>
5                    <overviewURL>
6                        http://www.myCompany.com/wsdlFiles/
weatherServiceImpl.wsdl
7                    </overviewURL>
8                </overviewDoc>
9                <instanceParms>
10                   <port name="weatherServicePort"
11                             binding="tns:weatherServiceSoapBinding"/>
12               </instanceParms>
13           </instanceDetails>
14       </tModelInstanceInfo>
15   </tModelInstanceDetails>
```

In this listing, we first direct the Web Services client through the overviewURL element to the weatherServiceImpl.wsdl document (lines 5–7) that contains the Web Services implementation information. The instanceParms element then directs the client to the matching port entry within the WSDL implementation document file.

Next, we briefly cover the two APIs that UDDI offers for searching for and registering Web Services.

Summary of UDDI APIs

The users of the UDDI registry interact with the registry using synchronous calls. For this purpose, SOAP is used as the message format and HTTP is used for the communication protocol. UDDI call-and-response structures are embedded in the SOAP message body as XML elements. Figure 14.6 illustrates the use of SOAP in the request and response from a UDDI registry call. Note that SOAP headers are not employed in UDDI registry calls. The SOAP message Fault element carries the UDDI registry's failure reports within its detail element.

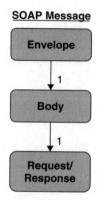

SOAP Message

Envelope

1

Body

1

Request/
Response

Figure 14.6   SOAP request and response from a UDDI registry call

Generally speaking, the UDDI Registry API supports two kinds of operations:

- **A publication API**   A Web Services provider uses this API to publish, update, or delete information about a Web Service it offers.
- **An inquiry API**   A Web Services consumer uses this API to search for information for a particular Web Service and to find an appropriate service provider who offers the required service.

UDDI Publishing API

There are two major call types in the inquiry API. They are of the form save_*xxx* and delete_*xxx*. The save_*xxx* call is used to create new information entities or to update existing information entities. An example of such a call is save_binding. Thus, this call type is used for publication. This type of call can take one or more information entities as input. An example of this type of call request and response is shown in Figure 14.7. In this example, bindingTemplates are being published.

In a similar manner, delete_*xxx* call types are used to remove or unpublish one or more information entities from the UDDI registry. This type of call can take as input one or more key attributes identifying the information entities to be removed. Figure 14.8 shows an example. In this sample call, a number of bindingTemplates are being removed from the UDDI registry.

UDDI Inquiry API

This API supports two major types of calls: find_*xxx* and get_*xxx*Detail. The find_*xxx* calls are used to locate registered information entities within the UDDI registry. This type of call may take as input *find qualifiers*

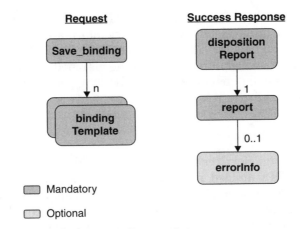

Figure 14.7   Publishing a call for a binding template

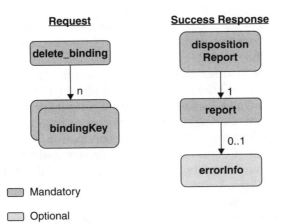

Figure 14.8   Removal of binding templates from the UDDI registry

(described later) that influence the result set. Most of these types of calls return summary information about information entities in the UDDI registry. This summary information includes the key of the found information entities. Examples of find call types are find_tModel, find_business, and find_service.

As mentioned previously, find qualifiers are used to narrow the search for information entities in the find_xxx call. The find qualifiers use a two-level structure in which the parent element findQualifiers serves as a container of the child element findQualifier. Each findQualifier element contains a findQualifier value. These values together determine the results returned.

Once the summary information about an information entity is obtained by the using the find_*xxx* call, the summary information, which includes the keys of the matched entities, is used in the get_*xxx*Detail call as the input to obtain detailed information on the matched entities. Examples of such types of calls include get_tModelDetail, get_serviceDetail, and get_businessDetail.

Commercial Products

Of the various Web Services standards discussed in this book, the adoption of the UDDI standard by the computer industry has been the most difficult because of some of its shortcomings. One of the major hurdles is that the classification system used in UDDI is a highly technical taxonomy that fails to capture the Web Service semantic required to fully exploit the potential of Web Services (that is, dynamic discovery, selection, and binding). The second important shortcoming is that UDDI does not provide a standard repository capable of storing artifacts, nor does it provide governance capabilities for managing the end-to-end life cycle of the various types of artifacts related to services.

The industry has tried to solve these problems in multiple ways. Some vendors have used extensions to UDDI in their products, whereas others have adopted a more independent path. In almost all cases, the functions of the registry have been combined with a repository in order to provide the storing of service artifacts and governance capabilities. For example, IBM's application server, WebSphere Application Server (WAS), still supports UDDI. However, IBM's service registry and repository product, WebSphere Service Registry and Repository (WSRR), does not rely on the UDDI standard. Currently, efforts are underway to develop new standards in this area.

Regardless of whether or not a product uses UDDI, the functionality for service discovery in these commercial products is still quite weak. This is because, in order to discover a particular service in one step, you have to know the exact service name or ID. This is undesirable for the following reasons:

- A goal of Web Services and Service-Oriented Architecture (SOA) is to decouple as much as possible the service provider from the service consumer. The service consumer is usually a programmer writing a client application, whereas the service provider is another programmer/developer who develops a service. Because consumer programmers can only discover a service through a registry, if they know the exact name or key, they must have a direct/indirect communication with the provider-side programmer/developer, thus forcing a strong coupling between the service provider and the service consumer developers.

This may be difficult given that all large corporations are spread across the globe.

- Guessing the exact name or key of a service without direct communication with the service provider is also made difficult by the fact that word usage varies depending on location. For example, the word "elevator" (commonly used in the U.S.) is replaced by the word "lift" in the U.K. In addition, even within the same locale, different words with the same meaning can be used. For example, the common word "get" can be replaced with "fetch' or "obtain." Similarly, instead of "car," one can also use "automobile" or "vehicle."

- The inability to guess the name or key, and therefore to discover the service definition, usually means that the service consumer programmer cannot incorporate the service in his code until the service provider programmer completes his work on the service and informs the programmer on the client side—either directly or indirectly—as to the specific name or key chosen for the service in order to register the service. This usually results in the delay of the development of consumer or client applications for a given service.

- The ability to discover a service definition without knowing the exact name or key also promotes the portability of client or consumer applications. As an illustration, consider car dealerships of different makes of cars, such as GM, Ford, Toyota, Mazda, and so on. Suppose each of these dealerships develops a service to get the price of its cars. They'll likely use slightly different names, such as getCarPrice, getVehiclePrice, getAutomobilePrice, obtainCarPrice, and so on. Having different names for essentially the same service means that separate consumer applications are needed for each of the brand-name dealerships using the present registries. However, if a registry was able to recognize that all these names refer to the same service, it would be able to return the service definition even though the name in the registry and the client application do not match exactly. Thus, only one consumer application needs to be developed with any one of the obvious names and it will be able to serve all the dealerships.

Currently, efforts are underway at IBM to solve this problem. A particular solution has been identified, and IBM is waiting for related patents to be issued before incorporating such a solution into its products.

Conclusion

In this chapter, you learned about the UDDI registry, which is a central place where a consumer of a Web Service can find information about the service and the service provider. This information is needed by the consumer of the service to invoke the service. The UDDI registry is also the place where a service provider can publish information about itself and the services it offers.

We started out by discussing the basic data model of a UDDI registry. This basic model consists of five entities: businessEntity, businessService, bindingTemplate, publisherAssertion, and tModel. A businessEntity is used to store information about a service provider such as its name and address. Nontechnical information about a service is stored in the structure businessService. Technical information related to a service and its end point is stored in the entity bindingTemplate. Perhaps the most important entity is the tModel, which serves the dual purpose of providing a technical fingerprint of a service and an abstract namespace. You also learned how to store categorization and identification information in a tModel using categoryBag and identifierBag containers. We also covered how to author or partition a WSDL document related to a service so that it can be easily referenced in a bindingTemplate and a tModel. We also briefly discussed the two APIs offered by the UDDI specification for publishing and for inquiring about an existing service. Finally, we discussed the various commercial products available and some of the future directions for the improvement of these products.

With the completion of this chapter, we have reached the end of our discussion of the standards related to Web Services. These standards are XML, SOAP, WSDL, and UDDI. In addition to these standards, we discussed the WS-I Basic Profile, which provides more stringent requirements over and above the other four standards. The purpose of these additional requirements is to ensure the interoperability of Web Services across different platforms. Both application developers and platform vendors must follow the WS-I Basic Profile to guarantee interoperability.

In the next chapter, you will learn how to develop Web Services based on the standards that we have discussed in this and the last three chapters. In the next chapter we will describe two different approaches for developing Web Services: a top-down approach and a bottom-up approach. In the top-down approach WSDL is developed first and then the skeleton for the service providers, and the service client is obtained through the use of an automated tool. The developer then completes the skeleton for the service provider according to the design. In the bottom-up approach Java Classes or Components are developed first and then a WSDL document is derived from these classes and components.

Web Services Implementation

In the last four chapters, we discussed the various standards that constitute the Web Services. In this chapter, we discuss how these standards are put to use in developing Web Services. In particular, we will employ XML, the related XML schemas, WSDL, and SOAP for developing these services.

Because all the messages in the Web Services are exchanged through SOAP, we start with a discussion of the two major choices for a SOAP engine. A SOAP engine is simply a framework for constructing SOAP processors such as clients, servers, and gateways. These two choices are Apache SOAP 2.3 and the JAX-RPC implementation, which includes the Apache Axis engine. JAX-RPC stands for *Java API for XML remote procedure call.* In this chapter, we only briefly discuss the Apache SOAP engine because the use of this engine has been deprecated due to poor performance when large documents are involved. This poor performance is the result of the use of the DOM parser in the Apache SOAP engine. Next, we discuss the JAX-RPC implementations of the SOAP engine, including the Apache Axis engine. The Axis engine employs the SAX parser instead of the DOM parser in order to obtain much better performance when large XML documents need to be processed. Another advantage of the JAX-RPC implementation is that the structure of the SOAP engine is highly modular, as you will see in the next section. We also discuss JSR 109, which is an extension of the JAX-RPC specification to the J2EE environment.

After discussing SOAP engines, we turn our attention to the main subject of this chapter—how to develop Web Services and their clients. For this purpose, one of two approaches is usually employed: the top-down approach or the bottom-up approach. In the top-down approach, a WSDL document containing the Web Service description is constructed first and then an automated tool is used to generate the code both for the client side and the server side. The top-down approach is the recommended approach for developing Web Services, and we will discuss this approach in detail, including the various files generated by the automated tool. In the bottom-up approach, Java classes or EJBs are developed first and then automated tools are employed to expose these classes as Web Services. These tools also generate the required WSDL documents. We will only briefly mention this method of developing Web Services because it is not the recommended approach for constructing Web Services. We will deal only with Java-based services because Java is the most common environment for developing services. However, it should be noted that there are other ways of developing Web Services, including services based on .NET or C++.

Finally, at the end of this chapter, we discuss some of the commercial tools available for developing services.

Implementation Choices

When it comes to implementing Web Services and their clients, you first must choose a SOAP engine. A SOAP engine is a framework for constructing SOAP processors such as clients, servers, gateways, and so on. In general, the two most common choices are

- Apache SOAP 2.3

- The JAX-RPC implementation, including Apache Axis.

The Apache SOAP 2.3 is based on IBM's donated code for SOAP4J. This code was donated to the Apache Foundation by IBM. It includes an implementation of SOAP 1.1, and has been used in the past as the core SOAP engine for a number of past WebSphere releases.

Figure 15.1 shows the architecture for Apache SOAP. The engine provides two servlets that are deployed in the application server's web container. One of the servlets handles RPC-style calls whereas the other handles messaging-type calls. The servlets call the SOAP engine, which looks for the name of the configuration manager in the file soap.xml. The default configuration manager provided with the distribution is org.apache.soap.server.XMLConfigurationManager. The manager is designed to look for the file dds.xml, which is the deployment descriptor for the services implemented in the web application. A graphical interface is also provided to simplify the maintenance of this file through a browser.

The Apache SOAP distribution also provides a client API, which is based on the class org.apache.soap.rpc.Call. This API provides a simple mechanism for the developer to use when creating RPC-style SOAP requests without requiring the developer to understand the schema for the SOAP message in any detail.

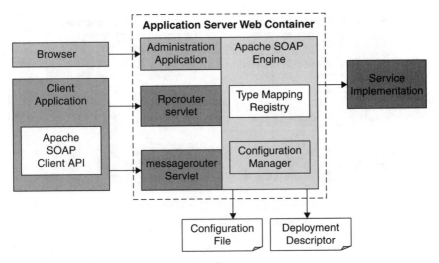

Figure 15.1   SOAP Apache structure overview

The major disadvantage of Apache SOAP is that it uses a DOM-based XML parser, which is not well suited for large XML documents because it causes poor performance when large documents are processed. IBM has deprecated Apache SOAP in favor of the second choice, which we are about to discuss. This second SOAP engine uses a SAX parser for improved performance.

The second implementation approach is based on an API known as Java API for XML Remote Procedure Call (JAX-RPC). This API allows all clients to use javax.xml.rpc.Call instead of a specific implementation such as org.apache.soap.rpc.Call. We discuss this API in detail later in this section. It is expected that all future Web Services implementations will provide interfaces based on the JAX-RPC standard.

To address some of the shortcomings of the Apache SOAP engine, the Apache organization decided to develop a new SOAP engine. It is called Apache eXtensible Interaction System (Axis). The most important new aspect of this SOAP engine is that it uses a SAX XML parser instead of a DOM XML parser. The SAX parser provides performance advantages when dealing with large XML documents. Axis also supports many extensions to provide for different invocation mechanisms and protocols.

The basic structure of Axis is shown in Figure 15.2. The figure shows that the Axis architecture is highly modular. Different handlers, which process different SOAP headers, are connected in chains. The handler chains can be defined at different levels, such as the transport, global, and service levels. It is important to note that the Axis engine can be

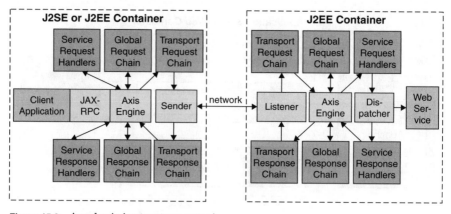

Figure 15.2   Apache Axis structure overview

used both in the role of service requester and service provider. This dual-purpose engine provides the benefit of using similar implementations for tasks such as XML encryption, XML signature, and authentication on both the service provider and service consumer sides.

Next we discuss the JAX-RPC API is detail. The Java API for XML Remote Procedure Call (JAX-RPC) includes a standard interface for developers to use when building both the client-side service requesters and the server-side service providers. JAX-RPC also defines the contract between a Web Service runtime container and a service implementation. A schematic view of JAX-RPC is shown in Figure 15.3.

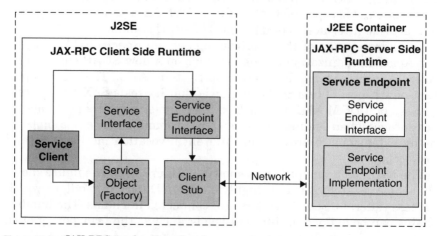

Figure 15.3   JAX-RPC implementation view

TABLE 15.1   JAX-RPC Terms

New Term	Description
Service end point	A collection of artifacts that provides the implementation of the service provider
Service end point interface	A Java interface that defines all the methods exposed by the Web Service. This interface extends java.rmi.Remote.
Service end point implementation	A Java class that provides the implementation of the service and implements a service point interface
Service interface	A Java interface that extends javax.xml.rpc.Service. It defines the factory methods to instantiate the service end point interface.
Service object	A Java class that provides the implementation of the factory methods and implements the service interface
Client stub	A vendor-supplied class that provides a client-side stub for the service end point interface
Service client	A Java class that calls the Web Service and is portable between JAX-RPC implementations

This figure introduces a number of new terms related to JAX-RPC. The meanings of these terms are summarized in Table 15.1. Almost all artifacts in this table are generated by the deployment tools provided with any JAX-RPC runtime. The exceptions are the service client and service end point implementations.

The JAX-RPC specification also defines a second invocation mechanism known as the *dynamic invocation interface (DII)*. The clients of DII use the service object to dynamically create an instance of a service end point interface. The methods and parameters of this interface can be discovered at runtime through inspection.

The JAX-RPC specification for Web Services has been extended for J2EE and is known as JSR 109. JSR 109 is an extension specification that defines how service definitions are declared within a J2EE application. A major advantage of using a J2EE container is that it allows the use of the JNDI naming service. This eliminates the need for the service consumer to invoke the service object factory class directly. Instead of using the factory class directly, the client applications use JNDI to look up the service reference. This ensures that the service client is completely portable between JSR-compliant runtimes.

In addition, JSR 109 defines both the client and server Web Service deployment descriptor formats. The files for these deployment descriptors are webservicesclient.xml and webservices.xml. These files define the JNDI service reference for the service client and the location of the service end point implementation for the service provider. The JSR 109 structure is shown schematically in Figure 15.4.

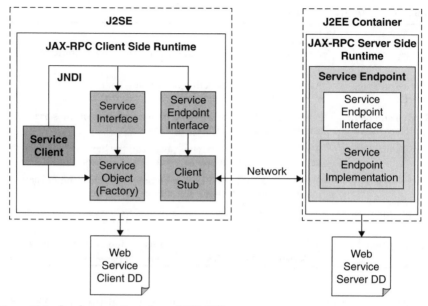

Figure 15.4 Implementation view of JSR 109

It is important to note that both that service requester and service provider, which are compliant with JSR 109, can interoperate with any other service implementation. In particular, JSR 109 does not preclude the service being invoked by a J2SE client using the default JAX-RPC mechanism.

In the case of JSR 109, the service requester could be a session EJB. The constraints imposed by JAX-RPC on the interfaces to be implemented and the exceptions thrown are somewhat relaxed by JSR 109. The only requirement is that the service implementation must implement all the operations of the service end point interface.

Building Web Service Clients

We first focus on the top-down approach to building Web Service clients, in which WSDL is constructed first and then a tool is used to generate the Web Service and the Web Service client. In discussing the files generated by the tool, we will only focus on the most basic structure of the files and ignore the other, more detailed structures that may be created by using the tool. Specifically, we will concentrate on the files generated by the tools WSDL2Java and Java2WSDL. The IBM-provided tools wrap these two tools to provide more functionality;

they should be used for production class Web Services. We use these tools in our discussion in order to focus on the most basic aspects of services files generation.

For this discussion we assume that a WSDL file called AddressBook .wsdl defines the interface and implementation portions of the Web Service, which corresponds to a telephone address book. WSDL was discussed in detail in Chapter 13. The service defines a single operation, addEntry(), that is used to enter a new phone address in the phone book along with a name.

The invocation command is shown in Listing 15-1. Note that this assumes you are in the directory that contains the WSDL file for the Web Service.

Listing 15-1

```
%java org.apache.axis.wsdl.WSDL2Java AddressBook.wsdl
```

The generated files would be put in a directory, which we will call AddressFetcher. The files are put in this particular directory because it is the target namespace from the WSDL file, and namespaces map to Java packages. Namespaces were discussed in Chapter 11.

Before we discuss the generated files that correspond to each section of the WSDL file, we need to note the standard mappings from WSDL to Java types. These mappings are summarized in Table 15.2.

Corresponding to each section, the tool generates one or more files. These generated files and the WSDL sections they correspond to are shown in Table 15.3.

TABLE 15.2   WSDL-to-Java Standard Mappings

WSDL Type	Java Type
xsd:boolean	boolean
xsd:int	int
xsd:integer	java.math.BigInteger
xsd:long	long
xsd:short	short
xsd:decimal	java.math.BigDecimal
xsd:float	float
xsd:double	double
xsd:string	java.lang.String
xsd:dateTime	java.util.Calendar

TABLE 15.3 Generated Classes Corresponding to the Different Sections of the WSDL Document

WSDL Section	Generated Java Class(es)
For each entry in the type section	A java class A holder class if this type is used as an inout or out parameter
For each portType	A java interface
For each binding	A stub class
For each service	A service interface A service implementation (the locator)

Next, we consider each section of the WSDL and the generated files that correspond to those sections, starting with the types section.

The types Section

For simplicity, we assume that this types section contains only one type, which is an XML complexType, as shown in Listing 15-2. The listing shows that the name attribute of the complexType is phone and the three elements correspond to the area code, telephone exchange, and number. Two of these elements are of the xsd:string type, and the third element is of type xsd:int.

Listing 15-2

```
<xsd:complexType name="phoneNumber">
        <xsd:all>
                <xsd:element name="areaCode" type="xsd:int"/>
                <xsd:element name="exchange" type="xsd:
string"/>
                <xsd:element name="number" type="xsd:string"/>
        </xsd:all>
</xsd:complexType>
```

WSDL2Java would create the class shown in Listing 15-3, which in this case is a bean (as is typically the case) from the preceding section of the WSDL file.

Listing 15-3

```
public class PhoneNumber implements java.io.Serializable {
    private int areaCode;
    private java.lang.String exchange;
    private java.lang.String number;
    public int getAreaCode ( ) {
        return areaCode;     }
```

```
        public void setAreaCode ( int areaCode) {
            this.areaCode=areaCode;                                    }
        public java.lang.String getExchange () {
            return exchange;        }
        public void setExchange ( java.lang.String exchange) {
            this.exchange=exchange; }
        public java.lang.String getNumber () {
            return number;      }
        public void setNumber ( java.lang.String number )   {
            this.number = number ;        }
        public boolean equals (Object obj) {   …..}
        public int hashCode () {  ….. }
}
```

The first thing to notice in the generated code is that the class name is Phone, whereas the XML name was phone. Therefore, the tool has capitalized the first letter of the name to match the Java convention that class names begin with an uppercase letter. The second thing to notice from the generated code that corresponds to the three elements of the complexType in XML, is that the bean has three properties. The types of these elements are mapped according to Table 15.2. All three properties of the bean have getter and setter methods. Finally, notice that this bean implements the java.io.serializable interface so that the bean can be transported over the network.

In addition to this bean, the tool also generates a holder class from the types section of the WSDL file, as shown in Listing 15-4. This holder class is typically used as an inout or out parameter. This is because Java does not have the concept of inout/out parameters. In order to achieve this behavior, JAX-RPC specifies the use of the holder class. (A holder class is simply a class that contains an instance of its type.) The holder for the Phone class is shown in Listing 15-4.

Listing 15-4

```
Public final class PhoneHolder implements javax.xml.rpc.
holders.Holder   {
        public Phone value;
        public PhoneHolder ()   {
        }
        public PhoneHolder () {
        }
        public PhoneHolder ( Phone value)   {
            this.value = value;
        }
}
```

A holder class is generated for a type if that type is used as an inout or out parameter. Note that the holder class has the suffix "Holder" appended to its name.

The portTypes Section

Next, we consider the tool-generated Java code that corresponds to the portType section of the WSDL service definition file. In this case, the tool generates a Java interface called Service Definition Interface (SDI) for each portType. For example, given the WSDL shown in Listing 15-5, the WSDL2Java tool will generate the Java code in Listing 15-6.

Listing 15-5

```
<message name="empty"/>
<message name="AddEntryRequest">
      <part name="name" type="xsd:string"/>
      <part name="address" type=types"address"/>
</message>
<portType   name="AddressBook">
       <operation name="addEntry">
              <input message="tns:AddEntryRequest"/>
              <output message="tns:empty"/>
       </operation>
</portType>
```

Listing 15-6

```
public interface AddressBook extends java.rmi.Remote {
      public void addEntry (String name, Address address)   throws
             java.rmi.RemoteException;
}
```

It is important to note that although the name of the SDI is typically the name of the portType, the WSDL2Java tool needs information from both the portType and the binding portion of the WSDL file. This feature adds some complexity, the discussion of which is beyond the scope of this chapter.

The binding Section

The WSDL2Java tool generates a stub class for each binding. This stub's name is the binding name with the suffix "Stub" appended. This stub class implements the SDI generated in the last subsection. The stub class contains the Java code that turns the method invocations into SOAP calls using the Axis Service and Call objects. The stub class stands in as a proxy for the remote service, allowing you to call the service as if it were a local object. In other words, you do not need to deal with the end point URL, namespace, or parameter arrays involved in the dynamic invocation via the Service and Call objects.

Listing 15-7 shows the binding section of a WSDL document.

Listing 15-7

```
<binding name="AddressBookSOAPBinding"  type="tns:AddressBook">
    ... .
</binding>
```

The tool WSDL2Java will generate the Java code in Listing 15-8.

Listing 15-8

```
public class AddressBookSOAPBindingStub extends
    org.apache.axis.client.stub  implements AddressBook
    public AddressBookSOAPBindingStub () throws
        org.apache.axis.AxisFault {   ...  }
   public AddressBookSOAPBindingStub ( URL endPointURL,
            javax.xml.rpc.Service service ) throws
        org.apache.axis.AxisFault {   ...  }
  public AddressBookSOAPBindingStub ( javax.xml.rpc.Service service )
        throws org.apache.axis.AxisFault {  ....  }
 public void addEntry ( String name, Address address )
        throws RemoteException {  ....  }
}
```

Note that three different constructors for this class are provided, in addition to a method that corresponds to the sole operation defined in the WSDL document, as shown in a previous subsection.

The service Section

Typically, a client program would not instantiate a stub class directly. Instead, it would instantiate a service locator and then call a method on the service locator that returns an instance of the stub class. This locator is derived from the service section of the WSDL document. The WSDL2Java tool generates two objects from a service section. Listing 15-9 shows the service section of a WSDL document.

Listing 15-9

```
<service name="AddressBookService">
   <port name="AddressBook"  binding="tns:
AddressBookSOAPBinding">
            <soap:address            location=http://
localhost:8080/axisServices/AddressBook/>
    </port>
</service>
```

Using this service section in the WSDL2Java tool would generate the service interface shown in Listing 15-10.

Listing 15-10

```
public interface AddressBookService extends javax.xml.rpc.Service {
     public String getAddressBook Address ();
     public AddressBook getAddressBook () throws
         javax.xml.rpc.ServiceException;
     public AddressBook getAddressBook (URL portAddress)
         throws javax.xml.rpc.ServiceException;
}
```

The WSDL2Java tool also creates a locator class that implements this interface, as shown in Listing 15-11.

Listing 15-11

```
public class AddressBookServiceLocator extends
     org.apache.axis.client.Service  implements AddressBookService {
....
....
}
```

For each port listed in the WSDL document, the tool generates a get method in this interface. The locator is the implementation of this service interface, and it implements these get methods. In other words, it serves as a locator of Stub class instances. Also note that the Service class, by default, will create a Stub class that points to the end point URL described in the WSDL file, but you may also specify a different URL when you ask for the portType.

The Java code in Listing 15-12 shows how the Stub class is typically used.

Listing 15-12

```
public class demo {
    public static void main (String [] arg) throws Exception
       {
            // create a service locator
           AddressBookService service= new AddressBookServiceLocator ();
           // use the service locator to obtain a stub
          AddressBook book = service.getAddressBook ();
          // invoke the real method on the stub
          Address address = new Address ( ... );
          book.addEntry ("John Smith", address);
    }
}
```

This concludes our discussion of the client-side code generated by WSDL2Java using the top-down (WSDL first) approach. Next, we consider the server-side code generated using the same approach and the same tool (that is, WSDL2Java).

Building Web Services

In the top-down approach, automated tools can also be used to generate server-side skeleton classes that represent the Web Services. The tool can generate a skeleton that is a Java framework. Once again, the tools provided by IBM are the best for producing production-class skeleton code. However, for simplicity's sake, in this section we will use the open-source tool WSDL2Java supplied by the Apache foundation.

In using the WSDL2Java tool to create server-side skeleton classes, you must specify the "—serverside –skeletonDeploy true" options. The command shown in Listing 15-13 is an example of how this tool can be used to create server-side skeleton classes using AddressBook.wsdl as input.

Listing 15-13

```
%java org.apache.axis.wsdl.WSDL2Java  --server-side  --skeletonDeploy true
     AddressBokk.wsdl
```

Table 15.4 provides all the additional files and classes generated by the tool when the preceding command is executed. This table also shows the section of the WSDL file that corresponds to the generated files and classes.

If the "—skeletonDeploy true" option is not specified, a skeleton will not be generated. Instead, the generated deploy.wsdd file will indicate that the implementation class is deployed directly. In this case, deploy.wsdd contains extra metadata describing the operation and the parameters of the implementation class. Note that *wsdd* stands for Web Services Deployment Descriptor.

Next, we briefly discuss each of the two classes generated corresponding to a binding section of the WSDL file.

Skeleton Class

The skeleton class is the class that sits between the Axis (SOAP) engine and the actual service implementation. The name of this skeleton class is the name of the binding with "Skeleton" appended at the end.

TABLE 15.4   Server-Side Files Generated by WSDL2Java

WSDL Section	Java Class(es) or Files Created
For each binding	A skeleton class An implementation template class
For all services	One deploy.wsdd file One undeploy.wsdd file

The skeleton class generated by the WSDL2Java tool would be similar to the one shown in the Listing 15-14.

Listing 15-14

```
public class AddressBookSOAPBindingSkeleton implements AddressBook
        org.apache.axis.wsdl.Skeleton {
        private AddressBook addressBook;

    public AddressBookSOAPBindingSkeleton () {
            this.addressBook = new AddressBOOKSOAPBindingImpl ();
    }
    public AdressBookSOAPBindingSkeleton (AddressBook impl)    {
            this.addressBook = impl;
    }
    public void addEntry (String name, Address address )
            throws java.rmi.RemoteException {
        addressBook.addEntry ( name, address);
    }
}
```

This skeleton contains an implementation of the AddressBook service. Either the implementation is passed into the skeleton upon invoking the constructor or an instance of the implementation is created. When the Axis(SOAP) engine calls the skeleton's addEntry method, it simply delegates the invocation to the real implementation's addEntry method.

Implementation Template

The WSDL2Java tool also generates an implementation template from the binding. This template can be used for the actual implementation. The template looks similar to the one shown in Listing 15-15.

Listing 15-15

```
public class AddressBookSOAPBindingImpl implements
    AddressBook    {
        public void addEntry (String name, Address address )
                throws java.rmi.RemoteException {
        }
}
```

The developer will fill out the addEntry method in this template to provide the real implementation of the service operation.

Deployment Descriptors

The WSDL2Java tool also generates deploy.wsdd and undeploy.wsdd files for each service. These files can be used to deploy the service once the developer has filled in the methods of the implementation class, compiled the code, and made the classes available to the Axis engine.

Bottom-Up Approach

In this approach, the developer either creates a Java interface (or class) or uses an existing Java class (or interface). Then the developer uses the automated tool, Java2WSDL, to generate a WSDL service description document. Finally, WSDL2Java is used to generate the binding and the artifacts needed on the server side and the client side.

We now briefly cover these steps using a simple example of a Java interface that provides two methods for setting and getting the price of a car model. The Java code for this interface is shown in Listing 15-16.

Listing 15-16

```
package example;
public interface CarPrice {
     public void setCarPrice (String modelName, string price);
     public String getCarPrice (String modelName);
}
```

The creation of this code for the Java interface constitutes the first step mentioned previously. We store this interface definition in the file CarPrice.java.

In the second step, we use the Java2WSDL interface definition file to generate a WSDL file that contains the service description. Listing 15-17 shows the command line use of the tool.

Listing 15-17

```
%java  org.apache.axis.wsdl.Java2WSDL -o carprice.wsdl  -l
http://localhost:8080/services/CarPrice  -n "urn:example" -p "examples"
"urn:example" examples.CarPrice
```

The various options used in this command line are summarized in Table 15.5.

TABLE 15.5   Explanation of the Options in Listing 15-17

Option	Description
-o	Specifies the name of the output WSDL file. In this case, we have chosen the name carprice.wsdl.
-l	This option describes the location of the service.
-n	This option specifies the namespace for the WSDL file.
-p	This option defines the mapping from the Java package name to a namespace. You can specify multiple mappings like the one shown.

TABLE 15.6   The Generated Files from Listing 15-18

Generated File	Description
CarPrice.java	A new interface that extends Java.rmi.remote.
CarPriceSOAPBindingImpl.java	The Java file containing the default server implementation of the CarPrice Web Service. The developer will need to modify the *SoapBindingImpl file.
CarPriceService.java	A Java file containing the client-side service interface.
CarPriceServiceLocator.java	This file contains client-side service implementation class.
CarPriceSOAPBindingSkeleton.java	This file contains the generated server-side skeleton.
CarPriceSOAPBinding Stub	This file contains the client-side service stub.
deploy.wsdd	The deployment descriptor file for the Web Service.
undeploy.wsdd	This file contains the descriptor for undeploying the Web Service.

The output WSDL document will contain the appropriate WSDL types, messages, portType, bindings, and service descriptions to support a SOAP RPC encoding Web Service.

In the third and the final step, we use the tool WSDL2Java to generate both the server-side and the client-side bindings. A typical invocation of this tool for our current example is shown in Listing 15-18.

Listing 15-18

```
%java org.apache.axis.wsdl.WSDL2Java -o . -d Session -s S true -N
urn:examples examples carprice.wsdl
```

This invocation will create a number of files. These files are described in Table 15.6.

This concludes our description of the bottom-up approach using the tools supplied by the Apache Axis engine. Next, we discuss some commercial tools that provide additional features for the development and deployment of Web Services.

Commercial Tools

Several commercial tools are available on the market that can be used to develop services and their clients. These are typically production-class tools and have additional features compared to open-source or free tools. We describe only the tools from IBM in this section for the sake of consistency—and because IBM tools may also be the best for the commercial development of Web Services and their clients. Two major tools are offered by IBM for the development of Web Services and services clients:

- The WSDK Toolset
- Rational Application Developer (RAD)

Our preferred implementation for JAX-RPC and JSR 109 is the WSDK Toolset. Therefore, we discuss it first.

WSDK stands for WebSphere Services Development Kit and is based on the Apache SOAP engine, Axis. This toolkit includes a number of command-line tools to help develop the Web Services using either one of the two approaches: top-down or bottom-up.

The two command-line tools for the bottom-up approach are Bean2WebService and EJB2WebService. The first is a utility for creating relevant artifacts to expose a bean as a Web Service. In addition, this utility creates all the files required for a service client. This utility is built on top of the Apache Axis command-line tool. The second utility, EJB2WebService, converts a session EJB into a Web Service using a bottom-up approach. This utility also wraps an Apache Axis command-line tool.

The third utility included in the WSDL toolset is WSDL2WebService. This utility uses a top-down approach to create a Web Service implementation skeleton for a given WSDL service specification. This utility is also built on top of Apache's Axis command-line tools.

In addition to the three aforementioned utilities, WSDK includes two other utilities that are needed for developing and testing Web Services. One of the command-line utilities is appserver. This utility is used to support the administration of the provided application server. This tool allows users to deploy, undeploy, and manage enterprise applications as well as to start and stop the application server itself. Another command-line utility included in the WSDK toolset is tcpmon. This utility provides a graphical TCP/IP monitor. Lastly, it is important to note that WSDK comes with a number of online tutorials and a graphical help system. Trial downloads of a full-featured WSDK are available from the IBM website to help serve as a starting point for your organization.

Although WSDK is our recommended toolset for developing and testing Web Services, Rational Application Developer (RAD) also provides a comprehensive set of wizards to develop both Web Services and their clients.

RAD offers the following features for developing services and related tasks:

- Create Web Services using a bottom-up approach either from a Java bean or from a stateless session EJB.
- Create Web Services using a top-down approach starting from a WSDL document and creating either a Java bean skeleton or a stateless session EJB.
- Create a SOAP message monitor.
- Deploy, run, test, and publish Web Services providers.

In addition, RAD also offers a wizard for creating Web Services clients. RAD supports the development of the following four kinds of Web Services clients:

- Standalone Java application
- Web client
- EJB client
- J2EE application client

RAD also offers tools for deploying, running, and testing Web Services clients. Note that with RAD version 6, you may not need to install a separate application server.

Conclusion

This chapter discussed the implementation of Web Services. We started out by describing the two SOAP engines that commonly form the basis of Web Services development. The first implementation is based on Apache SOAP 2.3. This implementation employs a DOM XML parser and therefore is not suitable when large XML documents are to be processed. As a result, the implementation based on this SOAP engine has been deprecated. The second implementation is based on the JAX-RPC and JSR 109 specifications. This implementation employs a SAX XML parser, which is very efficient for processing large XML documents. These implementations or SOAP engines also have a highly modular structure.

Following the discussion of the two SOAP engines, we described the two approaches for developing Web Services and their clients using the JAX-RPC and JSR 109 specifications. We described both the top-down approach and the bottom-up approach for developing Web Services and their clients. Both of these methods can employ automated tools for the development work. The top-down approach is the favored approach because it aligns very well with the overall SOA approach. In addition to the free tools available, we discussed some commercial tools that are suitable for production-class development. Among these, the premier tools are the WSDK toolset and Rational Application Developer from IBM. In the case of Java-based Web Services, the services can be based on either simple Java classes or stateless session EJBs. The Java clients of Web Services can be implemented in a number of different ways. In the case of Java-based development, we discussed how the various elements of the WSDL document map to the Java types, classes, and packages.

This chapter concludes our discussion of the Web Services standards and the approaches for developing Web Services and their clients. These Web Services standards included XML and XML schema, SOAP, WSDL, and UDDI, whereas the Web Services development approaches included top-down and bottom-up. However, our discussion of Web Services Clients is not yet complete. This is because the Web Services Clients we have discussed so far are suitable when the call to a service provider is simple and isolated. In many cases, such as business processes, this is not the case. We discuss the business process in the next chapter.

Integration Through Service Composition (BPEL)

In the last five chapters we discussed the standards that constitute Web Services and how to develop Web Services. In the last chapter, we discussed how to develop Web Services clients. In this development of the clients, we assumed that the interaction of the client application with the service provided would be isolated and simple. Such activities are stateless and result in uncorrelated service calls. If a program or application invokes Web Service A and following that invokes Web Service B, then Web Service B doesn't have any knowledge of what happened in Web Service A. Such is the case for many integration scenarios.

However, in many other scenarios the interaction of the client with the service is not so simple. Such is the case with many, and if not all, business processes. A *business process* is a collection of related, structured activities or tasks that produces a specific product (serves a particular goal) or service for a particular customer (or customers). A process begins with a customer's need and ends with the fulfillment of the need. Common examples of such business processes include planning business travel and purchasing.

Because a business process involves complex, related, and structured activities, it requires a stateful environment for invoking a chain of Web Services that implement the business process. Therefore, a model is needed for describing complex exchanges that characterize business interactions that includes sequences of peer-to-peer messages and stateful long-running interactions. An example of a business process that requires long-running interactions is a customer order for a product. This business process begins when the order is received and ends when the product is shipped. It may take hours, days, or weeks for the complete fulfillment of the order.

The Business Process Execution Language (BPEL) for Web Services (or BPEL4WS) is a language for describing such long-running, stateful interactions and executing these processes. In a BPEL representation, a business process is seen as a collection of coordinated service invocations and related activities that produces a result, either within a single enterprise or across several enterprises. An example of such complex interactions is shown in Figure 16.1, which describes a purchase order business process. This process invokes several services, including shipping service, invoice service, and production scheduling service.

Note: In this chapter, we will use the acronyms BPEL and BPEL4WS interchangeably.

We begin this chapter with an overview of the BPEL structure and the various types of activities, including primitive and structuring activities. This overview is followed by a somewhat detailed description of the various elements and structure of BPEL. Then we look at an example of a business process that illustrates how different primitive and structuring activities are used together to describe a business process in BPEL.

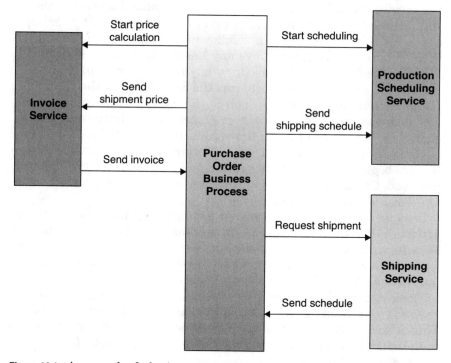

Figure 16.1   An example of a business process based on service composition

Overview

BPEL4WS, or simply BPEL, is based on three XML specifications: WSDL, XML schema, and XPath, as shown schematically in Figure 16.2. The data model used by BPEL processes is provided by WSDL messages and XML schema definitions. XPath provides support for data manipulation. All external resources and partners are represented as WSDL services. BPEL provides extensibility to accommodate future versions of these standards, specifically the XPath and related standards used in XML computation.

Primarily, two kinds of activities are defined in BPEL. Some activities are primitive activities, whereas others are structuring activities. Primitive activities help to define the basic tasks that make up the business process, whereas structuring activities help to define the control flow of the business process. Figure 16.3 shows the primitive and structuring activities separately.

In addition to primitive activities and structuring elements, BPEL also defines three more important elements: process, partnerLinks and variables. The process element is used to define various namespaces and provide a name to the business process. The partnerLinks element

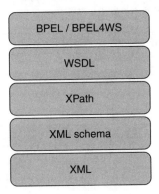

Figure 16.2   BPEL's relationships with XML, XML schema, XPath, and WSDL

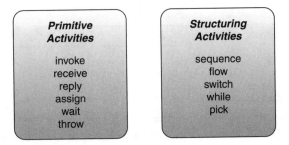

Figure 16.3   Primitive and structuring activities in BPEL

defines the different parties that interact with the BPEL process. These parties include all Web Services that will be invoked and the clients of the process. partnerLinks also specifies the different roles played by these interacting parties. The variables element is used to store, reformat, and transform messages. Generally, we use a variable for every message sent to and received from the Web Services. BPEL starts with the process declaration element (process), which is used to define the process name and namespaces. The typical arrangement of a BPEL document is depicted schematically in Figure 16.4. This figure will become clearer after we discuss each element in the next section.

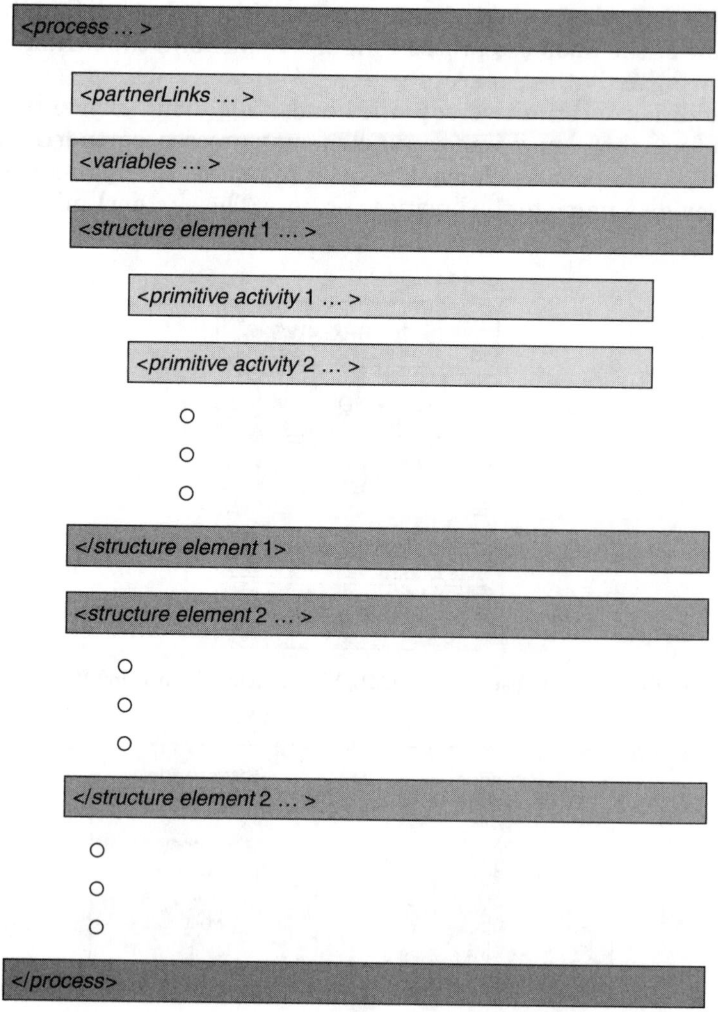

```
<process ... >
    <partnerLinks ... >
    <variables ... >
    <structure element 1 ... >
        <primitive activity 1 ... >
        <primitive activity 2 ... >
            O
            O
            O
    </structure element 1>
    <structure element 2 ... >
            O
            O
            O
    </structure element 2 ... >
        O
        O
        O
</process>
```

Figure 16.4   A typical arrangement of activities and other elements in a BPEL document

BPEL is similar to other programming languages but is geared toward the characteristics of a business process. BPEL provides a means to express complex flows, making it relatively easy to call asynchronous operations and wait for the callback. BPEL also provides event handlers and fault handlers.

From the client perspective, the BPEL process appears the same as any other Web Service because the BPEL process itself is described using WSDL. This is important because it allows Web Services to be composed into simple processes, simple processes into more complex processes, and so on.

To execute the instructions contained in a BPEL document for a business process, a runtime environment called BPEL server is required. A BPEL server usually provides control over process instances that are executing or have completed. It also provides support for long-running processes by dehydrating the process state (that is, by saving the state on the disk) to save resources. Some of BPEL servers may also provide control over process activities and allow their monitoring. Because all processes are deployed centrally, it eases the maintenance.

A number of commercial BPEL servers are available, including servers from IBM (WebSphere Business Process Server), Microsoft, and BEA. In addition, open-source BPEL servers include ActiveBPEL engine, Apache Agila, bexee, and FiveSight PXE.

Detailed Description

This section provides more detailed descriptions of various elements of BPEL. Three kinds of elements/activities were mentioned in the last section: primitive activities, structuring activities, and miscellaneous elements such as partnerLinks and variables. We now discuss the elements/activities contained in each of these categories, starting with the miscellaneous elements/activities.

Miscellaneous Elements

The elements in this category are usually the first few elements in a BPEL document. Therefore, we will discuss these elements first. We start out by discussing the process element.

The process Element   The process element is the first element of a BPEL document. It defines the name of the process and the various namespaces used in the BPEL document. An example of this element is shown in Listing 16-1. This process element has a name attribute that is used to specify the name of the process. In this listing, we have named the process BusinessTravel. The next attribute is the target namespace;

then we define the various namespaces we will need to complete the BPEL document.

Listing 16-1

```
Listing 16.1 : An example of process element
1    <process name="BusinessTravel"
2         targetNamespace=http://myCompany.com/bpel/businessTravel/
3         xmlns=http://schemas.xmlsoap.org/ws/2003/03/business-process/
4         xmlns:bpws=http://schemas.xmlsoap.org/ws/2003/03/business-process/
5         xmlns:travel=http://myCompany.com/bpel/travel/
6         xmlns:airline=http://myCompany.com/service/airline/>
```

The partnerLinks Element   This element is used to define the different parties that interact with the BPEL process. These parties include all the Web Services that will be invoked and the client of the process. The partnerLinks element can have one or more subelements called *partnerLinks*. Each of these subelements specifies one party with the name attribute. In addition, each of these subelements has two other attributes: myRole, which indicates the role of the business process itself, and partnerRole, which indicates the role of the party. Listing 16-2 provides an example of the partnerLinks element. This particular example has two subelements corresponding to two parties—the client and an airline.

Listing 16-2

```
Listing 16.2: Example of partnerLinks element
1    <partnerLinks>
2         <partnerLink name="client"
3              partnerLinkType="travel:travelLT"
4              myRole="travelService"
5              partnerRole="travelServiceClient"/>
6         <partnerLink name="myAirline"
7              partnerLinkType="airline:flightLT"
8              myRole="airlineCustomer"
9              partnerRole="airlineService"/>
10   </partnerLinks>
```

The variables Element   This element is used to define the variables used to store, reformat, and transform messages. Commonly one variable is defined for each message sent to or received from a Web Service. Note that variable is a subelement, and you can have as many of these subelements as you need. Listing 16-3 shows some sample code for this element. In this example, two variables are defined. Each of the subelements has two attributes: name, which is used to identify the variable, and messageType, which indicates the type of the message. The message types are usually defined separately, usually in a WSDL document or XML schema.

Listing 16-3

```
Listing 16.3: Sample code for element variables
1    <variables>
2       <variable name="TravelRequest"
3                     messageType="travel:TravelRequestMessage"/>
4       <variable name="FlightDetails"
5                     messageType="airline:FlightTicketRequestMessage"/>
6    </variables>
```

Primitive Activities

The various activities included in this category are invoke, receive, assign, throw, and wait, as shown earlier in Figure 16.3. We discuss each of these activities, starting with the invoke activity.

The invoke Activity   Invoking an operation on a service is a basic activity. Such an operation can be a synchronous request/response or an asynchronous one-way operation. BPEL4WS uses the same basic syntax for both, with some additional options for the synchronous operation. An asynchronous invocation requires only the input variable of the operation because it does not expect a response as part of the operation. A synchronous invocation requires both an input variable and an output variable. The basic syntax for the invoke activity is shown in the sample code of Listing 16-4. This sample code is used to synchronously invoke a service because both the inputVariable and outputVariable attributes are specified. The service operation name has to be specified as well as the portType attribute value. In addition, the partnerLink attribute value has to be specified.

Listing 16-4

```
Listing 16.4: Sample code for invoking a synchronous operation
on a service
1    <invoke partnerLink="employeeTravelStatus"
2            portType="employee:EmployeeTravelStatusPT"
3            operation="EmployeeTravelStatus"
4            inputVariable="EmployeeTravelStatusRequest"
5            outputVariable="EmployeeTravelStatusResponse" />
```

The receive Activity   A business process provides services to its partners through receive activities and corresponding reply activities. A receive activity specifies the partner link it expects to receive from, as well as the port type and operation it expects the partner to invoke. In addition, it may specify a variable that is to be used to receive the message data. However, this attribute is syntactically optional because it is absolutely required only in executable processes.

In addition, receive activities play a role in the life cycle of a business process. The only way to instantiate a business process in BPEL4WS is to annotate a receive activity with the createInstance attribute set to "yes." The default value of this attribute is "no." A receive activity annotated in this way must be an initial activity in the process—that is, the only other basic activities that may potentially be performed prior to or simultaneously with such a receive activity must be similarly annotated receive activities. Sample code for the receive activity is shown in Listing 16-5. In this sample code, the receive activity is used to receive the initial request from the client of the business process.

Listing 16-5

```
Listing 16.5: Sample code for receive activity
1    <receive partnerLink="client"
2            portType="travel:TravelApprovalPT"
3            operation="TravelApproval"
4            variable="TravelRequest"
5            createInstance="yes" />
```

The reply Activity   A reply activity is used to send a response to a request previously accepted through a receive activity. Such responses are only meaningful for synchronous interactions. An asynchronous response is always sent by invoking the corresponding one-way operation on the partner link. A reply activity may specify a variable that contains the message data to be sent in reply. However, this attribute is syntactically optional because it is absolutely required only in executable processes.

Note that the reply activity corresponding to a given request has two potential forms. If the response to the request is normal, the faultName attribute is not used and the variable attribute, when present, will indicate a variable of the normal response message type. If, on the other hand, the response indicates a fault, the faultName attribute is used and the variable attribute, when present, will indicate a variable of the message type for the corresponding fault. The syntax for the reply activity is shown in Listing 16-6. Note that a trailing question mark (?) indicates an optional attribute. Also note that "ncname" means name without qualification, and "qname" means qualified name.

Listing 16-6

```
Listing 16.6: Syntax for reply activity
1    <reply partnerLink="ncname"
2           portType="qname"
3           operation="ncname"
4           variable="ncname"?
5           faultName="qname"? />
```

The assign Activity   The assign activity can be used to copy data from one variable to another, as well as to construct and insert new data using expressions. The use of expressions is primarily motivated by the need to perform a simple computation (such as incrementing sequence numbers) that is required for describing the business protocol behavior. Expressions operate on message selections, properties, and literal constants to produce a new value for a variable property or selection. Finally, this activity can be used to copy end point references to and from partner links. Listing 16-7 shows two simple examples of copying the values of one variable into another.

Listing 16-7

```
Listing 16.7: example code for the assign activity
1    <assign>
2        <copy>
3            <from variable="c1"/>
4            <to variable="c2"/>
5        </copy>
6        <copy>
7            <from variable="c1" part = "address"/>
8            <to variable="c3"/>
9        </copy>
10   </assign>
```

The wait Activity   The wait activity allows a business process to specify a delay for a certain period of time or until a certain deadline is reached. A typical use of this activity is to invoke an operation at a certain time, as shown in Listing 16-8.

Listing 16-8

```
Listing 16.8: Example of the use of wait activity
1    <wait until="'2008-12-24T18:00+01:00'"/>
2    <invoke partnerLink="CallServer" portType="AutomaticPhoneCall"
3            operation="TextToSpeech"
4            inputVariable="seasonalGreeting">
5    </invoke>
```

The throw Activity   This activity is used by a business process to indicate an internal error. Every fault is required to have a globally unique QName. The throw activity is required to provide such a name for the fault and can optionally provide a variable of data that provides further information about the fault. A fault handler can use such data to analyze and handle the fault and also to populate any fault messages that need to be sent to other services.

Fault names are not required to be defined prior to their use. An application or process-specific fault name can be directly used by employing an appropriate QName as the value of the faultName attribute and providing a variable with the fault data if required. This provides a very lightweight mechanism to introduce application-specific faults. A simple example that does not provide a variable for the fault data is shown in Listing 16-9.

Listing 16-9

```
Listing 16.9: Simple example of throw activity
1    <throw
2      xmlns:tmp="http://company.com/faults"faultName="tmp:OutOfStock"/>
```

Structuring Activities

The simple primitive activities we just discussed are usually combined into more complex algorithms that specify the business process. For this purpose, BPEL supports many structuring activities. We now discuss some of the important structuring activities.

The sequence Activity A sequence activity is used for defining a set of activities that will be performed in an ordered sequence, which is determined by the order in which the activities are listed. This is depicted in a schematic manner in Figure 16.5. The sequence activity completes when the final activity in the sequence has completed. An example of the sequence activity is shown in Listing 16-10.

Listing 16-10

```
Listing 16.10 : Sample code for sequence activity
1    <sequence>
2        <invoke partnerLink="UnitedAirlines"
3                portType="airline:FlightAvailabilityPT"
4                operation="FlightAvailabilty"
5                inputVariable="FlightDetails"  />
6        <receive partnerLink="UnitedAirlines"
7                portType="airline:FlightCallbackPT"
8                operation="FlightTicketCallback"
9                variable="FlightResponse"  />
10   </sequence>
```

The flow Activity This activity is used to group a set of activities that will be performed in parallel, as shown schematically in Figure 16.6. The most fundamental semantic effect of grouping a set of activities in a flow is to enable concurrency. A flow completes when all the activities in the flow have completed. Sample code for a flow activity is shown in Listing 16-11.

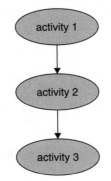

Figure 16.5   BPEL sequence element

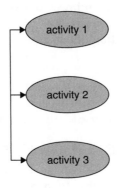

Figure 16.6   BPEL flow element

Listing 16-11

```
Listing 16.11: Sample code for flow activity
1    <sequence>
2        <flow>
3            <invoke partnerLink="Seller" .../>
4            <invoke partnerLink="Shipper" .../>
5        </flow>
6        <invoke partnerLink="Bank" .../>
7    </sequence>
```

The switch Activity   This activity is used for implementing branches, as shown schematically in Figure 16.7. This structuring activity has the same effect and construction as the switch statement in many programming languages such as Java and C/C++. This activity consists of an ordered list of one or more conditional branches defined by "case" elements, followed optionally by an "otherwise" branch. The case branches of the switch are considered in the order in which they appear. The first branch whose

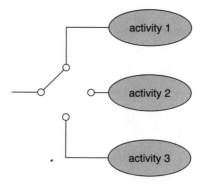

Figure 16.7   BPEL switch element

condition holds true is taken and provides the activity performed for the switch. If no branch with a condition is taken, then the otherwise branch is taken. A sample illustration of the use of the switch activity is shown in Listing 16-12.

Listing 16-12

```
Listing 16.12: Illustration of switch activity
1    <switch>
2          <case condition="boolean expression 1">
3                ......
4          </case>
5          <case condition="boolean expression 2">
6                ....... .
7          </case>
8          <otherwise>
9                ......
10         </otherwise>
11   </switch>
```

The while Activity   This activity defines a loop and also has the same effect as in other programming languages such as Java and C/C++. This activity supports repeated performance of a specified iterative activity. The iterative activity is performed until the given Boolean "while" condition no longer is true. The syntax of the while activity is shown in Listing 16-13.

Listing 16-13

```
Listing 16.13: Syntax for the BPEL while activity
1    <while condition="boolean expression" >
2          ....... .
3    </while>
```

The pick Activity   The pick activity awaits the occurrence of one of a set of events and then performs the activity associated with the event that occurred. The occurrence of the events is usually mutually exclusive in that the process will either receive an acceptance message or a rejection message, but not both. The form of pick is a set of branches of the form event/activity, and exactly one of the branches will be selected based on the occurrence of the event associated with it before any others. Note that after the pick activity has accepted an event for handling, the other events are no longer accepted by that pick. The possible events are the arrival of some message in the form of the invocation of an inbound one-way or request/response operation, or an "alarm" based on a timer (in the sense of an alarm clock). This particular scenario is illustrated in Listing 16-14.

Listing 16-14

```
Listing 16.14: Sample code for the use of pick activity
1    <pick>
2         <onMessage   ...>
3              activity 1
4         </onMessage>
5         <onAlarm>
6              activity 2
7         </onAlarm>
8    </pick>
```

Practical Example

We now demonstrate how the preceding constructs of BPEL come together with an example of a business process (see Listing 16-15). Note that this example is for illustration purposes only and is not meant for actual production use. This example is missing some important details, including any fault handling. In this example, we consider a business process for obtaining the best ticket offer from two airlines (United Airlines and US Airways) for a business traveler. The business process is shown in Figure 16.8, whereas the interactions of this business process with the customer and three other Web Services are depicted in Figure 16.9.

In the process shown, the business process customer (that is, the business traveler) obtains the best ticket offer from the business process through a synchronous call. For this purpose, the business process provides a portType to the customer, as shown on the left of the business process in Figure 16.9. After receiving a request from the customer, the business process makes an asynchronous call to the human resource Web Service to check the status of the customer as a business traveler. Then the process

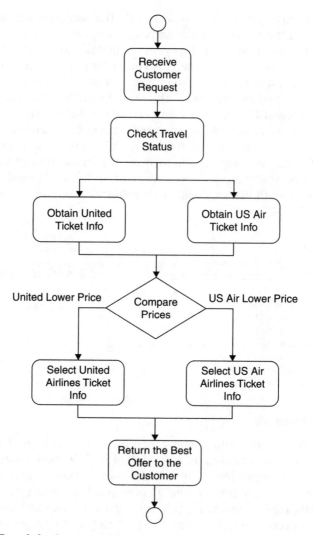

Figure 16.8   Sample business process

makes two asynchronous calls to obtain ticket information, including the price of the tickets from the two airlines. These two asynchronous calls are made at the same time. The replies from the two airlines are obtained by using callback operations. For these callback operations, the business process provides a portType to receive the ticket information. As a last step, the business process determines the lowest ticket offer and sends that offer to the customer.

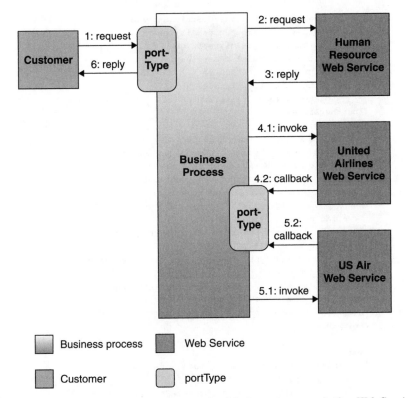

Figure 16.9 Interaction of the business process with the customer and other Web Services

Listing 16-15

```
Listing 16.15: Code of the example business process
1    <process name="BusinessTravel"
2         targetNamespace=http://myCompany.com/bpel/businesstravel/
3         xmlns=http://schemas.xmlsoap.org/ws/2003/03/business-process/
4         xmlns:bpws=http://schemas.xmlsoap.org/ws/2003/03/business-process/
5         xmlns:hr=http://myCompany,com/service/hr/
6         xmlns:line=http://myCompany.com/service/airline/
7         xmlns:go=http://myCompany/bpel/go/ >
8
9         <partnerLinks>
10             <partnerLink name="customer"
11                 partnerLinkType="go:goLT"
12                 myRole="travelService"
13                 partnerRole="travelServiceCustomer" />
14             <partnerLink name="workerGoStatus"
15                 partnerLinkType="hr:workerLT"
```

```
16                    partnerRole="workerGoStatusService" />
17              <partnerLink name="UnitedAirlines"
18               partnerLinkType="line:flightLT"
19               partnerRole="airlineService />
20            <partnerLink name="USAir"
21               partnerLinkType="line:flightLT"
22               partnerRole="airlineService" />
23          </partnerLinks>
24          <variables>
25            <variable name="CustomerRequest"
26                   messageType="go:CustomerRequestType" />
27            <variable name="WorkerGoStatusRequest"
28                   messageType="hr:WorkerGoStatusRequestType" />
29            <variable name="WorkerGoStatusResponse"
30                   messageType="hr:WorkerGoStatusResponseType"  />
31            <variable name="FlightDetails"
32                   messageType="line:FlightTicketRequestType"  />
33            <variable name="USAirFlightResponse"
34                   messageType="line:TravelTicketResponseType"  />
35            <variable name="UnitedAirlinesFlightResponse"
36                   messageType="line:TravelTicketResponseType"  />
37            <variable name="TravelResponse"
38                   messageType="line:TravelTicketResponseType" />
39          </variables>
40
41          <sequence>
42            <!—Initial request from the customer  -->
43              <receive partnerLink="Customer"
44                    portType="go:GoApprovalPT"
45                    operation=" GoApproval"
46                    variable="CustomerRequest"
47                    createInstance="yes"  />
48
49          <!-- Prepare  input for worker status check
50            <assign>
51              <copy>
52                  <from variable="CustomerRequest" part="worker />
53                  <to variable="WorkerGoStatusRequest" part="employee" />
54              </copy>
55            </assign>
56
57          <!—invoke the worker status check Web Service
58          <invoke partnerLink="WorkerGoSatus"
59                 portType="hr:WorkerGoSatusPT"
60                 operation="WorkerGoStatus"
61                 inputVariable="WorkerGoStatusRequest"
62                 outputVariable="WorkerGoStatusResponse" />
63
64  <!—Make parallel invocations to United Airlines and US Air Web Services
65        <flow>
66              <sequence>
67  <!--  make asynchronous invocation for United Airlines Web Service and
68                        wait  for the call back  -->
```

```
69          <invoke partnerLink="UnitedAirlines"
70                  portType="line:FlightAvailabilityPT"
71                  operation="FlightAvailability"
72                  inputVariable="FlightDetails" />
73
74          <receive partnerLInk="UnitedAirlines"
75                  portType="line:FlightCallbackPT"
76                  operation="FlightTicketCallback"
77                  variable="UnitedAirlinesFlightResponse" />
78       </sequence>
79
80       <sequence>
81        <!—Make similar asynchronous call to US Air Web Service and
82             wait for call back   -- >
83             <invoke partnerLink="USAir"
84                     portType="line:FlightAvaialbilityPT"
85                     operation="FlightAvailability"
86                     inputVariable="FlightDetails" />
87
88             <receive partnerLink="USAir"
89                     portType="line;FlightTicketCallbackPT"
90                     operation="FlightTicketCallback"
91                      variable="USAirFlightResponse" />
92        </sequence>
93       </flow>
94  <!--  Select the airline with lowest price (all details are not
     provided here)
95              -- >
96    <switch>
97        <case condition=
             "bpws:getVariableData('UnitedAirlinesFlightResponse',
98                  'confirmationData', 'confirmationData/line:Price')
99        <= bpws:getVariableData('USAirFlightResponse',
100                 'confirmationData', 'confirmationData/line:Price')">
101            <assign>
102                <copy>
103                     <from variable="UnitedAirlinesFlightResponse" />
104                     <to variable=" TravelResponse" />
105                </copy>
106            </assign>
107        <otherwise>
108            <assign>
109                <copy>
110                     <from variable="USAirFlightResponse" />
111                     <to variable=" TravelResponse" />
112                </copy>
113            </assign>
114        </otherwise>
115     </switch>
116     <!—Finally return a reply to the customer through a callback   -- >
117     <invoke partnerLink="Customer"
118          portType="go:CustomerCallback"
119          operation="CustomerCallback"
```

```
120                    inputVariable="TravelResponse" />
121        </sequence>
122    </process>
```

We now briefly discuss the important segments of the code from Listing 16-15.

Lines 1–7

In these lines, we define the top element (process) of this BPEL document. We specify the name (BusinessTravel) of the business process using the name attribute and then we define several namespaces. The most important namespace is that identified by "bpws," which corresponds to the BPEL schema and should be part of all BPEL process elements. We also define three additional namespaces specific to this example: hr, line, and go. These correspond to the employee status checking service, the airlines services, and the travel service.

Lines 9–23

These lines are used to define various parties interacting with the business process using the elements partnerLinks and partnerLink. In this sample code, four parties are identified, corresponding to the customer of the business process, the employee travel status service, and the two airlines services. Each partnerLinks element specifies up to two attributes: myRole (which indicates the role of the business process itself) and partnerRole (which indicates the role of the interacting party).

Lines 24–39

These lines are used to define variables that are used to store, reformat, and transform messages. Typically we need one variable for each message that is exchanged between a service and the business process. For each message, the message type must be specified. The choice of the message type is either a WSDL message type, an XML schema simple type, or an XML schema element. In this example, we only use WSDL message types for all variables.

Lines 41–47

Next we write the main body of the business process, which contains one top-level activity: a sequence. This top-level activity allows us to define several activities that will be performed in the order in which they are listed in the code. Within this structuring activity, the first activity is a receive activity, which is used to wait for the message that will start the business process. In our example, the message is from the customer.

The incoming message is specified by the partnerLink, the portType, the operation name, and, optionally, the variable that holds the received message. In this case, the variable that holds the incoming message is called CustomerRequest. An important thing to note is that the attribute createInstance is set to "yes." This means that every new message received will start a new instance of the business process.

Lines 49–55

In order to prepare the input for the employee travel status check service, we copy a part of the contents of the variable CustomerRequest to the variable WorkerGoStatusRequest. This second variable will be used as the input to the travel status check service request.

Lines 58–62

Next we synchronously invoke the Web Service to check the travel status of the worker by using the invoke activity. In order to invoke the service, we have to specify the port type, the operation name, and the input variable name. The input variable name here is WorkerGoStatusRequest. The output of this synchronous call is stored in the variable WorkerGoStatusResponse.

Lines 64–93

The code in these lines is used to make two asynchronous calls to the United Airlines and US Airways Web Services and then to receive the two callbacks from these services. These calls are made concurrently by using the flow structuring activity. For each of the two airlines, the invocation of the service consists of an invoke activity and a receive activity, which is used to wait for the callback. The structuring activity sequence is used to group these two activities. The results obtained through the receive activities are stored in two variables: UnitedAirlinesFlightResponse and USAirFlightResponse.

Lines 96–115

Next, a switch structuring activity is used to pick one of the two airlines by comparing the quoted prices and choosing the airline with the lowest price. The output of this activity is captured in the variable named TravelResponse.

Lines 116–122

The code in these lines is used to return the lowest offer to the customer through a callback and using an invoke activity. Once again, we have to specify the port type, the operation name, and the variable name that contains the input information for this callback.

Conclusion

This chapter covered the Business Process Execution Language (BPEL). BPEL is used to describe the composition of a business process from various services. A BPEL document can be used in a process server (such as IBM's WebSphere Process Server) to execute the business process. The interface to the business process itself is described using WSDL. The primary purpose of BPEL is to allow for a stateful environment that is required for long-running processes that involve a chain of Web Services invocations. BPEL is based on other standards, including XML, XML schema, XPath, and WSDL.

A very important advantage of BPEL is that new processes can be composed quickly from existing Web Services and then executed in a process server. This provides a more agile method of composing services compared to hard-coding the services in a programming language such as Java.

Appendixes

References

Common Database

1. Silbershatz, A., H.F. Korth, and S. Sudarshan. *Database System Concepts, Fifth Edition,* McGraw-Hill, 2005.
2. Elmasri, R. and S.B. Noble. *Fundamentals of Database Systems, Second Edition,* Addison-Wesley, 1994.

File-Based Data Sharing and FTP

1. Folk, M.J., B. Zoellick, and G. Riccardi. *File Structures: An Object-Oriented Approach with C++,* Addison-Wesley, 1998.
2. http://tools.ietf.org/rfc959 (J. Postel and J. Reynolds, 1985).
3. http://www.ftpplanet.com/ftprosources/basic.htm (FTP—New User Guide).

Sockets

1. Stevens, W.R., B. Fenner, and A.M. Rudoff. *Unix Network Programming: The Sockets Network API, Volume 1, Third Edition,* Addison-Wesley, 2004.

RPC (Remote Procedure Call)

1. *Unix Network Programming: Interprocess Communication, Volume 2, Second Edition,* Prentice-Hall, 1999.
2. Eddon, Guy. *RPC for NT,* Elsevier Science Ltd., 1994.
3. Bloomer, John. *Power Programming with RPC (Nutshell Handbooks),* O'Reilly & Associates, Inc., 1992.

CORBA and Java RMI

1. www.corba.org (CORBA home page).
2. www.omg.org (Object Management Group home page).
3. Rossenberger, J. *Teach Yourself CORBA in 14 Days,* Sams Publishing, 1999.
4. Brose, G., A. Vogel, and K. Duddy. *Java Programming with CORBA: Advanced Techniques for Building Distributed Applications, Third Edition,* Wiley, 2001.
5. Henning, M. and S. Vinoski. *Advanced CORBA Programming with C++,* Addison-Wesley, 1999.
6. http://java.sun.com/j2SE/docs/rmi/ (Java RMI).
7. http://java.sun.com/docs/book/tutorial/rmi/index.html (Java RMI tutorial).
8. http://www-0.1.ibm.com/software/webservers/appserv/wasproductline/ (WebSphere Application Server product information).
9. http://www.redbooks.ibm/abstracts/redp3918.html (technical information on IBM's WebSphere Application Server).

Messaging

1. Hohpe, G. and B. Woolf. *Enterprise Integration Patterns: Designing, Building, and Deploying Messaging Solutions,* Addison-Wesley, 2004.

2. http://www.ibm.com/software/integration.wmq (IBM's WebSphere MQ product information).
3. http://www.redbooks.ibm.com/abstracts/sg247128.html (IBM's red book of technical details on WebSphere MQ).
4. http://java.sun.com/products/jms/ (JMS API specification).
5. Yosuf, K. *Enterprise Messaging Using JMS and IBM WebSphere,* IBM Press, 2004.
6. Monson-Haefel, Richard. *Enterprise Java Beans, Third Edition,* O'Reilly, 2001 (message-driven beans).
7. http://java.sun.com/j2ee/tutorial/1_3-fcs/doc/MDB.html (a message-driven bean example).

XML

1. http://www.w3.org/TR/xml-infoset (XML Infoset, Second Edition).
2. Means W.S. and E.R. Harold. *XML in a Nutshell: A Desktop Quick Reference,* O'Reilly, 2001.
3. http://www.w3.org/TR/xmlschema-0/ (XML schema).
4. http://www.w3.org/TR/2004/REC-xmlschema-1-20041028/structures.html (XML Schema Part I: Structures, Second Edition).
5. http://www.w3.org/TR/2004/REC-xmlschema-2-20041028/datatypes.html (XML Schema Part II: Datatypes, Second Edition).
6. http://www.w3schools.com/schema/default.asp (XML schema tutorial).
7. http://www.w3.org/TR/xslt (XSLT specification).
8. http://www.w3schools.com/xsl/ (XSLT tutorial).
9. http://jcp.org/aboutjava/communityprocess/first/jsr173/ (StAX specification).
10. http://java.sun.com/j2ee/1.4/tutorial/doc/JAXPSAX.html (SAX tutorial).
11. http://www.w3.org/DOM/ (DOM specification).
12. http://java.sun.com/j2se/1.4.2/doc/api/org/w3c/dom/package-summary.html (Java API for DOM).
13. http://java.sun.com/j2se/1.4.2/doc/api/org/w3c/sax/package-summary.html (Java API for SAX).
14. http://www.saxproject.org/apidoc/overview-summary.html (overview of SAX API)
15. http://ws.apache.org/axis/java/user-guide.html (Apache Axis user guide).

SOAP

1. http://www.w3.org/TR/soap/ (latest version of SOAP).
2. http://schemas.xmlsoap.org/soap/envelope/ (SOAP schema).
3. http://www.w3schools.com/soap/default.asp (SOAP tutorial).

WSDL

1. http://www.w3.org/TR/wsdl (WSDL specification).
2. http://www.w3.org/TR/WSDL20/ (WSDL version 2.0).
3. http://www.w3schools.com/wsdl/default.asp (WSDL tutorial).

UDDI and SOA Registry

1. http://www.uddi.org/pubs/ProgrammersAPI-V2.04-Published-20020719.htm (UDDI API specification).
2. http://uddi.xml.org/ (online UDDI community).
3. http://www.w3schools.com/WSDL/wsdl_uddi.asp (UDDI tutorial).
4. http://www-0.1.ibm.com/software/integration/wsrr/ (WebSphere Registry and Repository [WSRR] information).
5. http://www.ibm.com/software/integration/library/faqs.html (frequently asked questions and answers related to WSRR).

Web Services Development Tools

1. http://www.ibm.com/software/awdtools/studioappdev/ (Rational Application Developer home page).
2. http://www.ibm.com/developerworks/library/library/ws-wsdk5/intro/ (WebSphere SDK for Web Services 5.1).
3. http://www.ibm.com/developerworks/rational/products/rad/ (Rational Application Developer).
4. http://www.redbooks.ibm.com/abstracts/sg247672.html (Rational Application Developer V7.5 programming guide).
5. http://ws.apache.org/axis/java/user-guide.html (Apache Axis user guide).
6. http://publib.boulder.ibm.com/infocenter/wsdoc400/v6r0/index.jsp?topic=/com.ibm.websphere.iseries.doc/info/ae/ae/rwbs_wsdl2java.html (WSDL2Java command).
7. http://publib.boulder.ibm.com/infocenter/wsdoc400/v6r0/index.jsp?topic=/com.ibm.websphere.iseries.doc/info/ae/ae/rwbs_wsdl2java.html (Java2WSDL command).
8. Zimmermann, O., M. Tomlinson and S. Peuser. *Perspectives on Web Services: Applying SOAP, WSDL and UDDI to Real-World Projects,* Springer, 2003.
9. Singh, I., S. Brydon, G. Murray, V. Ramachandran, T. Violleau, and B. Stearns. *Designing Web Services with the J2EE 1.4 Platform: JAX-RPC, SOAP, and XML Technologies,* Addison-Wesley, 2004.

Mainframe Application Integration

1. http://www.ibm.com/ims (IMS home page).
2. http://www.ibm.com/cics (CICS home page).
3. http://www.ibm.com/software/data/ims/toolkit/ (IMS Integration Suite).
4. http://wmq.boulder.ibm.com/training/techconf/2005mq/M39.pdf (IMS Bridge).
5. http://www.redbooks.ibm.com/redbooks/pdfs/sg245243.pdf (CICS Bridge).
6. http://www.ibm.com/software/data/ims/soap (IMS SOAP Gateway).
7. http://www.redbooks-ibm.com/abstracts/sg246794.html (IMS SOAP Gateway details).
8. http://www.redbooks.ibm.com/redbooks/pdfs/sg245466.pdf (Web Service support in CICS V3.1).
9. http://publib.boulder.ibm.com/infocenter/dzichelp/v2r2/index.jsp?topic=/com.ibm.etools.ims.tmra.doc/topics/tmresoverview.htm (IMS TM Resource Adapter).
10. http://www.ibm.com/software/data/ims/connect (IMS Connect).

Package Applications

1. http://w3.tap.ibm.com/w3ki/display/Adapters/Home (WebSphere application adapters).

BPEL

1. http://www-106.ibm.com/developerworks/library/ws-bpel (BPEL4WS specification).
2. Juric, M.B., B. Mathew and P. Sarang. *Business Process Execution Language for Web Services, Second Edition,* Packt Publishing, 2006.

Enterprise Service Bus

1. http://www-01.ibm.com/software/integration/wsesb (WebSphere Enterprise Service Bus [WESB] home page).
2. http://www.redbooks.ibm.com/abstracts/sg247212.html (Details of WESB, WESB red book).
3. http://www-01.ibm.com/software/integration/wbimessagebroker (WebSphere Message Broker home page).
4. http://www.redbooks.ibm.com/abstracts/sg247137.html (WebSphere Message Broker red book).

5. http://www-01.ibm.com/software/integration/datapower (WebSphere DataPower home page).
6. http://www.redbooks.ibm.com/abstracts/redp4327.html (WebSphere DataPower red book).

SOA (General References)

1. http://www.ibm.com/developerworks (an excellent source for up-to-date information on SOA, Web Services, and SOA-related topics).
2. Rosen, M., B. Lublinsky, K.T. Smith, and M.J. Balser. *Applied SOA: Service-Oriented Architecture and Design Strategies,* Wiley, 2008.
3. Earl, Thomas. *Service-Oriented Architecture: Concepts, Technology, and Design,* Prentice Hall, 2006.
4. Krafzig, D., K. Banke, and D. Slama. *Enterprise SOA: Service-Oriented Architecture Best Practices,* Prentice Hall, 2005.

Application Integration

1. Hohpe, G. and B. Woolf. *Enterprise Integration Patterns: Designing, Building, and Deploying Messaging Solutions,* Addison-Wesley, 2007.
2. Fowler, M. *Patterns of Enterprise Application Architecture,* Addison-Wesley, 2002.

Glossary

ALE ALE stands for *Application Linking and Enabling,* which is used in SAP applications integration. IDocs are the crux of ALE.

API API stands for *application programming interface,* which is employed by developers to interface with a given piece of code or software.

application The term *application* has been used with more than one meaning in the context of software. In this book, a restricted definition is used, where *application* means a computer program or an executable.

application integration *Application integration* (sometimes called *enterprise application integration* or *EAI)* is the process of bringing data or a function from one application program together with that of another application program.

architecture In the context of software, *architecture* refers to the policies and guidelines used in the design of software.

asynchronous message A message for which the receiving application is not obligated to send a response.

axis Axis is essentially a SOAP engine—a framework for constructing SOAP processors such as clients, servers, gateways, and so on. The current version of Axis is written in Java, but a C++ implementation of the client side of Axis is being developed.

B2B B2B is short for *business-to-business* and refers to commerce between two or more businesses.

B2C B2C stands for *business-to-consumer* and refers to a type of commerce where a company primarily sells directly to the consumer. Amazon.com is a good example of B2C.

Basic Object Adapter (BOA) A BOA's primary purpose is to interface an objects' implementation with its ORB. The BOA provides CORBA objects with a common set of methods for accessing ORB functions. These functions include user authentication, object activation, and object persistence.

BPEL   BPEL stands for *Business Process Execution Language.* In this book, BPEL is also used as a short form for BEPL4WS (BPEL for Web Services). BPEL is a language for composing Web Services into a business process. BPEL can be executed in a process server such as WebSphere process server.

CICS   *CICS (Customer Information Control System)* is a transaction server that runs primarily on IBM mainframe systems under z/OS and z/VSE. CICS is a transaction manager designed for rapid, high-volume online processing.

client/server   Same as remote procedure call (RPC).

correlationID   An identifier used to correlate the response message with the request message in simulating a synchronous call with asynchronous messaging.

CORBA   CORBA provides a standard mechanism for defining interfaces between components as well as some tools to facilitate the implementation of those interfaces using the developer's choice of languages. CORBA also provides language and platform independence.

CRM   Customer Relationship Management (CRM) consists of the processes a company uses to track and organize its contacts with its current and prospective customers. Typical CRM goals are to improve services provided to customers and to use customer contact information for targeted marketing.

DCOM   The Distributed Component Object Model (DCOM) from Microsoft offers capabilities similar to CORBA. However, it is mostly restricted to various Windows operating systems.

DOM   DOM stands for *Document Object Model.* It is a platform- and language-neutral interface that allows programs and scripts to dynamically access and update the content, structure, and style of XML documents.

doors   Doors is a form of restricted RPC. The limitation for the use of Doors is that the application communicating must be running on the same computer.

EJB   EJB stand for *Enterprise Java Beans.* This technology is the server-side component architecture for Java Platform, Enterprise Edition (Java EE). EJBs come in three different varieties, including entity beans, session beans (stateful and stateless), and message-driven beans.

encapsulation   Encapsulation is the central element of OOP and OOD. Data and behavior are encapsulated in classes. Classes provide data hiding. Access privileges can be managed and limited, which promotes modularity and robustness.

ERP   Enterprise Resource Planning (ERP) is an enterprise-wide information system designed to coordinate all the resources, information, and activities needed to complete business processes such as order fulfillment and billing.

ESB   ESB stands for *Enterprise Service Bus* and refers to a distributed middleware software system whose primary purpose is to allow the service provider and the service consumer to communicate even when they are not exactly matched in terms of their preferred communication protocols and message formats.

FTP   FTP stands for *File Transfer Protocol,* which is used to transfer a file from one computer to another computer over a network.

HTTP   HTTP stands for *Hypertext Transfer Protocol,* which is used most commonly by a web browser to communicate with a back-end server. It can also be used by applications to communicate among themselves over a network.

HTTPS   HTTPS is the secure form of the Hypertext Transfer Protocol.

IDocs   IDocs (Intermediate Documents) help with exchanging data between SAP R/3 and non-R/3 systems. As the name suggests, these documents act as intermediate storage of information, which can be sent bidirectionally.

IIOP   IIOP is an acronym of Internet Inter-ORB Protocol. IIOP's main purpose is to provide a standard protocol for ORBs from different vendors to communicate. All CORBA 2.0–compliant vendors must implement IIOP.

IMS   IBM Information Management System (IMS) is a joint hierarchical database and information management system with extensive transaction-processing capabilities. For this book, the transaction-processing part is the most important component and is also referred to as *IMS TM.*

inheritance   Inheritance in OOP and OOD refers to the fact that a new class can be derived from an existing class, called the *base class.*

This allows the creation of a hierarchy of related classes. This mechanism promotes code reuse.

Interface Definition Language (IDL) IDL specifies interfaces between CORBA objects, which ensure the language independence of CORBA. Interfaces defined in IDL can be mapped to any programming language; thus CORBA applications and components are independent of languages used to implement them. This allows a client written in Java to communicate with a server written in C/C++.

J2EE J2EE stands for *Java 2 Enterprise Edition.* Sun Microsystems has now simplified the name to JEE. The J2EE platform defines the standard for developing multitier enterprise applications. The J2EE platform simplifies enterprise applications by basing them on standardized modular components, providing a complete set of services to those components, and handling many details of application behavior automatically, without complex programming. Enterprise Edition adds full support for Enterprise Java Beans components, Java servlets API, Java Server Pages (JSP), and XML technology.

Java Remote Method Invocation (RMI) Java RMI is a very CORBA-like architecture but is restricted to programs written in Java.

Java RMI Registry Java RMI Registry is a simple remote objects registry that provides methods for storing and retrieving remote object references bound with arbitrary string names.

Java Server Page (JSP) Java Server Pages (JSP) is a Java technology that allows software developers to dynamically generate HTML, XML, or other types of documents in response to a web client request. The technology allows Java code and certain predefined actions to be embedded into static content.

JAXB Java Architecture for XML Binding (JAXB) allows Java developers to map Java classes to XML representations. JAXB provides two main features: the ability to marshal Java objects into XML and the inverse (that is, to unmarshal XML back into Java objects).

JAXP The Java API for XML Processing (JAXP; pronounced *Jacks-P)* is one of the Java XML programming APIs. It provides the capability to validate and parse XML documents, and as well provides three interfaces: DOM, SAX, and StAX.

JCA JCA is short for *Java EE Connecter Architecture,* which is a Java-based technology solution for connecting application servers and enterprise information systems (EIS) as part of enterprise application integration (EAI) solutions. Whereas JDBC is specifically used to connect Java EE applications to databases, JCA is a more generic architecture for connection to legacy systems (including databases).

JDBC Java Database Connectivity (JDBC) is an API for the Java programming language that defines how a client may access a database. It provides methods for querying and updating data in a database. JDBC is oriented toward relational databases.

JMS The Java Message Service (JMS) API is a messaging standard that allows application components based on J2EE to create, send, receive, and read messages. It is independent of specific implementations of the messaging system.

JNDI JNDI stands for *Java Naming and Directory Interface,* which is a Java API for a directory service that allows Java software clients to discover and look up data and objects via a name. Like all Java APIs that interface with host systems, JNDI is independent of the underlying implementation. Additionally, it specifies a service provider interface (SPI) that allows directory service implementations to be plugged in to the framework. The implementations may make use of a server, a flat file, or a database.

JSR 109 This specification defines the programming model and run-time architecture for implementing Web Services in Java.

marshalling (and unmarshalling) Marshalling refers to the transformation of the parameters of a method into a format that can be transmitted across a network. The transformed format is platform independent. Unmarshalling is the reverse of the marshalling process.

MessageListener MessageListener is a Java interface that is used to receive asynchronously delivered messages. This Java interface has a single method, onMessage(), that processes the received asynchronous message.

Message-Driven Bean (MDB) MDBs are stateless, server-side, transaction-aware components for processing asynchronous messages. These beans implement the Java MessageListener interface with a single method, onMessage(), for processing the received message.

MOM MOM stands for *message-oriented middleware,* which is software used to send and receive asynchronous messages, usually over a network. IBM's WebSphere MQ is the prime example of a MOM.

MQI   MQI stands for *Message Queue Interface* and is an API for sending and receiving asynchronous messages using IBM's WebSphere MQ messaging software.

Object Management Group (OMG)   OMG's charter is to provide a common architectural framework for object-oriented applications based on widely available interface specifications. OMG achieved its goal by establishing Object Management Architecture (OMA), of which CORBA is a part.

Object Request Broker (ORB)   An ORB provides the following functionality: When an application component wants to use a service provided by another component, it must first obtain the reference for the remote object providing the service. After an object reference is obtained, the component can call methods on the remote object, thus accessing the services provided by the remote object. In addition, ORB provides for marshalling and unmarshalling the parameters of the methods being called. See Chapter 5 for more information on marshalling and unmarshalling.

OOD   OOD stands for *Object-Oriented Design,* which is a process of planning interacting classes for the purpose of solving a software problem. OOD employs UML, and the output is a set of diagrams, including class and sequence diagrams.

OOP   OOP stands for *Object-Oriented Programming,* which is a programming style based on polymorphism, encapsulation, and inheritance. Generally speaking, these features are obtained by encapsulating data and behavior in classes and then using inheritance to build subclasses.

polymorphism   Polymorphism is a OO programming language feature that allows values of different data types to be handled by a uniform interface. The concept of polymorphism applies to both data types and functions. A polymorphic function, method, or operator has many forms or meanings. For example, polymorphic methods have the same name but different meanings, determined by the type of arguments provided.

registry   In the context of SOA, a registry is used by a service provider to register the services it offers. It is also used by the service consumer to find the services it needs. UDDI provides one standard way to register and discover these services.

Remote Procedure Call (RPC)   RPC is also known as *client/server architecture.* In RPC, one application, called the *client,* is able to invoke a function or procedure in another application, called the *server.* The client and server typically run on two different computers connected by a network. RPC is built on top of sockets and hides the low-level network programming from a developer.

repository   In the context of SOA, a repository holds the artifacts related to services. In particular, it is used as a governance tool that includes version control. Quite often the functions of a repository are combined with the functions of a registry in a single product. WebSphere Service Registry and Repository is the prime example of such a combined product.

SAX   SAX stands for *Simple API for XML* and is a more efficient alternative to the DOM parser. SAX is a serial XML parser and is used to retrieve information from an XML document.

servlet   Servlets are the Java counterpart to nonJava dynamic web content technologies such as PHP, CGI, and ASP.NET. Servlets can maintain state across many server transactions by using HTTP cookies, session variables, or URL rewriting.

SLA   SLA stands for *Service Level Agreement,* which describes a document that captures the agreement between the service consumer and service provider as it regards the quality of service. In other words, SLA captures the nonfunctional requirements for a service.

SOA   SOA stands for *Service-Oriented Architecture.* SOA provides methods for systems development and integration, where systems group functionality around business processes and package these as interoperable services. SOA also describes the IT infrastructure, which allows different applications to exchange data with one another as they participate in business processes. Service orientation aims for a loose coupling of services with operating systems, programming languages, and other technologies that underlie applications. SOA separates functions into distinct units, or services, that developers make accessible over a network so that users can combine and reuse them in the production of business applications.

SOAP   SOAP is a simple XML-based message format or protocol for exchanging information between applications.

SOAP engine   A SOAP engine (or processor) aids both consumers of Web Services and their providers to accomplish their tasks without having to worry about the intricacies of SOAP message handling. As far as the consumer is concerned, it invokes an operation in a way similar to how a remote procedure call is invoked. The Web Service provider needs to implement only the logic required by the business problem it solves. The consumer's SOAP processor converts the method invocation into a SOAP message.

socket   A socket is a data structure that allows programs to exchange data. It is generally used by computer programs running on different computers. Whenever different programs are communicating, sockets are always working in the background.

SQL   SQL stands for *Structured Query Language* and is a comprehensive database language. It has statements for data definition, query, and update operations. In addition, it has facilities for, among others things, embedding SQL statements in almost any programming language.

StAX   StAX stands for *Streaming API for XML*. StAX is a standard XML-processing API that allows you to stream XML data from and to your application.

synchronous message   A synchronous message is a message for which a response from the receiver is expected.

TCP/IP   TCP/IP is a set of low-level network protocols used to make connections on a computer network. TCP is an acronym for *Transmission Control Protocol,* and IP stands for *Internet Protocol*. TCP puts data into packets and provides reliable delivery across a network. IP delivers data packets across the network.

UDDI   UDDI stands for *Universal Description, Discovery, and Integration*. UDDI is a standards-based specification for Web Services registration, description, and discovery. Service providers register their services in a UDDI registry, and the service clients use the registry to find services.

UML   Unified Modeling Language (UML) is a standardized general-purpose modeling language in the field of software engineering. UML includes a set of graphical notation techniques to create abstract models of specific systems.

W3C   W3C is short for *World Wide Web Consortium*. W3C is an organization that coordinates standards for the World Wide Web.

WAS   IBM's WebSphere Application Server (WAS) is built using open standards such as Java EE, XML, and Web Services.

WebSphere MQ WebSphere MQ is the leading (asynchronous) messaging software from IBM. It can run on almost any platform.

WSDL WSDL stands for *Web Services Description Language,* which is an XML format for describing network services as a set of end points operating on messages containing either document-oriented or procedure-oriented information. The operations and messages are described abstractly and then bound to a concrete network protocol and message format to define an end point. Related concrete end points are combined into abstract end points (services).

WS-I Basic Profile WS-I Basic Profile is a set of specifications for Web Services that promotes interoperability between services on different platforms.

XDR XDR stands for *External Data Representation.* This data format is typically used for passing data between the RPC client and the server. The use of this format makes RPC platform independent.

XSD XSD stands for *XML Schema Definition.* XSD is an XML schema language standardized by W3C to describe XML documents.

XSL XSL stands for *Extendible Stylesheets Language.* XSL contains an XML vocabulary for specifying formatting semantics.

XSLT XSLT stands for *XSL Transformation.* It is a language for transforming one XML document into another.

Index